What's Ou Everton!

Mark O'Brien

The Parrs Wood Press
Manchester

First Published 2004

THE PARRS WOOD PRESS
St Wilfrid's Enterprise Centre
Royce Road, Manchester, M15 5BJ
www.parrswoodpress.com

© Mark O'Brien 2004

ISBN: 1 903158 54 0

Printed and bound by Biddles Ltd of King's Lynn

CONTENTS

ACKNOWLEDGEMENTS

I'd like to give thanks to:
Jan, my Mum and Dad, all the O'Briens, all the Schofields, all the Campbells, Graham Ennis, Phil Redmond (not him who did Brookside), Dave Swaffield, Dave Wiggins, Ste Connor, Phil Thornton, Peter Hooton, Oscar, Chris Darnton, Andy Searle, Mike Harris, Dan Davies, Ryan Herman, all the lads from the Butchers, the Stuart, the Albany and Orrys, everyone who has contributed to *When Skies Are Grey* - the fanzine and the website - over the years, all the slackers off the messageboard costing British industry millions, and anyone else who has ever made me laugh.

INTRODUCTION

This is a book about going to the match. More specifically, it's about going to the match to watch the unique and rather special club that is Everton Football Club.

I'm not going to bang on about supporting Everton being a passion or almost like a religion, as those terms have been flogged to death in recent years. Supporters of every club from Altrincham to Arsenal seem to think that they love their club more than anyone else, so we've ended up with this homogenised idea of what it means to be 'the average football fan'. It's an offensive notion, and thankfully there's not that much that's average about Everton. Except some of the players, perhaps.

I had the idea for a diary towards the end of the 2002/3 season when, inspired by a combination of our young manager, David Moyes, and a certain Wayne Rooney, we looked set for a place in the UEFA Cup at least. It never worked out that way though - we narrowly missed out - but wheels had been set in motion and it was decided that although I wouldn't be chronicling our jaunts across the Continent, just going home and away over the course of a domestic season would still provide plenty of material. And it did. In fact it actually ended up being a record-breaking season, but not in the way that any of us expected. And while I'm loath to spoil the ending, we didn't win the league. There, I've said it.

I suppose it will be looked back on as 'a hard season', but it's never that hard really, because there are few things in life Evertonians would rather do than go and watch Everton with their mates.

So, without further ado, let's cast our minds back to July 2003. Incidentally, I like to imagine everything going all wobbly at this point, like when they used to do flashbacks on television programmes years ago...

July

Chinese Rocks

Tuesday 15th July 2003

Well that's a good start. Wayne Rooney is the first casualty of the Blues' pre-season training camp in Austria. The teenage superstar has pulled his groin slightly and may have to rest for a day or two.

The whole Western world holds its breath.

Back home, there are reports that we're close to signing shaggy-haired ex-Liverpool winger Steve McManaman. He runs like John Gordon Sinclair in *Gregory's Girl* and he's on silly money at Real Madrid. I'd be surprised if he's the sort of player that Everton's manager, David Moyes, really wants.

Wednesday 16th July 2003

One of the perks of being involved with a fanzine, as I am, is that you occasionally get invited to interesting events. In this instance, I take a trip to London with Ste Connor, a mainstay of *When Skies Are Grey* and one of the lads I sit with at the match, for a screening of Irvine Welsh and Dean Kavanagh's short film, *Dose*.

There's a galaxy of minor celebrities on show at the 'premiere', including the one and only Mr Chesney Hawkes. Seriously, Chesney Hawkes. Cas Pennant, star of the seminal 80s documentary about West Ham's Inter City Firm, *Hooligan*, is also present and we toy with the idea of shouting out some of his infamous lines like, 'Kiddie firm, all facking mouth as usual' or 'Canning Town, city of thieves'. In the end, though, bottle out and plump for laughing at the shirt worn by the much smaller and less violent Paolo Hewitt.

WHAT'S OUR NAME? EVERTON!

Thursday 17th July 2003

Over in Austria, Everton cruise to a seven-nil victory over local side Bad Goisern. Seventeen-year-old Italian trialist Patrizio Pascucci scores a couple while Nick Chadwick goes one better with a hat-trick.

This coming season promises to be crucial for Chadwick and a number of Everton's other young reserves like Kevin McLeod and Leon Osman.

Chadwick has only made limited appearances for the first team and was even shipped out for a rather disappointing loan spell at Derby County last season. His physical, hardworking style does see him score a lot of goals for the second string but he needs to improve his technique and awareness quite considerably to hold down a regular place in the Premiership. In all honesty he looks eventually destined for a decent career in the lower leagues, but Everton's small squad and precarious financial state mean that for the time being we need to persevere and try to get the best out of him.

Friday 18th July 2003

It's looking increasingly unlikely that Moyes will secure his main transfer target, Sean Davis of Fulham. The West London club are apparently in financial trouble but they're unwilling to let Everton get one of their prize assets for a song. The player wants to come to us but Fulham are holding out for as long as possible, which seems the norm these days. They're probably hoping that someone with more poppy comes along and starts an auction. The latest rumour, almost inevitably, is that Middlesbrough are interested. Aren't they always?

An all-action midfielder like Davis would certainly improve our squad, but the existing lot don't do too badly in their second game over in Austria. They beat FC Schwann Schwannenstadt 4-1, with goals from Tomasz Radzinski, an own goal, one for Steve Watson and yet another for young Pascucci. He's knocking them in but experience tells us not to get too excited about these trialists before seeing them with our own eyes. David Prentice in the *Echo* even mentions a few famous ones of the past, such as

Ronnie Ekerlund, who scored in pre-season yet were tactfully deemed 'not quite what we're looking for at this moment'.

When Skies Are Grey, the fanzine I write for, also has a website and today on its messageboard there is much hilarity over the god-awful songs that the punters have been sending into the Liverpool FC official site in honour of their new fullback, Steve Finnan. The pick of the bunch has to be one to the Flintstones theme that uses the lines 'From the Irish Republic, he's the quickest thing we've ever seen'.

Pure gold.

Saturday 19th July 2003
It appears Mr Prentice had his finger on the pulse as it's announced that Pascucci will be taking his Diego Forlan hairstyle and Damon Albarn lovebeads back home to Italy. A couple of budding managers on the internet bemoan this fact - how can we let go a lad who has been prolific against the cream of the Austrian postal service?

It's increasingly common for football fans to become convinced that the player who can't get a game is actually the answer to all their team's ills, especially if he's a bit exotic. Never mind that the manager sees them in training and actually has an idea what they're like, a lot of fans just want to see change for change's sake.

A while ago at Everton it was lightweight Israeli winger Idan Tal who was 'never really given a chance to show what he could do', while Spurs fans famously had a love affair with ill-judged signing Sergei Rebrov. Last season, when Liverpool were struggling, the *Football Echo*'s letters pages were full of demands for their young winger Ritchie Partridge to be recalled from a loan spell at Coventry City and flung into first team action. This despite the fact Angry Armchair of Netherton wouldn't know him from Alan Partridge. Ah ha!

Sunday 20th July 2003
In an interview with Everton's official website, the Ghanaian midfielder Alex Nyarko says he can't wait for the season to start so he can put the past firmly behind him.

If he does end up getting another competitive game for the club it will mark an astonishing turnaround in fortunes for a man whose performances, following a £4.5 million transfer from Lens, were so abject that a disgruntled and rather hairy-backed fan, Stephen Price, confronted him on the pitch at Highbury and offered to swap shirts.

That was over two years ago, and Nyarko has since been out on loan to Monaco and Paris St. Germain. No permanent deal could be sorted with those clubs so the African, whose god-fearing personality would most politely be described as 'unique', has completed a volte-face and returned to see out the remaining two years of his contract with Everton, the club he vowed he'd never play for again.

It will be interesting to see if we really do end up viewing him like a new signing, a latter-day Lazarus, or more like a drain on the wage bill preventing us from bringing someone else in.

Elsewhere in the interview, Nyarko says he's looking forward to playing with Wayne Rooney, who reminds him of Ronaldinho, the Brazilian who has today turned down Manchester United in favour of a £21 million move to Barcelona.

"He obviously doesn't want to win anything, he just wants to fanny about in the sun," is my dad's verdict on the cartoon-faced forward. "Who can blame him," he adds. "Let's face it, when you've already won a World Cup and you're on that much money the prospect of a Premiership champions medal can hardly be that exciting. And anyway, it's fucking grim in Manchester."

Monday 21st July 2003

Huzzah! There's a spare ticket and a seat in a car going up to Glasgow on Saturday for our 'prestige friendly' - prestige meaning it's £17 to get in - with Glasgow Rangers. Everton's lack of European football has led to great store being put on pre-season games and the club have already had to ask the Gers for extra tickets, such is the interest.

Before then though, there is the matter of two friendlies being played simultaneously tomorrow evening: one at Rochdale and another at Crewe. Usually when this happens one game features the first team and the other an 'Everton XI' i.e. the reserves plus whoever is paying penance for upsetting the manager over the summer. In this case though, David Moyes has said he's splitting the squad down the middle, creating a quandary for the blokes who have never missed an Everton game since the Crimean War. A crisis meeting has been held to decide which game will be considered the official one in years to come. It's thought that some were considering chartering a helicopter to fly from Spotland to Gresty Road at half-time, inspired by Phil Collins' trans-Atlantic dash during *Live Aid*. The idea was rejected when it was discovered that you're not allowed to take a carryout onboard.

Tuesday 22nd July 2003

They announce the squads for the night's games and they do indeed appear to be split 50-50, well, possibly more 60-40 with the bias towards the tougher opposition at Crewe. Wayne Rooney, Joseph Yobo, Thomas Gravesen and Duncan Ferguson will all be at Gresty Road, while at Spotland assistant manager Alan Irvine will have the likes of Kevin Campbell, Tomasz Radzinski, Steve Watson and David Weir in his side.

The majority of Blues will go to Crewe, but our travelling party settle on Rochdale for the simple reason that none of us have ever been there before.

Everton obviously aren't big box office in this part of Lancashire, as the crowds seem pretty thin around the ground as we approach. Indeed, it's dead easy to get served in the club adjacent to the stadium, and a friendly little place it is too. Well, friendly to normal people that is, but one of our number, the diminutive, bespectacled Phil Redmond, assistant editor of *WSAG*, has his finely tuned hooli-antennae working overtime. Whenever we go anywhere out of the ordinary, for friendlies or in the cup, you can guarantee that as we draw near he will utter the immortal lines: "It could be a bit naughty here". In this instance he's convinced that some fat-necked weights freaks are giving us funny looks.

Thank God he's not coming to Rangers.

WHAT'S OUR NAME? EVERTON!

We almost make it into the ground without incident but unfortunately Weavers - a 30-year old Tim Robbins lookalike - gets bored queuing for the kids' entrance and tries to double-click in through the turnstile. He would have made it too if it wasn't for a Thora Hird lookalike in a luminous coat and club cap. The steward, moving with a savage grace belying her years, grabs him by the arm and tries to attract the attentions of a copper, but Weavers, ever the experienced jibber, offers up the right money and a look of bemused innocence that just about persuades her to let him through.

The game is the usual pre-season fare, i.e. painfully dull, and it's settled when Matthew Gilks in the Rochdale goal makes a mess of a simple backpass, allowing the little Lego man, Tomasz Radzinski, to tap home from two yards.

The Canadian international was far and away our best player last season, but still his position as first choice striker is far from assured. The reason for that is quite simple: Wayne Rooney. The wonder kid, the seventeen-year-old saviour of English football, plays in the same position as Radzinski in the Everton line-up - essentially the 'little fella' alongside a traditional target man.

Therefore, arguably our two best players, in a squad not overburdened with quality, are competing for the same position.

Rooney's the more naturally gifted of the two players - indeed he's more naturally gifted than just about anyone, anywhere - but it's undeniable that last season the team seemed to play better as a whole when the tireless, unselfish Radzinski started. It was great bringing Rooney on with half an hour to go, after Radzinski had softened the opposition up with his pace and persistence, but there's surely a limit to how long you can confine a talent like Rooney's to the bench.

Once again, this time around, the manager's biggest dilemma will be just how he best utilises the two of them. In fact, the success or otherwise of our whole season could well hinge on how he handles that very situation.

The other half of the squad dip 2-0 at Crewe, and we make it home without the need for a police escort.

Wednesday 23rd July 2003

David Moyes lets it be known in the morning papers that he's not happy with the way a number of the players performed at Crewe, and that he is expecting a lot more from them in the coming games. He does exclude Wayne Rooney from the criticism though, praising his contribution, especially as it was his first match of pre-season.

The photo of the seventeen-year-old accompanying the piece is truly horrific; he's had his head shaved down to the bone and looks like ex-presenter of *The Word*, Hufty.

Thursday 24th July 2003

Moyes is quoted in the papers as saying he won't pay over the odds for Chinese international, Li Tie. He reiterates that he would like the midfielder, who spent last season on loan with us, on a permanent basis but believes that £1 million, the value that his Chinese club Liaoning Bodao have put on him, is unreasonable in the present, depressed market.

Li Tie is one of several players at Everton who divide the opinion of the supporters down the middle. He came at the start of last season, along with countryman Li Wei Feng, as part of our sponsorship deal with the Asian electronics firm, Kejian. In all honesty the whole thing reeked of cheap publicity and marketing strategies to 'increase our profile in those growing Asian markets', but where Li Wei Feng was hardly seen, and eventually returned to China, Li Tie ended up pretty much a mainstay of the side. The big question though is whether that was more a reflection of his abilities or the limitations of the other midfielders at the club.

In his favour are his attitude and his fitness, he never stops running and chasing and working for his teammates. On the other hand there are times, especially when we're in possession, when it becomes apparent that he never grew up playing football at a consistently competitive level.

There is a school of thought that says he's bound to improve with a season under his belt, but Moyes only has a tiny transfer budget so can't afford to take a risk and pay over the odds for a player who is never destined to be anything other than 'a decent squad man'. Spending half a million too much on Li Tie could leave us short when trying to secure a player who would significantly improve us.

Friday 25th July 2003

Ahead of tomorrow's game at Ibrox, the *Daily Record* have run a story indicating that ex-Rangers striker and all round 'cult figure' Duncan Ferguson may not be the Everton captain for the coming campaign. Not unreasonably, they assert that someone like David Weir or Kevin Campbell, players who actually make it on to the pitch occasionally, might be given the role.

Ferguson is Everton's very own Norma Desmond, living on past, faded glories and prone to acts of random violence. This is his second spell at the club whose crest he has tattooed on his shoulder, the club whose fans hope desperately to see him regain just a fraction of his former potency, but who deep down know that it will never happen.

The Scot, in his pomp, was a uniquely Everton type of player. The club has a tradition of big number nines, from Graeme Sharpe, Bob Latchford and Joe Royle, back to Tommy Lawton and Dixie Dean, and the tall, powerful Ferguson is very much from that same mould.

However, it was more than just his physical prowess and awesome heading ability that made Blues' fans take him to their hearts when he first arrived in 1994. He came down to us from Rangers already with a reputation as a bad lad, overly fond of boozing and reluctant to walk away from trouble on and off the pitch. To Everton's predominantly working class support that swagger and recklessness was irresistible; he was living the life that the young men in the stands would live if they had his talent and his money.

When he scored his first goal for the club, in a famous 2-0 win over Liverpool, the supporters' imaginations ran riot as they tried to envisage his bacchanalian post-match celebrations. Add to the mix a forty-four day jail sentence, a refusal to speak to the press, and a knack of scoring in big games, particularly derbys, and it's no surprise that he became such an idol.

In 1998 our then chairman, the reviled Peter Johnson, sold Ferguson to Newcastle United for £8 million, reportedly without manager Walter Smith's knowledge. The ensuing uproar hastened Johnson's departure from the club, but in time it looked like an inspired piece of business, given that a series of injuries meant Ferguson hardly ever figured in a black and white shirt. However, Johnson's successor, the ever-emotional theatre impresario Bill Kenwright, simply couldn't help himself and brought the player back two years later.

Anyone with any sense could see that it was a decision based purely on sentiment, as a club with financial problems shelled out a £3.75 million transfer fee and thirty-odd grand a week in wages on, essentially, a crock. Could you imagine that happening at serious clubs like Manchester United or Arsenal?

Today we, the fans, are not so tolerant of Ferguson. His wild lifestyle and on the field petulance were somehow excusable when he was terrorising opposition defences and scoring goals, but last season there were more reported sightings of Elvis Presley and Osama Bin Laden in Walton than there were of our big striker. To make matters worse, when he did play against Aston Villa in one of the last games of the season, television cameras caught him elbowing Joey Gudjonsson in the face. So even if he does get himself fit and raring to go he is actually banned for the first three games of the new season. Things like that, the traits that were once thought of as part of his unpredictable, roguish charm, are now considered merely tiresome.

There are definitely more worthy candidates for the honour of the Everton captaincy.

Saturday 26th July 2003

Rangers is the first serious outing of the season. Ten o'clock in the car park of the Butchers Arms, Warrington, is the designated rendezvous, and amazingly everyone is bang on time and in one piece. It probably helps that there are only four of us going in this car - when there's a minibus-full the potential for mishaps increases exponentially. Another carload went at the ungodly hour of eight o'clock this morning, determined to get a decent afternoon's drinking in before the match. With no need to go and bang on doors and drag people out of their fetid pits, we're on the M6 and heading North in good time.

We look destined for a couple of hours in the bar ourselves until we reach the traffic jam that calls itself Hamilton. By the time we meet Bob the Bookie and the other lads at the Moathouse next to the SEC there's only half an hour to kick-off.

Bob, who runs a betting shop and permanently has his mobile phone to his ear while scribbling bets on the back of beer mats - hence the dead original nickname - has been to Glasgow once before and assures us that the ground is just a ten minute walk from the hotel. The distinct lack of replica-shirted people, or in fact any people at all, casts a certain doubt on this.

We head off in search of the ground, crossing the vast car parks around the SEC and Glasgow Science Centre, as the sun beats down and a vicious wind whips us with crisp bags. The whole area is eerily empty, like something from *The Day of the Dead*.

Glasgow was the European Capital of Culture in 1990, an award that Liverpool has won for the year 2008, to the great delight of everyone in the city. On the day of the announcement one emotional caller to a Radio Merseyside phone-in even declared: "We're not just best the city in the world, we're the best city in the universe!"

It will be interesting to see just what the award eventually means in real terms for the people of Liverpool though. Hopefully it won't just entail a load of spending on projects like this science centre, which looks like a Bacofoil facsimile of Thunderbird 2. Actually, more to the point, it looks like an empty Bacofoil facsimile of Thunderbird 2. Perhaps there's a reason for that - maybe all the big physics enthusiasts in the city support the Gers - but the last thing that cities like Liverpool and Glasgow need are vanity projects that look great on postcards but don't benefit the people that need help the most.

Only five hundred yards further on, we find ourselves slap-bang in the middle of an area that certainly looks like it could do with some assistance from somewhere. Dodgy looking scrapyards and grubby warehouses with smashed windows abound, and still no sign of the ground, any coppers, or indeed any indication at all that there's a match on.

Luckily, like latter-day Hansel and Gretels, we eventually pick up a trail of empty WKD bottles and Unionist graffiti that leads us to our destination just as the roar goes up to signify the start of the game. As we take our seats near the back of the lower Broomloan Stand the first thing we notice is that while Everton are wearing their amber away strip as expected, Rangers are modelling a quite hideous red and white striped number that makes them look like Paraguay or Stoke City. The second is that a bloke sitting directly in front of us is remonstrating with a bored-looking policeman.

"Why can't I hold my flag up?" he demands, waving an overstuffed carrier bag for effect.

"Cors issa trik'la," is the reply from the Bobby.

"They've all got flags," says our freedom fighter, indicating the vast banks of red, white and blue opposite.

"Iss diff'rent," is the final word.

The mates of the flag bearer persuade him that he has nothing to gain by pursuing the matter, and they're right of course. Once you're in the confines of a football stadium you forego all your rights and any attempt at putting forward a logical argument to the police is invariably treated as provocation. Let's face it, you've got more chance of being dealt with fairly in Guantanamo Bay than at the match. The boys in blue know that they don't even have to nick you and create hassle and paperwork for themselves, they can just eject you from the ground and balls up your day. If you don't like it, call Johnny Cochrane, see how you get on.

In terms of atmosphere and commitment this is certainly a step or two up from Rochdale. There's only a 28,000 crowd but the Everton end is packed and the noise is remarkable for a pre-season friendly.

Everyone knows that midfield is our weakest department, the one that the manager is most keen to strengthen, but in the opening exchanges of this game it's the defence that is all over the place. Our young Nigerian central defender, Joseph Yobo, is on international duty, leaving the veterans Alan Stubbs and David Weir to handle the lightning quick Peter Lovenkrands and the burly Stephen Thompson. They don't look comfortable at all and on twenty minutes Neil McCann skins our inexperienced fullback, Tony Hibbert, and crosses for Thompson to bullet home a header.

The goal is disappointing, but it's not the end of the world; what happens ten minutes later is far more significant. Wayne Rooney, playing up front alongside Tomasz Radzinski for a change, challenges for a loose ball with Bob Malcolm and then crumples to the floor, clutching his ankle. The physio is on immediately and within a minute he's signalling for a stretcher. The Everton section of the ground is a mass of slowly shaking heads as the stocky figure, on whose young shoulders so many hopes rest, is wrapped in a blanket and carried off.

Kevin Campbell replaces the stricken Rooney and makes an instant impact. He forged a good understanding with Radzinski last season and it shows here as they start to combine and push the home side back for the remainder of the half.

The veteran Campbell has been our highest goalscorer for four of the last five seasons but he still seems to have his fair share of critics. He looks sharp today though, and while he may get the odd unkind comment thrown his way, the stick he receives is nothing compared to that reserved for half-time substitute Niclas Alexandersson. The Swedish international winger is on the pitch for less than five minutes when the first shout of 'Take him on you faggot' rings out.

The Everton kangaroo court has decided that Alexandersson is lazy, useless and effete. They've also ruled that he's going to have to suddenly become a combination of Andrei Kanchelskis and Peter Reid if he's ever to win anyone around. In fairness, the stone-hearted Goodison faithful have hounded out far better players than the Swede before now, but even when he sets up two goals in quick succession he still only receives an ironic 'Ooh look, he thinks he's Maradona now'.

His first 'assist' is a pass to Radzinski that draws a foul from ex-Everton defender Michael Ball. The referee awards a spot kick and David Unsworth, whose general play is characterised by an ability to kick opponents and the ball as far as possible, sends Stefan Klos the wrong way and delicately strokes the penalty home.

The next goal is a thing of rare beauty. Li Tie has only been on as a substitute for a couple of minutes when, with Everton in possession, he bursts into the box like an oriental Bryan Robson. Alexandersson chips a ball into his path and Li, who has never so much as had a shot on target before now, lashes a volley into the roof of the net.

"Fucking hell!" is the general consensus.

The player looks even more amazed than the crowd as a huge smile beams from underneath his John Noakes fringe and he holds up one finger to indicate his relief at finally getting off the mark.

"That might persuade Moyes to stump up the extra money for him," is the somewhat predictable quip from one wag behind us.

Michael Mols capitalises on a horrible mix up at the back to equalise a minute later, but the jeering Rangers fans don't realise that the Dutchman has simply set up an hilarious finale.

In the last minute, with the score at 2-2, Everton are awarded a free-kick on the corner of the Rangers box. It's too wide for ex-Celtic defender Stubbs to try one of his Johnny Metgod type piledrivers, but the fans urge him to have a go anyway, just to annoy the Union Jack wavers who have booed him throughout. He obliges by attempting a tame, curling effort that Klos has covered...until Ball tries to head it clear, inadvertently diverting it into the net instead.

The succession of mis-shapen heads that appear from the stand above, to hurl obscenities and spittle, look absolutely gutted.

As the police are occupied with their efforts to keep us back at the final whistle, Flag Man wins a small moral victory by whipping his tricolour out of its bag and giving it a jaunty twirl above his head. At the same time, a young lad with his t-shirt sleeve rolled up to proudly display his Everton tattoo, decides to play an imaginary flute to the departing Rangers fans. As insulting mimes go it's hardly up there with aeroplane wings at Old Trafford.

When we're eventually allowed to leave the stadium we're horrified as, looking downhill, we see what appears to be a huge mob of Rangers massing outside a bookies that we need to pass. It's only as we draw tentatively closer that we discover that it's nothing more sinister than the queue for Ibrox tube station.

Redmond's paranoia must be contagious.

During the arduous drive home we ponder how unconvincing Weir and Stubbs looked, the fact that we still have no idea what our best midfield is, and obviously the biggest concern, Rooney's injury.

You should hear us when we lose.

Sunday July 27th 2003

Rooney's damaged ligaments in his ankle. He'll be out for at least four weeks, missing the opening games against Arsenal and Fulham. There's one less selection dilemma for Moyes at least.

And so much for Lazarus, Alex Nyarko has been told he is well down the pecking order and is away speaking to a couple of clubs in China who might be interested in yet another loan deal.

Monday July 28th 2003

We're linked with a bid for controversial Birmingham midfielder Robbie Savage. He is a horrible individual with his ridiculous long hair, penchant for leather trousers and, of all things, an Armani eagle tattooed on his arm. He is possibly the biggest whopper in football, and let's face it there's some serious competition.

However, there's no denying that he has an energy and a determination to win - possibly to compensate for his limited skill - that would probably improve most teams outside the top four or five in the Premiership.

Tuesday July 29th 2003

Rooney's injury is apparently healing well and he has an outside chance of recovering in time for what the papers like to call 'The Big Kick Off!'

First choice goalkeeper Richard Wright could be in contention for the opening day as well, depending on the extent of the shoulder injury he suffered while falling out of his parents' loft. That looks even more ridiculous written down.

Wednesday July 30th 2003
Tonight the first team plays at Dundee United. Fair play to anyone who goes up there on a Wednesday night, especially after Saturday's trip to Glasgow. I'm afraid I have to draw the line somewhere.

Thursday July 31st 2003
They dipped at Tannadice last night, courtesy of a goal by ex-Falkirk striker Colin Samuel. He was on trial at Goodison last season and this fact is not missed by a small number of fans who, desperate for fresh faces, are asking questions about Moyes' cautious approach to transfers.

When our outstanding young manager first arrived from Preston North End, one of their fans told us that he spends the club's money as if it's his own. Personally I think that's a strength, especially when you look at some of the characters who have picked up good money for doing very little for Everton over the years. However, with Chelsea and their new Russian owner Roman Abramovich spending like there's no tomorrow, it's easy to feel like hungry Dickensian orphans with our noses pressed up against the bakery window.

Patrizio Pascucci hasn't actually gone home yet, and scored the equaliser for the reserves at Rhyl, home of the world famous Sun Centre.

August

You Will You Won't

Friday August 1st 2003

How many uncles does Steve McManaman have? Scores of them or just one who can't keep his mouth shut in taxis? The latest from my cab-driving uncle Dave is that 'Macca' loves the lifestyle in Spain so much that if Madrid do pay up the remaining year of his contract he wants to move to another Primera Liga club and not crawl back over broken glass to Everton. This is obviously in stark contrast to the rumours that have him buying a house near Calderstones Park and putting his dogs in quarantine at Speke airport.

Saturday August 2nd 2003

A combination of blistering heat and blistering hangovers means that only four of us are fit for the short journey up the M6 for today's game against Preston North End.

During the season there's always bickering over whose turn it is to drive, so the canny ones try to get an easy one out the way early on. Gid McLean offers to come over from the Wirral and pick up Ray McKay, Phil Redmond and myself from Warrington.

Gid's in his twenties, has a good job, always has smart clobber and, according to him at least, often has to fight the women off with a shitty stick. Ray McKay, another little lad, could also do with a stick to fight off women, in particular teenage girls. Sadly for him, that's not a reference to his dashing good looks. Last year, while returning from the Grand National in an inebriated state, he was set upon by a band of young harpies who battered him in Warrington bus station. To add insult to injury, the police then arrested him, not his assailants, and we all refused to believe him when he claimed that it was the girls' boyfriends who actually snotted him.

Unfortunately for us, Gid could do with spending less money on CP Company and Paul Smith and more on his Peugeot 205, which overheats and splutters to a halt on the hard shoulder just short of Leyland.

The AA man takes exactly the allotted hour to arrive; we're convinced that he's been waiting around the corner reading the *Daily Star* and eating his egg butties thinking, "There's no point rushing to a job, you'll only get given another."

He fiddles under the bonnet for a bit and then tells us to drive a bit further up to the car park of the Leyland Hotel where he'll give it another look. While he's explaining to Gid in great detail the workings of the internal combustion engine, the rest of us, resplendent in shorts and polo shirts, gatecrash a wedding reception in search of shade and booze. The lobby is full of kids running around giving each other Chinese burns while squaddy types with moustaches shout at them and sweat profusely in their morning suits.

I'm sure we end up in the background of some wedding snaps when the bride arrives in the mandatory vintage jalopy. For years to come the happy couple are going to get sick of explaining that they have no idea who the three red-faced and irritated looking scruffs are.

Back under the bonnet, the words 'head gasket' and 'big job' indicate that Gid's wheels will not be making the last leg to Preston. Luckily for the rest of us, my dad, who is already in a pub near the ground, reluctantly agrees to come and get us while the unfortunate Gid is towed back to a garage in Warrington.

"You shower of useless twats", are my loving father's first words as he picks us up. "I'd just queued for ages and then had to give my two pints away."

And then, after all that fannying about, the Blues are absolutely shocking. Against his old club, David Moyes puts out his strongest available side, more or less the one that will start the season at Highbury, and they're appalling.

WHAT'S OUR NAME? EVERTON!

Last season's dramatic upturn in league form was down to hard work, keeping it simple and getting the basics right - when the opposition had the ball Everton closed them down as a group and forced them into making mistakes in dangerous areas. However, today you almost get the feeling that the players believe that it's beneath them to exert that much energy against lower league opposition.

One good thing about the Mediterranean temperatures is that there are an inordinate number of crop-topped honeys at the game. It's as if an awful lot of fellas have offered to take their better halves out for a drive, before heading into Lancashire and tentatively saying, "Er, I think Everton are playing up this way today. I could take you if you fancy," while casting furtive sideways glances to see if the lady in question has seen through such a feeble ruse.

On the other hand, the big drawback of the hot weather - apart from its contribution to the Everton players' apathy - is that everybody wants a drink at half-time, and the Deepdale catering facilities are woefully inadequate. It never ceases to amaze me that people are more than willing to be ripped off at football grounds, yet the clubs are absolutely hopeless at taking their money off them. You know that £2.50 or whatever for a plastic cup full of warm lager is taking the piss, but you accept it as part of the football fan's contract. Having to miss ten minutes of the first half to stand any chance of actually getting served though is what's most irritating. And that's not just at Preston, it's more or less everywhere.

Why not have one area selling cups of tea and Eccles cakes and another that just sells cans or plastic bottles of ale? They could even round the prices up and no one would be bothered. Surely that way more people could get served, more revenue would be taken and both the punters and the club would be happy, or is there some gaping flaw in my logic there?

Right at the start of the second half, while most of the visiting Everton fans are still trying to get a drink, Richard Cresswell scrambles a goal from a corner and Preston's annoying brass band strike up with the Pogues' *Fiesta* in celebration of what proves to be the winner.

Moyes makes six substitutions in the half but it does no good. Everton struggle to get a shot on target and for the last half-hour Preston, who know that they've got the game sewn up, start knocking the ball around like the Mighty Magyars.

The only Everton player to come out of the game with any credit whatsoever is Joseph Yobo. The young Nigerian central defender is world class: quick, strong and completely unflappable. When you see the likes of him or Rooney playing well it makes you realise how ordinary the majority of their teammates are.

They get booed off at the end - not exactly the most encouraging sign two weeks before the first league game of the season.

Sunday August 3rd 2003

An eagle-eyed *Sunday Mirror* journalist spots Stephen Price, the fan who had the altercation with Alex Nyarko at Highbury, in a photo of the crowd at Ibrox. Price received a three-year ban from every football ground in Great Britain, though he claims that it was reduced to two years. Highbury Corner magistrates seem to think he's trying to pull a fast one and Everton are apparently 'concerned' over this latest development. In truth, how easy is it to enforce a ban like that? Were Glasgow police expected to be on high alert, on the lookout for a middle-aged, balding man with a Scouse accent?

David Moyes says that there is no truth in the rumour that he's looking to buy Preston's Dickson Etuhu. We're always linked with the leggy Nigerian midfielder whenever it's a slow news day. In years gone by it was always Nathan Blake or Dean Saunders we were 'keeping tabs on' whenever there was a spare column inch to fill.

Monday August 4th 2003

Duncan Ferguson and Niclas Alexandersson, neither of whom even made the bench on Saturday, will play in the reserves against Southport at Haig Avenue tonight. The first team squad are in Holland tomorrow for a game against Roda JC, and Moyes has made it clear that there's no point in Ferguson playing as he needs to work with the strikers who will be starting the season. I'm no expert on man-management but that looks like a bit of a public humiliation, leaving a big name at home to play with the kids while the first team are abroad.

Ferguson isn't the only one who won't be going to the Netherlands for the game. The match was announced quite late, by which time I'd already made the arrangements for my stag weekend and my mates had booked flights, hotels and time off work. We all fly out this Thursday. To Amsterdam, naturally.

That's nothing; I thought I'd cunningly arranged my wedding in September to coincide with an international weekend. That was until the fixtures came out and it transpired that my walk down the aisle will actually be taking place on the day Everton play Newcastle at Goodison.

I'm sure this book's cursed.

Tuesday August 5th 2003

The reserves won 2-1 at Haig Avenue. Ferguson and Chadwick scored the goals just before half-time.

Due to visa issues Li Tie and Joseph Yobo can't travel for the game at Roda tonight, so at least we have an excuse if we get turned over again.

Meanwhile Gid's yet to hear from the garage about his car. He says that when the mechanics looked at it there was much pursing of lips and scratching of heads - sure signs that you're going to be landed with a mother of a bill.

Wednesday August 6th 2003

There are some seriously unhappy bunnies about after last night's 2-0 reverse in Holland. I must confess to an overwhelmingly selfish sense of 'Thank God I never changed all my plans and travelled over early for that' when I saw the result on the club's official website.

David Moyes said in his post-match interview that he was tempted to go over to the travelling supporters - including Bob the Bookie and Weavers - and apologise to them for the Blues' dire display.

AUGUST - YOU WILL YOU WON'T

These poor pre-season performances, combined with the lack of transfer activity, have produced an overwhelming sense of dread amongst the fans. Years ago no one took any notice of friendly results - in fact it was nigh on impossible to get hold of them at times, secreted as they were in tiny type in the corner of your morning paper. Now they show them on the telly, with the commentators invariably wheeling out phrases such as, "The real thing doesn't start for three weeks but Gareth Southgate was telling me beforehand that the players take these games very seriously and that they really want to win this mini-tournament. Ah, it looks like Boro are making a quintuple substitution."

As a result of this increased attention we now have the farcical situation where Sunday's final friendly, Colin Harvey's testimonial against Bologna, has taken on the mantle of a 'must win' game. If we don't we'll be dubbed 'Crisis Club Everton' at the start of August. A new record, even for us.

Thursday August 7th 2003
The Merry Pranksters fly out to Amsterdam for my stag weekend.

Friday August 8th 2003
Some sad bastard has had the result of Total Network Solutions versus an Everton XI texted out to him. The Blues apparently triumphed 3-1 and the sad bastard is roundly chastised for not finding out the scorers.

Sunday August 10th 2003
We're due to land at John Lennon Airport at 1.30pm, giving us just enough time to get our stuff and head straight to Goodison for the Bologna match. As we come through customs someone says there's a coach outside waiting to whisk the Bologna players to the game. Apparently their flight was delayed and the kick-off has been put back to 5pm.

Following three nights of intense revelry with Jamie the Red, the host with the most, we already look like the occupants of a World War One field hospital, so the thought of hanging around for over three hours to watch a testimonial hardly gets the juices flowing. So sorry Colin, but it's home and straight to bed for me.

Once the game got underway, Everton put on their first proficient display of the summer, comfortably dispatching the Italians 3-0, with goals from Radzinski, Chadwick and Pembridge. Richard Wright also played his second game in three days and looks set for next Saturday, which is a relief as his two immediate understudies, Paul Gerrard and Steve Simonsen, have stunk all summer. So bad have they been in fact that nineteen-year-old Iain Turner was given his debut in this game, replacing Wright for the last ten minutes.

The result will ease the pressure on Moyes and the players somewhat but it isn't all good news, far from it in fact, as Kevin Campbell limped off after 11 minutes with a hamstring injury.

Monday August 11th 2003

Bollocks. Campbell's out for at least a month. That leaves Radzinski and Chadwick as the only recognised strikers available for Saturday. Rooney's apparently making good progress but it's unlikely he'll be risked in a game that we have little chance of winning anyway. That's not me being unduly pessimistic by the way; it's just the way the Premiership is now. If, on the opening day, the team who finished 7th in the league last season wins at the home of the one who finished 2nd, it would be treated as a major upset.

One striker who has had better news than Campbell is Patrizio Pascucci. He must have done something to impress someone after the club initially said they didn't want him, as he's been offered a two-year deal. At the rate we're losing strikers he might end up playing at Highbury.

Around midday my head starts to feel like it belongs to my body again, so I check out the various rumours that have been circulating on the internet while I was away. Apart from all the usual staples we're now apparently interested in the thirty-seven-year-old Nigel Martyn for £400,000, Preston's gangly striker Ricardo Fuller and Michael Carrick of West Ham. Various waiters, head stewards and window cleaners lie at the source of these gems.

According to a slightly less reliable source, the *Sunday Mirror*, Wayne Rooney's new mate is none other than the self-pitying ex-Take That weirdo Robbie Williams. Williams apparently flew Rooney down to his gig at Knebworth last week, where he got the full VIP treatment. In return, Wayne has kindly promised 'the Robster' tickets to any Everton game he likes. Presumably not the derby though, as everyone wants them.

Tuesday August 12th 2003

David Moyes' patience has paid off as Li Tie has signed a three-year deal. Liaoning Bodao, his club in China, eventually caved in and accepted an 'undisclosed fee' - presumably considerably less than the £1.5 million they were originally asking for.

One midfielder not having such a great time is Scot Gemmill, Archie's lad. He's torn a thigh muscle in training and will be out of contention for the next four to six weeks. Most fans will probably shrug, as Gemmill is a player who is always used as an example of the paucity of our squad. It's like when someone tries to describe the ignominy of life in the lower leagues, they always mention playing on a wet Tuesday night at Grimsby. Well, for many people, Gemmill is Grimsby. Which is a little bit unfair; he's a clever footballer, in that typical ex-Nottingham Forest type way, but his Billy Casper physique means that he sometimes goes missing amongst the creatine-fuelled monsters who dominate the modern midfield.

The 'engine room', as has been mentioned several times, is our Achilles heel, despite the fact that we have an overabundance of candidates to play there. The problem is that, like Gemmill, they all have some good qualities but also some glaring weaknesses. No matter how Moyes shuffled them about last season he could never settle on a combination that looked particularly convincing.

Wednesday August 13th, 2003

We've apparently had an improved offer for Sean Davis rejected. However, Fulham are meant to be in talks with American international Claudio Reyna - he of the unfeasibly big head - who is a similar sort of player. Therefore it looks like they've resigned themselves to letting him go. Middlesbrough are the only other club still interested but they are said to be trying to get Gaizka Mendieta from Lazio. They must be mad, Mendieta had one good season with Valencia but since then he's stunk at Barcelona and in Italy.

Boro are a strange club, it's as if they know they'll never win anything so they placate their fans with a succession of fading yet famous names from the continent.

Everton, on the other hand, are trying out a somewhat less famous name in the shape of Frenchman Cyril Chapuis. The ex-Rennes and Marseilles striker is coming over for a week's trial. With a whole one goal in thirty-three games in the French league last season, he sounds a belter.

Thursday August 14th 2003

After yesterday's rejection, Fulham have now accepted bids for Sean Davis from Middlesbrough and Everton. All the signs seem to point towards him preferring a move to Goodison. If the deal comes off then Moyes' patience and determination to get his man must be applauded. To think that some people, including my barber, were starting to refer to him as 'Dithering Dave'.

Excuse the pun, but my barber does my head in. I've even tried to go elsewhere to avoid talking to him but he's only round the corner and with the temperature reaching record highs I'm in dire need of a shearing.

He's got loads of Everton memorabilia in the shop but as far as I can tell he's not been to a game since they scrapped the Zenith Data Systems Cup. He's always working you see. Cabbies are the same, they use work as an excuse for never going to the match but feel they can speak with some authority thanks to what they glean from Radio Merseyside and the TalkSport phone-in.

"They'll struggle this year, Everton," he says.

"Not necessarily. The players performed well last year; there's no reason why they can't do it again."

I can see him in the mirror giving a little shake of the head and pulling that 'I've just tasted sour milk' face that signifies that I don't know what I'm talking about.

"He can't attract the players and the competition are all strengthening."

"Like who?" I enquire.

"Well, just look at Blackburn."

"They've sold their two best players, Duff and Dunn, how's that strengthened them?"

"Ah, but they've got loads of money now though, they can go out and buy."

"Eh? Using that logic we would be best off selling Rooney for £30 million or whatever."

"That's right, we should."

Oh fuck off. The bastard's prices have gone up to £6 as well. I've got a good mind to grow a big Art Garfunkel bushy mop, just to spite him.

Friday August 15th 2003

Well, Cyril Chapuis didn't hang about. The Frenchman arrived at Bellefield, Everton's training ground, but said he didn't want to train. Moyes, who is not an individual to trifle with, told him to sling his hook. And that was that, apparently.

If today's big story is anything to go by though, we won't miss the shot-shy Frenchman as Moyes is apparently trying to sort a deal out with Arsenal to bring Francis Jeffers back to Goodison on a year's loan. Everyone seems really excited by the prospect, but I'm not so sure.

Jeffers was superb for Everton when he broke into the team as a teenager, but since his big money move to Arsenal he has suffered badly with injuries, and when he has been fit he's struggled to get into the first team. He's nowhere near as good as Rooney, and I don't think he's even as good as Radzinski, which would leave him more or less third choice if we're going to continue playing with a target man. I just think he's got an awful lot to prove, and we wouldn't even be considering him if it weren't for the fact that he's an Evertonian. I hope I'm proved wrong though.

The transport problems have started again. There are six of us going down to Highbury. That's a bad number, too many for one car. Weavers has even mentioned the dreaded 'V' word: Van.

WHAT'S OUR NAME? EVERTON!

Sitting in the back of some borrowed work's Transit, getting tangled up in oily blue ropes and impaled on chisels is good knockabout fun for about half an hour, but it soon gets tiresome, especially if Everton get beat, which they surely will in this instance.

Saturday August 16th 2003

A quick test drive of the van shows it to have somewhat dubious brakes; in fact the Ark Royal can stop quicker than this deathtrap. An executive decision is taken that involves me and Redmond going in his car while Bob the Bookie, Weavers, Alan Welsh and Kel, Alan's brother-in law, go in his. The plan is to liaise via the wonder of mobile phone and park somewhere near the ground.

We're making good time when, almost inevitably, a light starts flashing on the dashboard. It's in the shape of an oilcan so, remarkably, we deduce that it can only mean the car needs oil. Now I'm no mechanic, but Redmond truly sets the standard when it comes to technical incompetence. He's almost proud of the fact that he knows less than nothing about cars, informing me that as he's always had lease cars or company cars he's never had to trouble himself with trivialities like water or oil. This is all well and good I tell him, but it's not much consolation when we're stuck at a petrol station in Walsall. As if to prove that he's not exaggerating his ignorance, he even has to get the handbook out to find out how to open the bonnet.

We've got a little bit of the Dunkirk spirit though, and between us we eventually pick a bottle of oil from the hundreds of different varieties on offer and even work out how to get it into the engine without having to ask a grown-up. The light thankfully goes out on the dashboard so, feeling all gruff and manly with oil on our hands, we get back on the motorway and resume our journey.

Perhaps the curse has been lifted after all.

We get to North London with no more incident, and following right behind Kel's car we pass the Drayton Arms, which is surrounded by a big crowd of Everton supporters enjoying a drink in the sun. Without warning, Kel pulls into an alley right behind the pub and parks in a small courtyard surrounded by scruffy looking flats.

Bob spills from the car with a bottle of lager in his hand and indicates for us to park right next to them.

"It's a sound little speck this," he says proudly. "We've parked here for the last four years, right next to the boozer and the ground. Spot on."

Redmond is incredulous; there are signs everywhere that make it quite clear that parking is strictly for residents only. Bob assures us that those warnings are just there for show. Who are we to argue when we've got such a prime position? The alternative after all is to start shlepping around North London in search of some overpriced official car park.

In Bob we trust.

The Drayton is absolutely heaving. It's always the same in the designated away fans' alehouse, so normally we try to find somewhere off the beaten track. Today, though, no one has the energy to get a tube up to Highbury Corner where our London-based mates are drinking. Luckily there's a little shop selling cans next door so we stand outside drinking warm Red Stripe as the crowd continues to swell. By the time the Everton team coach drives past you would think that we were the home side. Most of the players look slightly bemused by the raucous cheer that greets them - only Wayne Rooney, with a massive grin on his face, gives a sly clenched-fist salute. You get the feeling that if he weren't a footballer himself he would be standing out here with us, up to his ankles in plastic glasses and the detritus from fruit and veg stalls that seems to litter every pavement in the capital.

Once inside the ground we locate our seats in the Lower West Stand, right at the end of a row, separated from the Arsenal fans by nothing but a low railing. Elsewhere in the country this could prove a bit nerve-wracking, but the home supporters across the barricade here are either clean cut Nick Hornby types or teenagers in replica shirts and Evisu jeans.

Not only do our tickets put us in gesticulating distance of the home fans, they also entitle us to an unobstructed view of a fucking big post - it's just like being at Goodison. Nevertheless, despite the obvious drawbacks that this old ground has, it will be a shame when the Gunners move to their proposed new stadium at Ashburton Grove. Places like this, with the entrances set between the houses and the fans right on top of the pitch, are what going to the game is about for those of us over thirty. It's got character, for want of a better word.

Today, Moyes' Toffees appear to have a bit of character too, starting much more purposefully than Arsene Wenger's aristocrats; we're closing them down quickly and forcing them to hit hopeful balls over the top for Thierry Henry to chase. With Yobo in the team we can defend against that all day.

Our Danish international midfielder, Thomas Gravesen, is also playing particularly well in these early stages, outshining even the majestic Patrick Vieira. While there are several players who divide opinion amongst the Everton fans, none does so more than the baldy Scandinavian schemer. There's no doubting he's got tons of ability in terms of his control, his vision and his passing, and when he's playing well he seems to have hours on the ball while everyone else is running around like a headless chicken. Crucially, he's also the only one of our midfielders whose instinct is to go forward and take responsibility for pushing the team on, and it's for that reason that Moyes is forced to tolerate his shortcomings and make him almost a mainstay of the side.

You see, for all his skills on the ball, when things aren't going our way, Gravesen, or 'Mad Dog' as he is sometimes known, can be an utter liability. For instance, he may look like Grant Mitchell, with his shaven skull and bulging temples, but he tackles more like Peggy, and frequently gets booked for the stupidest of challenges. When he gets frustrated he's also prone to shooting from ridiculous positions and attempting impossible, infuriating passes. But what really rankles with some fans is his tendency to showboat and act as a cheerleader, demanding more noise from the crowd and pumping his fists in the air. That sort of behaviour may be acceptable if you're having a great game, but this barmpot does it even when he's having a nightmare. Believe me, there's nothing more galling than watching someone fanny about, getting the runaround off Chris Marsden or Kevin Horlock, and then having him gurn at you and beat his chest like King Kong as he's about to take a corner.

This isn't one of those days though, and we almost open the scoring when the Dane's through-ball releases Radzinski down the right and his low cross is met in turn by Nick Chadwick. Unfortunately, Arsenal's new German keeper, the unconvincing-looking Jens Lehmann, gets a foot to the ball and keeps the shot out. Things start to look even more promising when Gravesen picks a ball up in the centre-circle and heads straight for the heart of the Arsenal defence, eluding a challenge from Kolo Touré, only to be upended by Sol Campbell on the edge of the box. The England defender has denied Gravesen a clear goalscoring opportunity, which referee Mark Halsey acknowledges, brandishing a red card.

While most of the Everton fans give a big cheer and a wave to Campbell, I turn to Redmond and say: "All this means is that they'll be able to sing 'We only had ten men' when they beat us now."

And my pessimism is proved well founded as Arsenal come to life in the face of adversity. Vieira is suddenly everywhere, likewise Robert Pires. They're all so quick and sharp, and what's also noticeable is that most of them, especially the French players, are extremely two-footed. When space is at such a premium, as it is in games like this, the ability to play with either foot gives them a considerable advantage. Alessandro Pistone, the ex-Inter Milan fullback, is the only Everton player on show who has this ability, which is just one of the reasons why Arsenal will be challenging for the title and we won't, I suppose.

Arsenal slowly start to build momentum and it's no surprise when they take the lead half an hour in. Henry flicks the ball on to Alan Stubbs' elbow and Halsey points straight to the spot. The decision still looks a bit harsh from where we are.

Henry takes the kick himself, sending his ex-team-mate Richard Wright the wrong way. For some reason the striker then goes berserk, peeling off his shirt and running straight towards the Everton fans behind the goal, gesturing like some sort of loon. Pandemonium breaks out as the stewards tangle with angry fans and Henry is showered with assorted beverages and pastries. Things get a bit fraught by us too as a family of fat lads in front start jumping on their seats and screaming abuse at the Arsenal supporters to our left, paying particular attention to one who is the double of Nicolas Anelka. That's all par for the course I suppose, but when coins, spit and racial abuse start to get hurled across, enough is enough. We voice our objections and the tubbies look at us stunned, as if they can't understand why we'd be upset by the way they're acting. They stop though, which is the important thing.

We get to half-time without conceding another, despite Gravesen marring his performance by playing a slack pass across the back that gifts Gilberto Silva a free run on goal. Luckily, the most un-Brazilian of Brazilians completely mis-controls with only Wright to beat.

During the break, after the big screen replay shows that Stubbs clearly meant the handball for the penalty, Nicolas Anelka starts talking to Redmond across the railing. He's a dead nice lad, Arsenal through and through, and is surprisingly philosophical about the abuse off the empty-heads. His only concern is that a stray coin might hit someone's kid. That doesn't stop us being embarrassed and apologetic.

In the second half Arsenal are just as dominant, with Pires doubling their lead on the hour after a brilliant double save from Wright. It's only near the end, with Rooney and Li Tie on as substitutes, that we begin to look like possibly getting something as their ten men begin to tire. Radzinski scores with six minutes remaining and suddenly Arsenal are wobbling. We're pouring forward and even when Li Tie gets dismissed for two bookings in quick succession, an equaliser still looks possible.

In the dying seconds a corner is worked to Pistone whose cross dips invitingly towards Joseph Yobo, unmarked on the penalty spot. The young Nigerian rises and connects firmly, too firmly in fact, and his header flashes a foot over the bar. And so it finishes, 2-1, and as predicted we get our rendition of 'We only had ten men' as we file out.

One consolation is that we'll be able get an early dart seeing as we're parked so handy. Maybe we'll even have time to stop for a pint somewhere on the way back. As we get to the corner of the road though we see Kel at the entrance to the alleyway, slowly shaking his head.

Two cars. Both clamped. £85 a piece.

Bob and Weavers look like whipped dogs. They apologise so profusely that in the end we have to almost absolve them of the blame, saying things like, "Well, we never had to park here. It's the driver's responsibility at the end of the day" when what we actually mean is "You pair of stupid bastards. Why did we ever trust you?".

If the fees for getting the clamps removed weren't steep enough, we spend another small fortune in the Drayton while we wait for the men from 'You Northern Muppets Security' to come and release us. Even a wave from David Moyes, leaving the ground in his Mercedes, does little to lift the mood.

We're meant to be going to Charlton a week on Tuesday in Weavers' Arkansas Chug-a-Bug. God knows what the curse is going to throw up for that one.

Sunday August 17th 2003

During yesterday's excitement we forgot that the draw had been made for the competition formerly known as the League Cup - we're at home to Stockport County. Our record in this competition, particularly against lower league opposition, is truly awful, so I'm not counting any chickens.

As sure as death and taxes, Redmond will say, "I really hope we win it this year." He does every year, and we never do; it's the one domestic honour that still eludes us.

Today's *Observer* features a big article about Duncan Ferguson that's based mainly on comments from a 'senior Everton insider'. It doesn't tell us anything we don't already know in terms of how much Ferguson costs us and how little he puts back in terms of scoring goals and spending time on the pitch, but what is interesting is that 'the insider' claims that Ferguson doesn't really care about football any more, especially since

Wayne Rooney took over as the Goodison hero. He adds that Moyes wants to try and get him out on the pitch as much as possible to prove to the supporters that he's not up to the rigours of the Premiership any more. In essence, the piece calls Ferguson a conman.

There's no point in pretending that we'll ever see our former idol back to his best, and his wages, along with those of several other big earners at the club, are obviously a big drain. However, nobody put a gun to Bill Kenwright's head and forced him to give any of these players these big deals. It was Everton who went to Ferguson at Newcastle and offered him the earth to come back. What's he meant to do now, ask for a pay cut because his injuries have stopped him from performing?

Obviously this present situation isn't ideal by any stretch, but do we really need some sort of smear campaign to try and force Ferguson out? The player himself will probably not be that bothered - thirty-seven grand a week will dull the pain - but is this sort of thing any good for the image of the club and the mood of the supporters?

The parties involved need to act like grown-ups and try and sort something out in private. Sneaking to the press just seems cheap, although Everton have plenty of experience of doing it in recent years. Whenever they want to offload a crowd favourite, for instance Francis Jeffers, Michael Ball or Don Hutchison, they always leak just enough dirt to the media to turn the fans against them first.

Almost every decent player we've had in the last decade has left under a cloud - at this rate the Hall of Fame dinners in twenty years time will just be opportunities to sing 'One Greedy Bastard' and 'Judas'.

Chelsea beat Liverpool 2-1 at Anfield, live on the telly. For all Roman Abramovich's spending, Chelsea don't look any better than last season. Their most significant deal of the summer was letting Gianfranco Zola go. Liverpool, for their part, are appalling. How can a club who have spent close to one hundred million pounds kick the season off with Igor Biscan and Bruno Cheyrou in the starting line-up?

AUGUST - YOU WILL YOU WON'T

Monday August 18th 2003

Mark Halsey apparently included something in his report about Thierry Henry's celebrations on Saturday, but the FA have chosen not to take any action against him. I'm glad. All sorts of people were phoning Alan Green on *606* straight after the game, demanding at least a public flogging. It's funny, football fans give some unmerciful stick to players yet as soon as they react you get people acting like right sensitive little souls. Last season we had Liverpool fans running to the police falsely accusing Rooney of spitting at them at Goodison. It's a relatively modern, unpleasant phenomenon.

Young winger Kevin McLeod has signed for second division Queens Park Rangers for a quarter of a million pounds. At one point it looked as if he would be a cracker for us but he seemed to stagnate in the reserves and hasn't really had much of a look-in since Moyes arrived. Given that the manager has been pretty fair with other young players, like Tony Hibbert and Wayne Rooney, it would seem that he believes McLeod simply isn't up to Premiership standard.

Tuesday August 19th 2003

Alex Nyarko couldn't sort a deal out in China so he's coming back to Goodison again. Moyes is unhappy that he was out there for two and a half weeks and has made it clear that he will be looking to get him farmed out to someone else as soon as possible. *The Echo* have intimated that Everton need him off the wage bill in order to make a move for McManaman possible. That must be in case the Ghanaian's not unpopular enough already.

The Jeffers deal appears to have reached an impasse as well, with Arsenal wanting Everton to commit to buying him after the initial one-year loan. Obviously the Blues aren't going for that given the player's poor fitness record. I will be surprised if we don't get him on our terms though, as we seem to hold all the cards in the negotiations given Arsene Wenger's obvious desperation to get him off the payroll.

Jeffers' only regular football seems to be for the England 21s and tonight he starts in a televised friendly for them against Croatia at

Upton Park. For all England's star names, young millionaires like Jeffers, Jermain Defoe, Glen Johnson and Jermaine Jenas, they are taught a comprehensive footballing lesson by the Croatians who cruise to a 3-0 victory. In injury time, at the end of a brilliant passing move, their left-back scores a chip that would have had Michel Platini screaming, "Pick le bones out of that". It's difficult to imagine his opposite number, Paul Konchesky, showing the same sort of poise and imagination.

Wednesday August 20th 2003

Someone rings from the *Daily Post* to ask my opinion on Everton's announcement that plans for a new stadium are now on the back-burner. I'm tempted to give a quite concise reply: "No shit."

Most of us just want to consign the whole sorry ground move thing to history now. Peter Johnson originally mooted the idea of moving from Goodison in the mid-nineties. His original idea of a super-stadium on the site of Kirkby golf course never got beyond the artist's impression stage because he couldn't get permission from the council to build there. Before he could look at any alternatives he'd been ousted, but his successor, Bill Kenwright, still liked the idea and so we were sold the grand plan: a multi-purpose arena at the Kings Dock.

The scale models and the videos used to promote the scheme did look really impressive. It was going to have a sliding roof like the Amsterdam Arena and a retractable pitch that allowed the venue to be used for pop concerts, exhibitions and whatever else people want to do in a really, really big room.

You have to remember that this was pushed at a time when things on the field were truly horrible and the club's finances were even worse. As the results and performances deteriorated under Walter Smith we were constantly told that things would pick up once we had the new stadium. The Kings Dock was the key to everything, the light at the end of the tunnel, the pot of gold at the end of the rainbow.

Got beat three-nil at home by Charlton? Don't worry about it, wait until we've got the Kings Dock, Madonna and U2 will be playing there every other week and with all that non-football revenue we'll be able to rebuild the team and put Everton at the pinnacle of European football.

Seriously, that was the dream.

Occasionally, someone would ask why the money that was to be spent on the stadium couldn't be spent on the team instead. The answer was always that it was different money - we could attract investment on the strength of the stadium and the future revenues it would generate, but those investors weren't interested in giving us money to throw at players.

The whole planning and bidding process dragged on interminably, with Everton gaining preferred bidder status for the site and looking for some time to be in pole position. However, when push came to shove it transpired that we simply couldn't raise our portion of the money required to get the project off the ground. 'Spiralling construction costs' were cited as the reason for us dropping out at a late stage, but the basic fact seemed to be that a club twenty million pounds or so in debt simply cannot afford to fund any part of a major civil engineering project.

A lot of Evertonians probably aren't that bothered. For us there isn't a better ground in the world than Goodison, it's where our fathers and grandfathers came to watch Everton after all, but in selling the concept of a new ground so forcefully the powers that be also pushed the idea that Goodison is somehow second rate. By raising expectations in the manner they did and then failing to deliver, they have saddled themselves with the label of the board that messed up the Kings Dock and forced us to stay at a decrepit old ground. While things are now looking a lot better on the pitch thanks to David Moyes, this will be overlooked to a certain extent. However, if things start to go wrong and we begin to struggle in the league you can guarantee that the Kings Dock will be the first stick the supporters beat them with, especially if Liverpool's plans to move to a new stadium go ahead.

According to the bloke at the *Post*, Everton have said that now they're not looking to pursue plans for an alternative site they will be able to concentrate on giving David Moyes the backing he needs. Obviously this doesn't exactly tally with their long-held assertion that a new stadium would not affect any money going to the manager.

Chelsea's young striker Carlton Cole has joined Charlton Athletic on a year's loan. He was reportedly offered to us first but we didn't accept the offer because there is no chance of an option to sign him permanently. The exact opposite of the Jeffers situation then.

I trust Moyes but Cole looks brilliant - he could have formed a fearsome partnership with Rooney, even if it had been only for a season. He's also a nap to score against us on Tuesday now.

Thursday August 21st 2003

After looking great against Arsenal, Thomas Gravesen picked up a knee injury playing for Denmark last night. The initial prognosis was that he'll be missing for two weeks at least, but then a scan revealed no serious damage, making him a possibility for Saturday's home game against Fulham. If he's missing, the central midfield pairing will be Li Tie and Tobias Linderoth - we'll never cross the halfway line.

A group of Evertonians are holding a service at the Hillsborough memorial at Anfield on Saturday. The Reverend Harry Ross, the Everton vicar, is conducting it and former Everton captain Dave Watson will be in attendance. They're hoping that it will heal some of the wounds caused by the idiots from both clubs who vandalised that memorial and the Dixie Dean statue at Goodison in recent seasons.

Let's face it, the spiteful little twats who do the paint throwing couldn't care less about the service, and no doubt there will be more vandalism in the future. However, what's important about acts of respect like this is that they show that the vast majority of decent people who follow both clubs won't allow these incidents to cloud their judgement. It's up to the press, and in this case fanzines and fans' websites bear a particular responsibility, to emphasise the fact that the vandalism is perpetrated by a handful of horrible inadequates. It's important that the 'typical Everton/Kopite scum' line is never allowed to become the norm, because if it does then we've let the vindictive minority win.

Friday August 22nd 2003

Sean Davis is reported to be at Bellefield sorting a deal out. The mere mention of his name now makes me lose the will to live. He had better be good after all this.

He's not the only one at the training ground though as we're reported to be giving three players trials. What is the collective noun for a group of trialists? A 'panic' perhaps?

The first of the three is Seville's Mexican midfielder Gerardo Torrado. Phillipe Delaye, a French defender and headline writer's dream is next, and then finally Alexandre Nelson, a goalkeeper from Sporting Lisbon.

There's only a week left until the summer transfer window closes, so we can probably expect all sorts of mad deals to be rushed through soon.

We pick up the new copy of the fanzine from the printers and it looks smart. No matter how many issues we produce, and this is number 102, it's still dead exciting opening up a brand new copy.

A young graphic designer, Nick Jones, has been given free rein to design the covers and he's certainly made a great job of the first one. Unfortunately our proofreading isn't quite up to the same high standards and a 'Jordan-sized gaping hole' has become a 'Jordan-sized raping hole' in one article.

Saturday August 23rd 2003

Fulham at home. These games are your bread and butter if you're going to do well in the league. We finished seventh last season because hardly anyone beat us at Goodison. There were some great away wins too but you treat them as bonuses, likewise a win against one of the top teams. While last season's injury-time winner against reigning champions Arsenal will live long in the memory, it was still only three points. If anything, the points we took from the likes of Southampton and Charlton had more impact on our final placing, given that those sides ended up immediately below us.

Fulham have got some good footballers, especially in midfield, but they're the epitome of the soft Southern ponces who don't like it up 'em, so to speak. Players such as Steed Malbranque and Sylvain Legwinski will pass you to death if you let them, but put them under any sort of concerted pressure and they buckle.

On the way to the ground, Redmond and I discuss games that evoke memories of intimate interludes. The pick of the bunch is a tale involving one of his mates and the much-missed *Football Italia* on Channel 4. On the Sunday afternoon in question the lad and his lady friend were apparently enjoying what is sometimes known as a 'matinee', with the telly on in the background. The seeds of the young couple's eventual break-up were sown at the point when the chap sat up, leaned to one side for a better view of the box and politely asked for a brief respite from their lovemaking while he awaited the outcome of a penalty in the Milan derby.

Women are funny about stuff like that.

Once we're at Goodison the sun starts shining and we enjoy a pleasant couple of hours selling the magazine. At the opening home game you always see loads of familiar faces sporting their holiday suntans and box-fresh sneakers, and invariably everyone is in a buoyant mood. You're always war-weary by the end of a season, but there's only so many weekends traipsing around Ikea or squabbling in a caravan in North Wales you can tolerate before you start to itch for the familiar sights and smells of Goodison Road.

Word filters from the ground that Wayne Rooney, despite being some way off full fitness, will start the game up front with Tomasz Radzinski. Mark Pembridge, the Merthyr Maradona, will start in central midfield in place of Thomas Gravesen - Li Tie is only on the bench.

Despite this somewhat patched up team, Everton get right into Fulham from the first whistle and, true to form, the Londoners bottle it. We're deservedly three-nil up at half-time - a scoreline that is a tribute to the less glamorous members of the Everton squad. Before the game few people would have pinpointed Gary Naysmith, a fullback playing on the left side of midfield, as a key figure, but the wan-faced Scottish international has a hand in all three goals.

He drives home the first himself on seven minutes and then heads the ball down from a free-kick for Wayne Rooney to set up Steve Watson for the third. Sandwiched between those two is a David Unsworth strike that comes at the end of a move that the 1970 Brazil side would have been proud of. It starts when Rooney casually plucks a ball from the air out by the right touchline and cuts inside the Fulham fullback. At this point there seems little danger, but the youngster fires a pass to the edge of the box that Naysmith instinctively backheels to Pembridge, who in turn feeds the marauding Unsworth. The big left-back takes one touch and drills the ball low past Edwin van der Sar - or Wurzel Gummidge as one wit refers to the lanky Dutchman.

Add to this goalfest an Alan Stubbs free-kick that strikes a post and it's safe to say that an under-strength Toffees' side has earned its half-time ovation. Not everyone is happy though. Ste Connor comes back from the toilets during the break shaking his shaven head in disbelief.

"You'll never guess what I've just heard in there," he says.

Nobody even tries.

"The bloke next to me said 'I'd be happier if one of the strikers got on the scoresheet.'"

As is so often the case when teams have a big lead, Everton relax a bit too much in the second half and Fulham, with the burly Barry Hayles on as sub, put up a bit of a fight. A knackered Rooney tries unsuccessfully to chip the eleven-foot van der Sar before Hayles grabs a consolation, causing us to shift uncomfortably in our seats for a few minutes, faced with the prospect of a dramatic comeback. It's happened on countless occasions in the past but this Everton side is made of stern stuff. Pembridge and the dogged Swede, Tobias Linderoth, immediately reassert themselves on Legwinski and Lee Clark in the midfield and any hopes of a Fulham revival fizzle out.

We're famous for doing things the hard way, so it's quite refreshing to watch such a controlled, professional performance so early on in the season. After the game Chris Coleman, Fulham's young manager, says that he hopes his side can eventually emulate David Moyes' Everton.

WHAT'S OUR NAME? EVERTON!

While waiting for our goals on *The Premiership* in the evening it's hilarious to see Frank Lampard being interviewed following Chelsea's narrow defeat of Leicester. The midfielder looked like he had a good game but all the interviewer is interested in talking about is their new signing, Adrian Mutu. Lampard uses the time-honoured phrase: 'He showed some nice touches'. That roughly translates as: 'He's an absolute fanny merchant'.

Sunday August 24th 2003

David Moyes confirms the unlikely-looking story that he's interested in Glasgow Rangers' captain Barry Ferguson. He goes on to state that he doesn't think we can raise the sort of money that the Gers would be looking for, although they have confirmed that they will consider any offers. Liverpool have come out and said that they're definitely not one of the clubs interested, so the smart money would appear to be on Blackburn Rovers. Even if we really pushed the boat out and everyone emptied their piggy banks, Graeme Souness would surely be able to trump any bid with the mountains of cash he received for David Dunn and Damien Duff. I'm never going to be able to show my face in that barber's now.

Our very own Tomasz Radzinski is also linked with a move to Ewood Park. I hope that's as preposterous as it sounds.

Monday August 25th 2003

After all this time the Sean Davis deal has now collapsed.

Apparently a second scan of his injured knee has shown that he's actually done damage to his cruciate ligaments and will be out for at least two months. It remains to be seen whether we now move for someone else in the next few days or sit tight and sign Davis when the transfer window re-opens in mid-season.

Claudio Reyna's been mentioned as an alternative as he is yet to complete his move to Fulham. The thought of hijacking that transfer doesn't exactly get the pulse racing.

Tuesday August 26th 2003

"Once we get through the Blackwall Tunnel we're laughing."

"Where's that though, Neil?" Weavers, Gid and I ask in unison.

"It's got to be around here somewhere," is our navigator's rather unconvincing reply.

We're back in London and our not so trusty guide is Neil McKeown, a resident of New Cross who has been visiting his parents in Warrington. He leapt at the offer of a lift back, assuring us there was no need to get directions to the ground off the internet as he has 'the knowledge'.

When we go past the same Money Shop in Stratford twice we eventually have to concede that we're lost. London's multi-ethnic blend is what makes it one of the most vibrant and culturally significant cities in the world. However, that's of little consolation when Everton are about to kick off in little over an hour and you need to ask someone for directions. We eventually find someone who doesn't look at us as if we're visitors from Mars and he directs us to the Blackwall Tunnel. In fairness to Neil, once we emerge south of the river he does manage to guide us the remaining three hundred yards without a hitch.

Conscious of the Arsenal clamping, we park at an Asda where a family of Charlton fans assures us we'll be fine. One of the first things you notice in the streets and the pubs around The Valley is just how many families there are. There doesn't seem to be any groups of young lads at all, apart from the ones outside the Rose of Denmark and the Antigallican, and their shaven heads and Lacoste tracksuits mark them down quite clearly as Evertonians. It has to be the most friendly ground in the country; even the police are dead polite. In fact their hospitality appears to have no bounds as when we approach the ground itself there are no turnstiles and very few stewards checking tickets. We just walk in unmolested - for £25 I want at least a pat-down search.

Everton have got three thousand supporters there on a Tuesday night. I don't really go in for all that pointless 'we're better supporters than you' type stuff that fans of the North East and Manchester clubs seem so fond of, but it does feel a little bit special when you're at an away ground and your end is packed. I'm not really much of a singer either, but nonetheless it makes the hairs stand up on the back of your neck when the home fans are drowned out by a chorus of 'It's a grand old team to play for'.

By the time that last throaty roar of 'Come on!' goes up it feels as if Everton simply can't lose.

Unfortunately the players don't seem quite as confident as the fans in the early stages, as Charlton's talented midfield take hold of the game. In many ways the Addicks are similar to us in that they work hard for each other and they've got a number of extremely talented players, most notably Scott Parker, but they're not quite the complete package. Where we fall short in midfield, their strongest area, they are not very convincing at the back, with Mark Fish and Hermann Hreidarsson looking vulnerable on the occasions when Wayne Rooney or Tomasz Radzinski gets a chance to run at them.

The hosts open the scoring when David Unsworth brings down Parker at the end of a clever passing move on the edge of our box. The Everton players seem to think that Unsworth got a foot on the ball, but from where we are it looks pretty clear cut. Jason Euell calmly strokes the penalty home.

Two minutes later, however, Everton are level. Steve Watson, whose bursts into the box from the right-hand side of midfield are an important weapon for us, makes a clever diagonal run, latches on to a Mark Pembridge pass and delicately flicks the ball over Dean Kiely and into the net.

Early in the second half Charlton regain the lead when they're awarded another spot kick. This time it's Hreidarsson who makes a surge into the Everton box and Joseph Yobo, normally so assured, sticks out a leg and invites the big Icelandic defender to go down. He duly obliges and Euell again makes no mistake from the spot. Instead of throwing the towel in though, as Everton teams of the past might have, the Blues step up a gear and absolutely hammer Charlton for the remainder of the half. Unfortunately, for all our pressure, we only manage to score one goal to earn a point, but what a goal it is.

Saturday's star, Gary Naysmith, gathers a ball on the left and beats a player before looking up and firing in an awkward waist-high pass to Rooney. Despite the close attentions of Mark Fish, the young striker kills the ball in one movement, spins away from the defender and smashes a shot - with his left foot, his 'weak' one - into the roof of the net. From the moment the ball reaches him, he moves so quickly and so instinctively that it's almost as if he's playing at 78rpm while everyone else is stuck at 33.

He's only been playing first team football for a year and yet he's already given us more 'shake your head in stunned disbelief' moments than most players produce in a lifetime. And he's still only seventeen. We forget sometimes, we just expect him to be head and shoulders above everyone else, which is unfair when he's still just a kid and he's up against grizzled veterans who play this game in order to put food on the table.

However, one drawback about being such a young, precocious talent is that referees seem to have it in for him. That's the opinion of David Moyes anyway, as tonight's official, Steve Dunn, incenses him by booking the youngster for an innocuous challenge on Parker late in the game. Moyes is so annoyed that after the game he announces that he intends to speak to the head of the referees, Philip Don, before the situation gets any further out of hand.

On the way home Redmond rings on the mobile to say that Moyes has again confirmed in his post-match interview that he wants to bring Barry Ferguson to Goodison if he can. We all agree it's not like him to announce stuff like that if he's not confident it can be achieved.

We arrive home at two in the morning, tired but happy with a point and quietly excited by the thought of what can only be described as a big name signing. We haven't had one of them for some time.

Wednesday August 27th 2003

The morning papers are full of Barry Ferguson stuff. Blackburn are reported to be getting fed up with having their bids rejected and it appears Everton lead the way with a £6 million offer. That would make Ferguson our costliest signing ever, and would push our spending right to the limit.

Thursday August 28th 2003

Finally, we've signed someone. Not Barry Ferguson though. David Moyes was in Copenhagen last night watching Rangers progress to the group stages of the Champions League, but the papers say he didn't have any talks with Rangers officials.

No, the man to sign is the Potuguese goalkeeper, Alexandre Nelson. He is on a one-year loan but he might be forced to make his debut this Saturday, in the first Merseyside derby of the season. With having the midweek match, nobody has had much chance to think about the home game against Liverpool until now. The Reds drew 0-0 at Anfield against Spurs last night and have only two points from their first three games. Their fans are getting increasingly fed up with Gerard Houllier, but they have a knack of getting themselves back on track against us. And while many of us still have doubts about Richard Wright, we hope that he's fit for Saturday as the thought of facing Michael Owen with a debutant foreign keeper is not one we relish.

I have horrible visions of Nelson wearing tracksuit bottoms and trying to punch every ball that comes into the box. These games are not for the faint-hearted.

Friday August 29th 2003

The arse has fallen out of our bid for Barry Ferguson. After some deliberation it seems that the Blackburn board have agreed to offer £6 million up front plus more dependent on appearances. Our offer would only have eventually risen to £6 million, and that was us pushing the boat out. The player's reportedly going to earn thirty-seven grand a week as well. There was just no way we could compete with that.

Not discouraged by this latest setback though, we are apparently in talks with Valencia's lanky Norwegian striker John Carew. Again we're looking to get him on one of our trusty loan deals. He won't come, and he's rubbish anyway. A big yard-dog as my dad would say.

Saturday August 30th 2003

A big thank you to Sky for dictating that the derby kicks off at twelve-thirty. Bob and Weavers, ever the sticklers for tradition, can't face the derby sober and are going to some alehouse in West Derby that is opening ridiculously early. Maybe I'm just getting too sensible in my thirties, but I can't face getting bladdered before breakfast. Instead I wake up at 6am and pace around like a caged animal until Redmond picks me up at nine-thirty, much to my girlfriend's relief.

After picking up Graham Ennis, editor-in-chief and driving force behind the fanzine for the past ten years, and setting up our t-shirt stall in St. Luke's Church, we have time for a couple of sherberts in the homely surroundings of the Stuart Hotel.

I always expect the worst from derby games but there are plenty of people about who are in bullish mood.

"Liverpool are shite", "They've not scored in open play" and "That Houllier hasn't got a clue" are just some of the reasons why we're going to tonk them everywhere.

"We must be due to beat them," is the best I can add. The last time we did was at Anfield in 1999 when Kevin Campbell scored the winner and three players were sent off. The last time we beat them at Goodison was in 1997 - the goalscorers were Danny Cadamarteri and Neil Ruddock with an oggy. Yes, Neil Ruddock, that's how long ago it was.

Goodison Road is chocker as everyone tries to maximise their drinking time and the unique, heady derby day atmosphere is stirred further by the police helicopters hovering menacingly low over the ground. The whole stadium is buzzing as we take our seats in the Park End, disappointed to see that the Liverpool fans haven't brought any new banners.

If ever a set of supporters believed their own press, it's this lot. For instance, they're always trying to outdo each other with the most obtuse slogans on their flags - the more pretentious the better it seems. A good old Shanks quote always went down well, but in recent years they've become even more bizarre, the most notable being the one telling the late Princess Diana that she'd never walk alone. Another classic said, 'Wine For My Men, We Ride at Dawn'. What on earth is that meant to mean?

And then of course there's Doctor Fun and those two moustachioed weirdos who wear the waistcoats festooned with Liverpool badges. It really is a freakshow on the Kop these days. Normal Liverpudlians are even embarrassed by the attention seeking 'did you see me on Sky with my scarf in the air and taking photos of the corner-takers?' types they now attract in their droves.

Apart from the injured Richard Wright we start with the same side that did well at Charlton. The goalkeeper's replacement is actually Steve Simonsen, not Alexandre Nelson, as even the Portuguese keeper doesn't want to play for us, citing the catch-all 'personal reasons' for his change of heart.

Liverpool's confidence looks shaky after a run of poor results and we force them on to the back foot for the opening quarter of an hour or so. However, during this period of early dominance we fail to score, with Tomasz Radzinski dragging a shot wide and Mark Pembridge firing a free-kick just off target. Slowly the Reds see more possession as it becomes apparent that we are running out of ideas after our initial burst of energy. We're actually making them look good - for the first time this season - by playing too many sloppy passes and wasting free-kicks and throw-ins in potentially dangerous areas. They can't believe their luck.

Five minutes before half-time, Liverpool move the ball unopposed from one end of the pitch to the other before new signing Harry Kewell mis-hits a shot that breaks to Michael Owen. Unlike our strikers, he keeps his cool and tucks the opener in off the post.

Almost immediately we break up the other end and Steve Watson, deadly in midweek, has a golden opportunity to blast a shot past Jerzy Dudek in the Liverpool goal. Against anyone else he wouldn't hesitate but the occasion seems to get to him and he tries to be too deliberate, squaring the ball to Wayne Rooney. The youngster, desperate to score, miscontrols and the grateful Dudek clears the danger.

You just cannot afford to spurn chances like that.

The game's pretty much over as a contest early in the second half when Joseph Yobo, who is having a horrible game, allows Milan Baros to muscle past him and square for Owen, who again makes no mistake. We're all over the place; Liverpool have got the freedom of midfield and know that as long as they don't do anything stupid then the three points are theirs.

Incredibly, despite the fact that we're resorting to just lumping the ball aimlessly forward, we still manage to create more opportunities. At the crucial moments though, Dudek shows his class, denying a point-blank Rooney header and another thunderous Pembridge shot. Perhaps if substitute Duncan Ferguson's free-kick had gone in off the crossbar Liverpool might have buckled but, almost inevitably, it merely rattles the woodwork and bounces away to safety. Then, with ten minutes to go, a long ball into our box causes a panic that eventually leaves Kewell with an empty net into which he slots his first goal for his new club.

Three-nil. Rubbish.

After the game, there are some lame excuses that the referee swung it their way or that the only difference was the finishing, but there was more to it than that. Even Moyes, in his post-match comments, says that there is a gap between us and the top teams. While Liverpool aren't a patch on Arsenal, and certainly not a shadow of their own great sides of the past, they've got more good players than us and, crucially, they all played well today.

It's churlish to suggest otherwise, and much more sensible to try and be philosophical while getting extremely drunk.

Sunday August 31st 2003

Horrible, horrible hangover.

With the transfer deadline tomorrow, it's reported that Moyes was straight on to the phone to Steve Bruce after yesterday's defeat, hoping to get Robbie Savage. It's not surprising that he wants to get someone a bit more dynamic in straight away after watching Steven Gerrard being given the freedom to operate completely unopposed in Liverpool's midfield yesterday.

Quelle surprise though, both clubs seem to differ in their valuation of the player - with Birmingham describing our offer as 'derisory' - so of all the deals that have been suggested in the last few weeks the only one that actually looks certain is the one to bring Nigel Martyn from Leeds.

Despite picking up yet another booking in the derby, this time for stupidly kicking the ball away, Wayne Rooney has been called up to the England squad for the upcoming games against Macedonia and Liechtenstein. While I'm happy for him that he's getting international recognition I'd much prefer him to be safely tucked up in Croxteth instead of risking injury playing for a country whose press have been less than supportive of him lately. Irked by Everton's policy of not allowing him to talk to reporters for the time being, some sectors of the media have taken it upon themselves to portray the seventeen-year-old as some sort of ignorant, fat thug. To anyone with any sense he is obviously just a shy young lad who is freakishly good at football. Surely he doesn't need to have photos taken of him and his family on the beach, or even more bizarrely, reporters asking chippy owners just what meals he eats. That last particular piece of insightful journalism was from the *Sunday Mirror* - a story entitled 'Wayne Ballooney'.

If it's true that we get the press we deserve, then Britain must be populated by a right shower of thick twats.

September

Join Our Club

Monday September 1st 2003

Transfers are like buses. You wait forever for them and then they all come at once… and you can never be quite sure whether you've got on the right one. Or something like that.

With just one day to secure new players the whole transfer situation goes mental and, as events unfold, I can't help imagining scenes reminiscent of Orson Welles' 1938 *War of the Worlds* broadcast, with pensive looking Evertonians everywhere gathered around their wireless sets.

At breakfast time - or 'early doors' as it's known in football parlance - it's revealed that the Francis Jeffers deal has indeed been resurrected and he will be back with us for at least a year-long loan.

Slightly more surprising is that we have one outgoing player, Mark Pembridge, who rejoins his old Welsh teammate Chris Coleman at Fulham. Perversely, Pembridge has been having one of his best spells since he's been with us, thanks mainly to the fact that he's been deployed in the centre of midfield instead of stuck out wide. Admittedly his style of play and scuttling run have never been the most pleasing on the eye, but you couldn't ask for a more wholehearted player, and one who can deliver a mean dead-ball too. But, when you're in our position, half a million pounds or so can't be sniffed at, especially for a player in his thirties.

All day there are rumours that we're still trying to get Robbie Savage and that he's desperate to play for Everton, but the next signing, Motherwell's twenty-year-old striker James McFadden, takes everyone by surprise. We have been linked with him in the past but, as is already quite apparent from this diary, that means little in this day and age.

According to the Motherwell supporters who venture on to the *WSAG* messageboard, and various other people who know a bit about Scottish football, McFadden is the most exciting thing from North of the Border since Owen Paul. They absolutely rave about his ability and think he's a bargain at just over a million pounds, although there are some questions over his attitude and temperament. Some photos on the internet show him sporting a selection of Freddie Ljungberg-style wacky haircuts; if he wants that sort of thing to be tolerated in Walton then he will have to be every bit as good as Pat Nevin and Dominik Diamond reckon.

Everyone seems genuinely excited by the capture of the young Scot, but the mood is dampened somewhat by yet another deal that is announced with only twenty minutes to go before the deadline.

Kevin Kilbane, Sunderland's left-winger, is the final addition to the squad, sparking outrage on the various Everton websites. To be fair to Kilbane, the last time I saw him play was at Goodison when he scored a cracker, and I've not really seen much more of him to make a fair judgement. However, the Sunderland fans despised him and some Irish Evertonians on the website are absolutely traumatised, saying that it's bad enough watching him for their country without having to see him at Goodison as well.

It doesn't exactly bode well. However, he's our player now, and David Moyes must rate him, so he should at least be given a chance to show what he can do. My worry is that the first thing he does wrong will be greeted with the patented 'Goodison groan' and a resounding cry of "I told you he was shit" and we'll have yet another Niclas Alexandersson on our hands.

So, four new players in, although no new central midfielder. We've certainly got more options up front now, an embarrassment even, and Richard Wright will have to improve if he's going to keep the ever-dependable Nigel Martyn out of the side. But only time will tell how Moyes plans to use these new players and just how much they will improve us.

Tuesday 2nd September 2003

David Moyes confirms that he hopes to be going back to sign Sean Davis when the transfer window re-opens on January 1st. He also says that he knows he has Bill Kenwright's full backing.

Thursday 4th September 2003

Whilst doing a bit of shopping in Liverpool city centre I can't help but notice that the Prada-clad, 'no visible means of income' brigade, who frequent the menswear emporiums and coffee-shops of Cavern Walks, are all engrossed in the *Echo*'s cover story concerning John Hyland. The big news is that the local boxing promoter has been arrested and charged with blackmailing Wayne Rooney's agent, Paul Stretford.

A couple of months ago the Sunday newspapers reported that Stretford was being put under pressure from individuals wanting a share of the spoils that his company, Proactive Sports Management, are set to make from handling the young starlet.

According to a crime journalist I spoke to a while ago this sort of thing is rife in football - after all there's a lot of easy money to be had in the murky and unregulated arena of the transfer market. Add to this the fact that players have plenty of cash and spend a lot of time in nightclubs and it's little surprise that 'well-known local businessmen' have become an intrinsic part of the whole football world.

He went on to tell me about the Premiership star who apparently owns a chain of brothels back in his home country. Now there's something they don't talk about on *Soccer AM*.

Friday 5th September 2003

The *Daily Post* shows a picture of Liverpool's El Hadji Diouf entering Glasgow Sheriff's Court to face charges arising from his spitting at Celtic fans during last season's UEFA Cup game at Parkhead. He is wearing what can only be described as a brown polyester suit, replete with big pockets on the kecks, as well as a hooded top and a pair of brown Puma bumpers.

WHAT'S OUR NAME? EVERTON!

The Sheriff, or whoever, should lock him up and throw away the key for his crimes against fashion if nothing else.

To my shock and horror there is a book coming out entitled 'Wayne Rooney - The Story of Football's Wonder Kid'. Jesus wept, he's only seventeen. It was bad enough having to endure the horrible documentary that Sky made about him at the end of last season. The book's written by curly-haired hack, Harry Harris, as well. What a thought-provoking tome it promises to be.

Saturday 6th September 2003

After shopping for wedding rings, crates of ale and party quiches in the morning, I feign an injury so as to be allowed to go home and lie on the couch for what promises to be a feast of international football. The qualifiers for Euro 2004 are reaching the crucial stages now and all the home nations are being featured on the telly.

Scotland are first up and they manage to make hard work of a home game against the nine foot fishermen of the Faroe Islands. After getting over my initial shock at the sight of Stevie Crawford's sidies, I realise that I've never set eyes on half of the Scotland players before now.

One who is familiar is Barry Ferguson and on this showing he demonstrates that you don't get a great deal for £7 million these days. Were we really ready to blow our whole transfer budget on him? A player with any sort of class about him should dominate against the likes of the Faroes, but Ferguson looks very ordinary. Maybe he's just having an off day, but his midfield partner, Colin Cameron of Wolves, looks a better player.

In the second half our new signing, James McFadden, comes on and scores a tap-in to make it 3-1 and seal the victory.

I then catch half an hour of the Republic of Ireland against Russia and only see enough of Kevin Kilbane to note that if nothing else he's quite energetic. I'm feeling in a glass-is-half-full mood.

Next up is England away to Macedonia, with Wayne Rooney up front alongside rugby-ball head, Michael Owen. The first half is shocking, with Macedonia scoring a comical goal and England humping the ball anywhere.

The television pictures show Emile Heskey lining up with Owen to kick off in the second half so I assume that Rooney's been hawked off. It wouldn't have been a surprise if he had, as he must have touched the ball three times in the first period. However, to my surprise he's still on, deployed in a sort of free role at the expense of Frank Lampard.

Early in the half David Beckham, the only player to look anything like world class, knocks forward a long ball that Heskey heads down to the edge of the box. Rooney, making a run from deep, connects with it first time and slots in the bottom corner.

I must confess to a whoop and a holler.

That goal makes Rooney the youngest-ever scorer for England - at this rate Harry Harris is going to need a bigger safe for his royalties.

I am genuinely made up for Rooney, but when I see him play for England it does stir feelings of jealousy. I want him all for us, for Everton, I don't want Halifax fatties in Burberry caps chanting his name. On the other hand I also get annoyed when he gets criticised for having a bad game for his country, usually by Southampton fans who see his every error as further proof that farmhand James Beattie should be the England number nine.

The replay shows that the Macedonian keeper would have saved the shot had he deigned to actually stick his hand out, but nevertheless the kid scored and yet again made history. The papers will like him again for a few days now, and most of them will probably ignore the fact that apart from the goal he didn't have a very good game at all.

The final game of the day is the best, with Mark Hughes' Wales facing Italy in the San Siro. The match eventually ends up 4-0 to the magnificent Azzurri, but for most of the first half the Welsh have them worried.

Unlike England, Wales have no delusions of grandeur; they play to their strengths and, a bit like Everton, know that they must work hard to bridge the gap between themselves and the more star-studded sides. Robbie Savage encapsulates that work ethic as much as anyone, but I must admit that for the second time today I feel slightly relieved that we missed out on a player. For a supposed hard man, Savage simply can't tackle. He spends most of the game barging into the back of players and giving away the stupidest free-kicks. Eventually he picks up the inevitable booking that will see him miss Wales' next game. He's an idiot, worse than Gravesen.

By the time all the football's finished the couch has a me-shaped indentation in it, like the one Wile E Coyote leaves in the canyon floor when he's fallen off a cliff.

Sunday 7th September 2003

Apparently a couple of Nationwide League clubs want to take Duncan Ferguson on loan. Ipswich will be one - Joe Royle's the manager there and Ferguson enjoyed his best spell at Everton when he was in charge.

Would he go though? If he's as disinterested in football as some say then there's no chance he's going to put himself out to play in a lower league, especially if it's for a club at the other end of the country.

Redmond, a lover of the sleazy Sundays, tells me that one paper's featuring a fashion shoot with Wayne Rooney's girlfriend, Colleen McLoughlin.

Sweet baby Jesus and the orphans.

Monday 8th September 2003

The only story that's more reliable than a link to Dickson Etuhu is the groundshare one. This time the 'debate' has been sparked off by a suggestion from the North West Development Agency that the city's sporting facilities need improving ahead of the 2008 City of Culture shenanigans, and that a shared football ground for Everton and Liverpool would make sense.

We all know it makes sense, financial sense at least, to pool resources and have one stadium that's more efficiently utilised, but since when has football been just about what makes sense?

If you take the financial prudence argument to its logical conclusion, wouldn't it make more sense to merge teams altogether and have just the one Merseyside Uber-outfit with seventy or eighty thousand for every home game?

I don't want to share with them, or anyone else for that matter, and I don't give two hoots whether it works fine in Milan or not. Football's about identity, and despite the Sky generation's attempts to make matchgoing a generic experience - "look at us in our near-identical replica kits singing the same songs as you in our faceless concrete bowl next to a Toys R Us in some fucking retail park 'just off the motorway'" - some of us would like our clubs to retain their sense of individuality.

Tuesday 9th September 2003

The unique stadium that is Goodison hosts the England under 21s' make or break European Championships qualifier against Portugal. It's only a tenner to get in but due to personal reasons, i.e. overwhelming apathy, I elect not to go, preferring to watch it from the comfort of the couch instead.

It's meant to be the game where Francis Jeffers nets the winner back on home turf and breaks Alan Shearer's under 21s scoring record. However, they lose 2-1 and feel mightily aggrieved that the late winner comes off Helder Postiga's arm. In truth, just like the Croatians, the Portuguese look miles ahead of England in terms of technique and awareness. If they hadn't insisted on showboating they could have won much more comfortably.

Jeffers works hard, but I still have my doubts about whether he is genuinely top class.

Wednesday 10th September 2003

My best man, Chris, offers to meet me in Liverpool city centre for a couple of pints in the afternoon, our last chance to have a few before I get married. We set up camp in the excellent La'Go and, at £1.30 a pint, a couple rather predictably turns into a few, then into a load and on to a skin-full. We must be bevvied as Chris, a cycling fan of all things, even agrees to walk up to another pub, the Brewery, to watch England versus Liechtenstein on their big screen.

It ends up being Wayne Rooney's most impressive performance for England to date - I just wish I could remember it properly. Sven-Goran Eriksson plays him in that phoney 'behind the front two' position favoured by the Nick Barmbys and Nigel Cloughs of this world - players too slow for up front and too weak for midfield - but against a bunch of part-timers Rooney has a field day. While James Beattie lumbers about hopelessly and even David Beckham and Michael Owen struggle - this is what I was told afterwards anyway - everything Rooney does oozes class.

Through the haze I do recall him whipping in a cross from the left that Beckham poked on to the post, and also nonchalantly chesting a pass about twenty yards to a teammate. Then, early in the second half, after Owen opens the scoring, Rooney meets a Steven Gerrard header first time and drills a low shot through a crowd of players and into the net for his second international goal in less than a week.

He leaves the pitch on sixty-nine minutes to a rapturous ovation from the full house at Old Trafford.

I fall over.

Thursday 11th September 2003

West Ham have taken Niclas Alexandersson on a month's loan. If I had a penny for every person who said, "Do they want to take that fucking Nyarko as well?" I'd have about 7p.

And in the wake of yesterday's game, Harry Harris is rumoured to have put a deposit down on Tokyo.

Friday 12th September 2003

While running around trying to sort out caterers and florists and all that wedding cack, I get a phone call from the *Daily Post* asking for my reaction to a poll they ran asking would people be willing to accept a groundshare scheme. The results of their rather unscientific survey indicated that 47% would, while 53% are, like me, appalled by the notion.

They want to know whether I'm surprised that it was so close. To be honest, I'm not. Once people accepted the notion of moving away from Goodison - to our very own state of the art Mega-Colisseum on the Mersey - then a big taboo was broken and the way was paved for any manner of schemes.

Nowadays, many modern fans seem only too willing to accept the idea that their clubs are solely businesses, and we all know there's no room for sentiment in business. Therefore, if there's a promise of increased revenue then sod it, discard years of history and sell your soul to the highest bidder, all in the hope of what? Maybe playing in the tiresome Champions League?

I accept that improvements need to be made to Goodison, and I eventually even got my head around the idea of the Kings Dock, which was sold to us as such a magnificent once-in-a-lifetime opportunity, but you have to draw the line somewhere.

In my opinion, sharing a stadium with Liverpool would be the death knell for Everton. We, the fans, keep going to watch them, despite their lack of success since the mid-eighties, because we have a bond that draws us to Goodison. And when times have been really tough - when we've faced relegation with absolutely shocking teams - those fans have rallied around, made the ground a bear-pit and played a huge part in keeping us in the top division.

Would that happen if we played in some neutral concrete bowl somewhere, with the cleaners on standby at the final whistle to get the place spick and span for Liverpool's midweek UEFA cup tie against Slovan Obscure?

At just what point do we stop being Everton? Will it be when a mobile phone company offers us £10 million to play in orange perhaps? "Hey, we could get a quality midfielder with that money…"

Football is all about sentiment; if it weren't then we'd all support Manchester United.

Saturday 13th September 2003

"It was the happiest day of my life" is only slightly less sickly than "You'll understand when you have kids of your own, it changes everything", but it's true. Janice Campbell becomes Janice O'Brien and, ever the japester, my Grandad, keeps shaking his head and whispering to me, "Everton are two down already" despite the fact the game is more than two hours from kick-off.

By three o'clock my dad simply can't contain himself any longer and has to go indoors and switch the telly on to watch that Sky Sports live update thing while everyone else loosens their ties, takes off their new shoes and gets merrily pissed in the garden.

By the time I've finished charging around refilling glasses and smiling for photographs with people I'm sure have just walked in off the street, Newcastle are 2-1 up at Goodison and both sides are down to ten men.

I sit down with my Dad to watch the last five minutes and he fills in the details. Rooney, the all-conquering idol of English football, is off injured, the referee Rob Styles is going mental, booking everything that moves, including substitute Duncan Ferguson for aggressive pogoing, Laurent Robert has been dismissed for two soft bookings, Gary Naysmith for a professional foul, Alan Shearer has scored two penalties and Tomasz Radzinski has slotted for us.

As he relays all this to me, Sky switches suddenly to Alan McInally at Goodison. "Another penalty," he reports, "and it's to Everton."

With only two minutes to go, Jermaine Jenas had bundled Radzinski over in the box and the man to take the kick in the absence of David Unsworth is none other than big Duncan.

I groan, he's bound to miss against his old club and the Geordies will take great delight in pointing out what a big piss-taking waste of money he is and always has been.

"He steps up," says McInally, and before he can relay the outcome of the kick the crowd behind him erupt. The highlights later show Ferguson confidently striding up, doing a little Aldridge shuffle and then smashing the ball into the top corner. The man 'the insider' reckons doesn't care any more looks mightily pleased as he runs to the Gwladys Street Stand, hiking up the sleeve of his shirt and pointing to his Everton tattoo.

At the night do, all my mates - who I had considerately not invited to the ceremony so as to save them the bother of making excuses so they could sneak to the game - reckon that it was awful. Neither side played any football and Styles, who handed out eleven yellow cards as well as the two reds, apparently gave the most inept refereeing performance seen at Goodison for a long time.

Sunday 14th September 2003

While going through the wedding cards in the morning one immediately stands out, having a load of signatures on it. At first glance I don't recognise any of the names until I see that the first one, in the same handwriting as the best wishes message, is that of David Moyes. It turns out that my mate Alan Welsh, bass player of Liverpool indie outfit the Sunday Drivers, had sent the Everton manager the card and a stamped addressed envelope and asked him to sign it for me. He in turn got the players to sign it as well.

I'm like a little kid; how nice a gesture is that?

For the record, Leon Osman and Nigel Martyn have got impeccable handwriting, but I don't remember us signing anyone called Usgfe Kloo or FkloP Zaanbak.

Monday 15th September 2003

Jan and I fly out to Southern Italy for our honeymoon and a break from football. As our coach drives through Naples, the Thomsons rep points out the ominous Mount Vesuvius looming ahead. I'm too knackered to really care, but when I see a load of floodlit seven-a-side matches I'm rubbernecking in a manner normally reserved for unsupported female joggers.

The new trouble and strife just rolls her eyes in dismay.

Saturday 20th September 2003

Everton aren't playing until tomorrow, when they visit the Riverside, but I visit the awful faux-Irish pub, Chaplin's, in Sorrento to catch the day's Premiership scores. Rather alarmingly, Southampton have won 3-1 at White Hart Lane and Birmingham have beaten Leeds at Elland Road thanks to two Robbie Savage goals.

Middlesbrough are yet to win this season, so we really need to be looking at getting a point at the very least from tomorrow's game, otherwise we're going to start losing touch with the other UEFA Cup hopefuls.

Sunday 21st September 2003

We've booked a trip to the island of Capri - where the tour rep reckons we could bump into celebrities such as Steve Spielberg, Michael Douglas and Dale Winton - so I won't even get a chance to watch the Middlesbrough game on the telly.

A couple of years ago, we went on a coach to the Riverside for the televised FA Cup tie where the nation saw us hammered three-nil, a result which finally precipitated the departure of Walter Smith. The team weren't the only ones humiliated that day though, thanks to an incident in Thirsk on the way home.

All the Everton coaches stopped at this little market town to allow their occupants a couple of hours drinking in the pubs on the main square, and as a result there was quite a heavy police presence. As we made our way back to the coach from the cosy warmth of the pub, Ray McKay and I both suffered that peculiar male phenomenon of suddenly wanting a piss as soon as you've walked just far enough for it to be a pain to go back and use the toilets. In time-honoured fashion we nipped down an alleyway - hey, I'm not proud of this - and quickly raised some clouds of steam. Unfortunately, as we re-emerged on to the main street we were followed by two lazy snakes of frothing urine.

"Hey, you there, that's disgusting!" yelled an elderly woman walking with her husband.

She was right of course, so rather than stay and discuss the matter, we just started walking towards our coach.

"Come here!" she shouted, and at that point she started to head towards us.

"Just keep walking," said Ray, and we increased the length of our stride.

Imagine our horror when a glance over the shoulder revealed that our accuser had broken into a run. Situations like these require a rapid assessment of the situation and split-second decision-making, qualities not normally associated with a full day on the ale. I had visions of her grabbing one of us while she tried to attract the attentions of a copper, a brief struggle ensuing and then a fall to the pavement followed by the full shattered hip scenario.

So we legged it.

The lads already on the bus: Alan Welsh, Gid and Redmond initially thought we were being pursued by a mob of knife-wielding Smoggies as we burst on to the car park at full tilt. But that wasn't the end of it though. Not only did we have the shame of being 'run all over Thirsk' by a senior citizen, we then had to duck down in our seats as the old bat dragged some young policeman around, peering in the windows trying to find us.

Happy days.

Monday 22nd September 2003

We return from honeymoon and I watch a video of the Middlesbrough game despite knowing that we dipped one-nil.

The first half is appalling as we struggle to cope with the world-renowned strike partnership of Malcom Christie and goalscorer Joseph Desire-Job. Alan Stubbs looks like he's running in sand most of the time while at the other end the frustrated Wayne Rooney is constantly remonstrating with the referee.

There's a vast improvement in the second half, when we completely dominate possession but still fail to create many clear-cut opportunities. The only bright spots are the performances of the late substitutes, Duncan Ferguson and James McFadden. The new addition to the squad is only on for ten minutes, but even in that short time he beats the fullback more times than Kevin Kilbane did in the previous eighty. We've all vowed to give the ex-Sunderland boo-boy a chance but it's already apparent why few fans have a good word to say about him.

In injury time, David Moyes and ruddy-faced Boro manager Steve McLaren almost go toe to toe on the touchline. It's far and away the most exciting incident of the game.

WHAT'S OUR NAME? EVERTON!

Tuesday 23rd September 2003

This ground share thing is still rumbling on - it looks like this time there's more substance to the idea than when it's been mooted in the past. From what I can gather, both Liverpool and Everton need a large amount of public funding to complete any stadium move of their own. The NWDA and the local council seem to be intimating that they would release funds for one big, prestigious stadium but not two separate, presumably smaller ones. From their point of view that makes sense, especially with the whole City of Culture thing looming.

Liverpool's Chief Executive, Rick Parry, is not keen on the idea though, as the Reds are already three years down the line towards building their own new ground in Stanley Park. Let's face it, why do they need us? If a new ground would generate extra revenue from non-football related activities such as concerts and conference facilities then Liverpool are hardly going to be in a rush to split it with Everton.

The silence from Goodison is deafening. With the Kings Dock dead in the water, so to speak, is a shared stadium the only game in town for the Blues?

Wednesday 24th September 2003

Stockport County in the Carling Cup. Even Everton, with their hideous record of upsets in this competition, couldn't make a balls up of this tie against a struggling second division side who have only recently sacked their manager, Carlton Palmer.

Moyes makes a number of changes to the side that played so miserably in the first half against Boro, most notably Nick Chadwick and Duncan Ferguson starting up front and James McFadden replacing the cup-tied Kilbane.

It ends up a straightforward three-nil win, with Ferguson scoring a couple and Chadwick grabbing the other. The star of the show though is McFadden. Granted, the opposition are hopeless, but still the Scot has undoubtedly got talent, most notably exquisite ball control.

The crowd take to him immediately, they love his willingness to get hold of the ball and take people on. The highlight of the night is when he bursts past three defenders down the left and squares the ball for Ferguson to slot the final goal of the night.

Both of them, McFadden and Ferguson, must be certs to start against Leeds on Sunday after their performances tonight and at the weekend.

Thursday 25th September 2003

In possibly the most bizarre news story of the year the *Echo* reveals that Frank Bruno was wandering around Walton, knocking on doors and looking for an old friend, a couple of days before being sectioned under the Mental Health Act. They've even got pictures of the hapless heavyweight posing with little kids in the street.

I'm no Carl Jung, but Bruno's obviously got serious problems given that he apparently thinks he's the jockey Frankie Dettori - has no one tried the 'mirror test' on him? One of the first things I saw when I got back from Italy was the Sun's sympathetic headline 'Bonkers Bruno'. You certainly don't get that quality of journalism in the *Corriere della Serra*.

The reserves triumph 2-1 at Sunderland, with the recovering Kevin Campbell netting. With Duncan Ferguson already looking lean and mean, there's going to be some serious competition for places up front at this rate.

Friday 26th September 2003

James McFadden gives an interview to the official site saying the usual 'they're a great bunch of lads here' and 'the supporters have been great to me' type stuff. He also intimates that he thinks he'll be on the bench on Sunday.

He should start.

Saturday 27th September 2003

We're not playing until tomorrow because, of all things, the bloody Tall Ships are in town and the police don't want to deal with that and a game on the same day.

I end up watching a typically robust Yorkshire derby, Bradford City versus Sheffield United, on the telly. To my great delight the lantern jawed Dean Windass gets sent off in injury time. I dislike most players, but having encountered this ignorant fool in the flesh he is definitely in my top five.

It was during my short-lived career as a DJ when me and my mate played a little gig on a Thursday night in some college near Crewe. We were merrily spinning a few tunes in the bar of this place when a group of blokes, clearly too old to be students, swaggered in, acting as if they owned the place. The fact that they were nearly all wearing flip-flops, shorts and polo shirts with the collars turned up marked them out immediately as professional footballers. Amongst their number were Windass, Peter Schmeichel and the man that many consider the worst ever to don an Everton shirt, Brett Angell.

In fairness to Angell and Schmeichel, who smoked like a nervous beagle, they were pretty quiet and unassuming, but Windass and his coterie of gel-headed sycophants were just downright obnoxious, particularly towards the student bar staff. At one point the ignorant bastard even started clicking his fingers and shouting over to me: "Hey you, play Slim Shady!"

I studiously ignored him until he collared my mate who eventually relented. Half an hour later one of his slimy little mates came over and asked again would I play Slim Shady for Dean.

"We've played it already," I explained.

"Did you?" he asked.

"Yes."

"Oh, can you play it again then?"

Wankers.

We've drawn Charlton at home in the Carling Cup.

Sunday 28th September 2003

The legend 'Champions League Semi-Finalists 2000' emblazoned across the chest of a Leeds United fan's t-shirt tells you all you need to know about today's opponents. Their fans are the worst sort of comedy Yorkshiremen, regaling us with all the old favourites such as 'You'll Never Get a Job', 'Yarkshire! Yarkshire!', 'You Only Sing When You're Thieving' and even, bizarrely, 'Who's That Dying on the Runway'.

It's strange that all the 'scouse thieves' or 'scouse smackhead' songs and comments always seem to be most popular with supporters from places like Newcastle, Manchester or Leeds. None of them exactly Xanadu themselves.

If the antics of the Leeds supporters are laughable, they are nothing compared to the performance of their team, and in particular their on-loan central defender Roque Junior. In a game where several Everton players give utterly brilliant performances - any one of four could have been man of the match - everyone ends up talking about the Brazilian World Cup winner's embarrassing attempt at impersonating a professional footballer. He is absolutely awful, panicking and lashing the ball anywhere as Everton start the game as if they really mean business.

While Leeds are awful, we, on the other hand, are majestic. Contrary to his comments in the week, James McFadden continues on the left and, if anything, plays even better than he did against Stockport, tormenting two or three Leeds players at a time with his pace and mazy dribbling.

Duncan Ferguson is also outstanding. Nobody ever expected to see him play like this again. He wins everything in the air, which you expect, but his all-round play is reminiscent of when he first arrived at Everton from Rangers - he looks sharp and hungry and, quite simply, awesome.

As for Steve Watson, well, for a full-back converted to a winger he doesn't do too badly at all, scoring a remarkable hat-trick.

His first comes as something of a relief, after nearly half an hour of spurned chances. Usually when a team are so wasteful in front of goal they start to lose a bit of momentum and allow the opposition back into the game, but thankfully Tomasz Radzinski pressures Roque Junior into a mistake that allows Watson to play a one-two with Ferguson before smashing an angled volley into the top corner of Paul Robinson's net.

Less than ten minutes later he scores his second, the pick of the bunch. McFadden, in a tight spot near the Everton penalty area, turns away from Jermaine Pennant and launches a peach of a pass downfield for the ever-willing Radzinski to chase. Robinson, one of the best keepers in the league, rushes out of his area to clear but mis-kicks the ball towards Watson on the edge the centre-circle. The 'genial Geordie' looks up and sends it back goalwards with a first time chip that sails in a lazy arc over the back-tracking keeper and finds the bottom corner of the net in a most satisfying fashion.

Then, five minutes before the interval, with the whole side brimming with confidence, Tony Hibbert knocks the ball past Lamine Sakho before floating a perfect cross to the far post. Duncan Ferguson, charging in like some unstoppable force of nature, almost bursts the net with his header. Again the shirt comes off as he celebrates and the crowd burst into a chorus of a song that brings back so many great memories. It's cheesy as anything, but I defy any Evertonian to not feel a swell of emotion when they hear 'Duncan, Duncan Ferguson' being belted out to the tune of gay anthem 'Go West'.

Peter Reid makes a triple substitution in the second half but amazingly Roque Junior stays on the field. Mark Viduka manages to force one save from Nigel Martyn, but that is the sum total of the Leeds attacks. Less than ten minutes in and Watson completes his hat-trick, controlling a deep ball from Unsworth on his head and then sending a lob over Robinson and into the net from an almost impossibly tight angle.

A badly dressed Leeds fan makes a pathetic attempt at a pitch invasion while the rest of the wacky funsters start singing 'We're going to win 5-4'. That's the sort of behaviour you expect from the likes of Derby County, who Leeds will surely be playing next season barring some sort of miracle.

What makes Everton's performance all the more impressive is that for all but the last twenty minutes the England number nine is only on the bench. When he does get a run out, Wayne Rooney almost scores with his first touch, forcing a great save from Robinson with a powerful volley. Then, in the final minute, he finds himself clean through but pauses to check that the linesman's flag isn't raised before dragging his shot narrowly wide.

In Orry's wine bar (it's sound, but not nearly as grandiose as the name suggests) after the game, Weavers reveals that he had a fiver on us to win 5-0, at odds of 40 to 1.

"You must be gutted with Rooney's miss then," says Ray McKay.

"What miss?" asks Weavers.

"The one at the death when he was clean through."

"Oh, I left a couple of minutes before the end." There's a long pause and a slow furrowing of the brow. "The little twat!"

Monday 29th September 2003

David Moyes is full of praise for the team following yesterday's game, hailing it the most creative performance since he's been in charge. He singles out Steve Watson, obviously, and also Duncan Ferguson. He notes that it was pleasing to see the team getting good crosses in to him and varying their play rather than just humping long balls towards him as they have done in the past.

Tuesday 30th September 2003

The Sun have run a story alleging that eight Premiership footballers raped a seventeen-year-old girl in a London hotel at the weekend. The amount of potentially libellous speculation on the messageboards of the Rivals network - the people who host the *WSAG* website - led the company to take the rather drastic measure of shutting all their football sites down overnight to avoid the chance of any legal repercussion.

Serious stuff.

October

Safe European Home

Wednesday 1st October 2003

Kevin Campbell is not only celebrating his return to fitness, he is also apparently chuffed at being the first professional footballer to own a record label. His is the woefully named '2 Wikid Records', and their first star signing is Leicester's very own R and B legend, Mark Morrisson. Remember him, the handcuff-sporting weirdo who sang *Return of the Mack* and then got sent down for trying to take a stun gun on an aeroplane?

Another slightly lesser-known pop phenomenon, Alan Welsh, is trying to sort out the transport for Saturday's away game at Spurs. There are six of us again and the man with the van is on holiday, so our self-appointed head of logistics has got his work cut out.

Thursday 2nd October 2003

Since Leeds United's Sunday thrashing at Goodison, their manager, Peter Reid, has been the subject of much press speculation concerning his future at the club. In a bizarre twist, their eccentric-looking chairman, Professor John McKenzie, has said that Reid won't be sacked, and that the board have reached that decision after consultation with the fans.

Now just how realistic is that little scenario? Is it not more likely that they had a look at how much compensation they'd have to pay to Reid, on the back of what they've shelled out to Terry Venables and David O'Leary, and the fact that no one with any sense - and certainly no one actually in a job - would be willing to replace him?

Even if a club did want to include fans in decision-making processes, how would you actually go about it? Which ones do you ask? Fanzine writers and supporters club organisers perhaps? What makes them qualified to decide stuff on behalf of 'the fans' per se? Personally I'd be mortified if, for instance, Everton wanted my advice on an important matter. I'd hope that my club is run by people who are better informed and cleverer then me.

Friday 3rd October 2003

We've narrowly avoided a Saturday morning stand-off - the one that we have when we see who cracks first and agrees to jockey - as Alan has booked us a people carrier and he's the only one insured to drive it. These things cost a fortune to hire normally, but he's got a special offer that works out at thirty pounds each, including juice. Not bad, all things considered.

Saturday 4th October 2003

Now this is the way to travel.

We look like Aerosmith or Big Brother contestants as we're whisked up the motorway in our brand spanking new, tinted-windowed Volkswagen seven-seater. With a case of Fosters left over from my wedding, numerous newspapers, Echo and the Bunnymen on the stereo and a bag of sarnies, we are indeed living la vida loca as Alan wellies it towards London and a Wetherspoons in Edmonton that is showing the Liverpool versus Arsenal game.

You can say what you like about the soulless McPub atmosphere of the JD Wetherspoon chain, but when it comes to drinking in London they are veritable oases of reasonable pricing. Hence they are always chocker, and this gaff on Tottenham High Road is no exception. We're only in there for five minutes, taking the first sips from our student union-style plastic pint glasses, when ninety per cent of the clientele go mental, cheering Harry Kewell's sweetly struck opener at Anfield.

WHAT'S OUR NAME? EVERTON!

Twenty minutes later though, the other ten per cent of us get some evil stares as we applaud Sammi Hyypia's unlucky own goal at the other end. All's well though, as by the time Robert Pires curls home a delightful winner for the Gunners we're already deep in conversation with the Tottenham grocks who had looked ready to lynch us. They're rather ominously predicting that we'll thrash them, basically because Spurs are without a manager since Glenn Hoddle got sacked while Everton, on the other hand, are on the back of that champagne football display against Leeds.

Sacking Hoddle might work in their favour though. If he was still around then the players, who obviously didn't like him, would continue to lack motivation, and the fans would be more willing to get on their backs. Also, bear in mind the fact that we've not won here in the league since 1985 and you can see why, although we're all quietly confident, none of us Evertonians think the result is a foregone conclusion.

However, we stagger down towards the Lane knowing that, with Liverpool beaten, a win will take us level in the table with our dear neighbours.

For some reason there seem to be hundreds of police around the ground, and behind one turnstile there is apparently even a sniffer dog on drugs duty. The poor canine must be going berserk, given the number of Evertonians who need artificial stimulants to get them through ninety minutes nowadays. There is a school of thought that says the explosion of drug use at Everton games coincided with the reign of Walter Smith and some of the most boring football the School of Science has ever endured. Whether that's true or not, it's undeniable that the stench of skunk and the sight of gangs of runny-nosed lads crammed into toilet cubicles are as much a part of the modern matchday experience as bobble hats and Bovril were in more innocent times.

Instead of leaping all over glassy-eyed teenagers though, perhaps the dog would have been better employed in the Everton changing rooms, searching for the big stash of Temazepam the team appear to have ingested prior to kick-off. How else can their shocking performance be explained?

Again, as against Liverpool and Middlesbrough, opponents who have been struggling badly cannot believe their luck as we afford them far too much time and space to knock the ball about and steady their nerves. As we approach the interval, the likes of Robbie Keane, Darren Anderton and the seventy-five year old Gus Poyet are finding absolutely acres of space in midfield.

I'm halfway down the stairs, hoping to beat the queue for a drink when, unchallenged, Poyet cushions a header towards Frederic Kanoute who lets the ball bounce once before thrashing a thirty-five yard screamer into Nigel Martyn's top left-hand corner. It's a magnificent strike, but how were they allowed so much space in the build up? Lee Carsley and Thomas Gravesen looked so solid in the middle of midfield against Leeds - it looked like we'd finally found our best combination in that troublesome area - but here they're not even getting close to their opposite numbers.

Our one hope as we sip our half-time tea - no ale for away supporters at Tottenham - is that Moyes will work his now customary magic and we'll see a more purposeful Everton in the second half.

Before we've even taken our seats, however, Poyet glances home a header from the edge of the box to make it two to Spurs. And while the inquest goes on into that body blow, Robbie Keane finds a massive hole in the centre of our defence, tears the back out of David Unsworth, and then pokes the ball into the bottom corner of the net.

That's three goals in six minutes. More than a handful of people take that as their cue to get out and beat the traffic. What a bargain: £34 for less than fifty minutes of football.

The ineffectual James McFadden and Tomasz Radzinski make way for Kevin Kilbane and Wayne Rooney with just over half an hour to go, but they're fighting a lost cause by this point. To Rooney's credit he looks like the one player who will not accept such a defeat lying down, but all his charging about does is get him increasingly wound up until, red faced and snarling, he ends up giving referee Dermot Gallagher little choice but to book him for dissent.

It's rare that we leave a game before the final whistle, but when some Evertonians start making the whole afternoon even more depressing with their spiteful gas chamber hissing we decide to make this an exception.

We cut dejected figures as we trudge back to the people mover and hardly anyone speaks other than to make the standard observation that applies in these situations: "Another great afternoon ruined by Everton."

Sunday 5th October 2003

David Moyes' quotes in the papers are brutally honest, as ever. He basically says that there were no positives to be taken from yesterday's game. Not only did we lose, but Alan Stubbs and Duncan Ferguson both picked up groin strains as well.

The only happy news is that, according to the *Sunday People*, Wayne Rooney's gone and got engaged to his long-standing girlfriend, 'the lovely Colleen', as she is now known in the press.

"Engaged? At seventeen? With all that money? Is he fucking mad?" comments my father, the old romantic.

Monday 6th October 2003

'Kop Star Shot' screams the *Liverpool Echo*. The star in question is none other than Jon Otsemobor. No, none of the Liverpool supporters have heard of him either.

The young defender, with one first team appearance to his name, received slight injuries to his arse, while two of his mates were more seriously wounded, when some loon opened fire in the infamous Slater Street. Imagine Matthew Street's sinister cousin - less hen nights from Clitheroe and more shaven-headed psychotics from Huyton - and you'll get the picture.

It's just the latest in a series of crazy incidents in the city centre in the last few weeks, although shootings are almost passé these days. You see, Liverpool has an uncanny knack of always going one better than everywhere else, with gangland figures recently blowing up a car outside the 051 club and throwing a nail bomb into Dickie Lewis' Pub. They'll be carpet-bombing Bold Street and sending smackhead suicide bombers into the Newz Bar next. Just you see.

Tuesday 7th October 2003

Ahead of England's Euro 2004 qualifier in Istanbul on Saturday all the experts in the papers and on the radio are debating whether Wayne Rooney has the right temperament to play. This is all because he received his fifth yellow card of the season on Saturday. Given his last two performances for England, for whom he's never even looked like getting booked, it seems highly unlikely that Sven-Goran Eriksson will drop him.

The same pundits who complain about referees giving cards out like confetti are the ones trying to make out that Rooney is some sort of wild-eyed maniac.

One player Eriksson won't even be considering though, is Rio Ferdinand. The breaking story has it that he failed to take a random drugs test - he says he forgot - and as far as the FA are concerned that's a doping offence even though he did produce a negative sample thirty-six hours later. He could face a two-year ban.

Wednesday 8th October 2003

Girls Aloud! The world's gone mad.

There's still an ongoing investigation into the alleged gang rape by a group of Premiership footballers - whose names everyone knows but are too scared of litigation to mention - and now two Leeds United players are apparently being questioned about another serious sexual assault.

Given all this, it probably wasn't particularly wise of the England squad to threaten to go on strike in support of Rio Ferdinand. 'Ill-judged' is putting it mildly as the radio phone-ins go berserk with people wanting to know just exactly who these players think they are. Pampered, spoilt and arrogant are just some of the words being used to describe them - I just can't believe it's taken people this long to notice.

They'll never strike though. Solidarity is one thing, but as soon as they realise that failure to play against Turkey will cost them their international careers, and therefore millions of pounds in endorsements, it will be a unanimous "Fuck Rio".

And top it all, as you don't get much madder than this, Arnold Schwarzenegger has been voted governor of California.

Thursday 9th October 2003

Fancy that, the players decided not to strike after all, and instead released some whining, wheedling statement about how they feel disappointed with the FA but don't want to let down their magnificent fans, especially as Rio rang them and begged them to play.

Behave. They realised that public opinion was against them and that they had backed themselves into a corner. After years of living under New Labour rule the British public are spin-savvy enough to see right through this damage limitation exercise.

Meanwhile, Leeds United have suspended the horrible Jody Morris. How bad can things get there? Peter Reid must be wishing that he'd been given the sack after all.

Back at the ranch, it's not good news for Everton, as Alan Stubbs' groin strain is serious and will see him out for at least a month. Alessandro Pistone's also having surgery on a hernia, meaning he will be out even longer. The Italian is the only Everton player that gets called 'sicknote' by Duncan Ferguson.

David Weir will now return to the first team in Stubbs' place. Hopefully he will start playing better than he did when he came on as sub on Saturday, as he was utter cack.

Friday 10th October 2003

Everton's accounts for the year have been leaked and, depending on who you listen to or how you interpret the figures, the club are either slightly in profit or massively in debt. As far as I can see though, the fact that David Moyes has been allowed to recruit new players in the last month would indicate that while we're not Real Madrid, we're not quite on the point of asking players to get two cups from every teabag in the Bellefield canteen just yet.

Saturday 11th October 2003

Thankfully, these are more or less the last of the Euro 2004 qualifying matches. After this weekend the domestic season will get going properly and we'll have a good run of games.

Sky are showing a double-header, starting with Scotland against Lithuania. James McFadden starts on the left with his Everton compatriot Gary Naysmith. There seems to be some SFA rule that dictates that at least one of their players has to have some sort of disturbing facial hair. Against the Faroes it was Steve Crawford's Del Amitri sidies; this time it's Naysmith and a full beard that makes him look something off the cover of a Sven Hassel novel.

Inevitably the Jocks struggle, but the two Everton players combine to set up Manchester United's Darren Fletcher for a late winner that sees them in Monday's draw for the play-offs. I've always had a soft spot for Scotland, as Jan's family are all from up there, and in recent years Everton have had quite a few players representing them.

Next up is the one the nation has been waiting for: England versus Turkey in Istanbul.

Surprisingly, it's the Turkish players who seem most affected by the atmosphere. They seem incapable of playing their normal patient passing game and it's England, with Rooney and Steven Gerrard running the show, who look most like scoring.

Just on the stroke of half-time the tabloids and their xenophobic readers get what they've been longing for. England are awarded a penalty, but the normally reliable David Beckham slips as he takes his run up and balloons his kick ridiculously high and wide. Aston Villa's Ozalan Alpay screams in the England captain's face and a minor fracas breaks out that continues as the players leave the field.

Sky's Geoff Shreeves, speaking in a grave tone normally reserved for state funerals, then reports mayhem in the tunnel.

Despite all this drama there is little incident in the second half and England get the draw that they need to top their group and qualify automatically for the finals in Portugal.

Sunday 12th October 2003

Predictably, Alpay is being cast as some sort of pantomime villain. The consensus from the boneheads who roam the internet and ring the phone-ins is that 'the dirty Turkish scum' should be hounded out of English football. Even ex-players like Dennis Mortimer are saying Villa should sack him.

This country does hysteria better than anyone. Alpay shouted at Beckham and then gave him a poke in the face - big deal. Given the accusations being made about several homegrown Premiership stars at the moment, this is all a little bit rich.

Monday 13th October 2003

Everton have offered a new, improved contract to eighteen-year-old goalkeeper Iain Turner. He only signed from Stirling Albion in January, but David Moyes says he's very pleased with his progress.

And Scotland draw Holland as their opponents in the Euro 2004 play-off. They were a nap to get either them or Spain, not Latvia or Slovenia.

Oh, and *The Sun* award Rooney eleven out of ten for his performance against Turkey, as they have been led to believe that the youngster punched Alpay in the tunnel. Grow up.

Tuesday 14th October 2003

James McFadden has been criticised by the Glasgow police after an incident with a steward at the end of Saturday's game. Despite his reputation as a nutter, he has the public's sympathy in this case as he was apparently trying to fulfil a promise and give his shirt to a little lad with cerebral palsy when the steward stepped in and tried to usher him down the tunnel.

You wouldn't fancy being Rock Steady Security's PR man after a story like that.

Wednesday 15th October 2003

Everton have started looking at players' contracts, with Leon Osman signing a twelve month extension, preliminary talks starting with David Unsworth, and rumours circulating of a new, improved five year deal for Rooney to be sorted before Christmas.

Osman's a great little player, head and shoulders above everyone else in the reserves, but he hasn't really had a sniff of the first team, primarily because of his physique. Unfortunately his exquisite touch and vision are seriously undermined by the fact that he's even skinnier and shorter than Scot Gemmill.

Unsworth, on the other hand, is quite the opposite. While he's often lauded as a 'great servant' and a 'true blue' the fact remains that he is the weak link in our side. He was a cracker when he burst into the side ten years ago: quick, strong and really mobile - for a while he really was the new Kevin Ratcliffe. His career peaked with the 1995 Cup final win though, when he was arguably man of the match, giving the then awesome Mark Hughes one of the hardest games of his career.

Unsworth was called up for one game for England but then suffered a serious injury. After that he piled on weight, lost his pace and never recaptured that early form. He left to go to West Ham for a while and then returned via Aston Villa during Walter Smith's first transfer spree. He's now shifted out to left-back from central defence but, despite his wholeheartedness, he is just too slow and his distribution so inadequate that we can't seriously want to keep him. Redmond refers to him as the benchmark: while he's still getting a game then we really haven't moved forward as far as we'd like to think.

That's seen as heresy in some quarters, due to Unsworth's all-round good bloke persona, but he struggles to hold his own at the top level any more.

The reserves draw 1-1 with West Brom. Francis Jeffers plays after reportedly being laid low with a virus that has also struck Alex Nyarko and Duncan Ferguson. The rumour from my uncle at the weekend was that the reason Jeffers has hardly played since returning is because he was at the wrong end of a beating in town. You hear stuff like that all the time though, especially about the local players.

Friday October 17th 2003

An interview with Chelsea's chief executive, Paul Smith, on Radio 4 is being reported as confirmation that the West Londoners are preparing a bid for Wayne Rooney. How that's possible when he actually uses the words "There are no plans to pursue Rooney, but we never rule anything out or anything in" is beyond me. Elsewhere he says that they never set an upper limit on what they're prepared to pay for the right players. Naturally that is interpreted as 'Chelsea prepared to pay anything to get Rooney'.

David Moyes actually calls the rumours 'shite'.

Saturday October 18th 2003

If we beat Southampton at Goodison tomorrow we will go level with Liverpool as they've lost at Portsmouth, their third straight league reverse. This is usually a bad omen. Whenever we have the chance to catch them we almost invariably make a balls of it.

Sunday October 19th 2003

Well then, can we break with tradition and take advantage of Liverpool's recent poor form and catch them in the league? Our record against the Saints at Goodison is excellent, and they're without the suspended Kevin Phillips, so this is as good a chance as any to take three points.

There's no Wayne Rooney, as he sits the game out with his one match ban, and Duncan Ferguson hasn't recovered from his chest infection either. To make matters worse, at the last minute it's revealed that Tomasz Radzinski has succumbed to a calf strain picked up in training. That leaves us with Kevin Campbell and Francis Jeffers up front - hardly ideal given how little first team football they've played this season.

As there are no fanzines to sell, I take the chance to go and have a drink with my dad before the game. I always have a laugh with him and the motley crew he drinks with in the Albany, the friendliest matchday boozer bar none, but the amount of ale I end up lashing down my neck to keep up with them always leaves the game itself something of a blur.

One of the fellas he drinks with, Tony, was on the train back to Aintree after the Goodison derby last season, seething at the now customary Everton capitulation, when a trio of Liverpudlians started singing some song or other. When he told them to shut up they quite understandably refused, but then one of them made the mistake of standing up and pointing his finger in defiance. A left hook persuaded him to sit back down before all hell broke loose and the four of them ended up grappling in a mad, whirling Sylvester and Tweety Pie type scenario. Luckily for Tony the train pulled into Aintree station as he was beginning to tire, allowing him to break free and make a dash for it.

No one pursued him, so he nipped straight into the toilets of the Old Roan pub to survey his war wounds. To his delight he looked in the mirror and saw only a little cut on his lip and a slightly mussed barnet - a quick wash and a comb had him looking right as rain. Feeling good, he decided to have a quick pint before going home.

As he stood at the bar waiting to be served he became aware of people whispering and casting sidelong glances at him.

"What's up, what are you staring at?" he eventually asked the table of old blokes sitting nearest to him.

"Sorry lad," they replied. "We were just wondering why you've got no back in your shirt. Is it a new fashion or something?"

Two and a half hours of solid boozing later I lurch to the ground, trying to avoid the scores of kids asking for a "Penny for the Guy". Since when did putting an Everton shirt or a Lacoste jumper on a cuddly elephant constitute a Guy? Try telling these little gangsters that though, or even worse, try giving them an actual penny.

It takes only a few minutes of the actual game before it becomes apparent that Southampton aren't going to be the victims of a post-Tottenham backlash. In fact, Sky couldn't have picked a worse game to televise than this - it's absolutely dreadful. Both sides work hard, but there is a desperate lack of imagination or flair. Quite frankly, without Rooney or Radzinski, we look laboured and pedestrian. Jeffers and Campbell graft but they don't look particularly sharp, although they're not helped by the lack of service from the midfield.

When Steve Watson heads wide with the goal at his mercy in the second half, it becomes painfully clear that a point is the best we can expect.

The crowd are getting increasingly restless, particularly with Thomas Gravesen, whose passing is atrocious, although in fairness to the Dane he gets the blame even when his doppelganger, Lee Carsley, makes a mistake.

The final straw comes when, with minutes remaining, the referee, unhappy about a Southampton player's backchat, moves an Everton free-kick to the left hand edge of their box. As the players jostle and manoeuvre in the six-yard box, expecting a low kick into their midst, Gravesen takes a run up like Fred Trueman and thrashes the ball into the top tier of the Bullens Road Stand. There ensues a cacophony of groans and clanking seats as hundreds of punters stand up and walk out in disgust.

Moyes will no doubt be livid again, but his options are very limited. I can see him starting with Rooney at Aston Villa next week though, and then leaving him in the team come what may.

On the way to Orrys for a post-match shandy I search in vain for a cuddly elephant to boot the stuffing out of.

Monday 20th October 2003

The internet is full of anti-Gravesen stuff. The only person in sport less popular is Steve Bartman, that tit who tried to catch the ball and cost the Chicago Cubs a place in the World Series. The Dane isn't playing well, but he gets more stick than his teammates as he's the one who looks for the ball even when we're struggling. There's any number of players who go missing or pass the buck yet continually escape the wrath of the crowd because, by being so unadventurous, they avoid making any obvious, glaring errors.

And while we're on the subject of whipping boys, Niclas Alexandersson has turned down the chance to extend his loan spell with West Ham. He basically says he's happy to fanny about in Everton's reserves for the remainder of the season before returning to Sweden.

Wednesday 22nd October 2003

We're once again linked with a £5 million move for Scott Parker. The *WSAG* website is full of offers from Evertonians to display assorted parts of their anatomies in various shop windows if that deal ever materialises.

Another one of our forgotten men, Alex Nyarko, scores a thirty-yard Bobby Dazzler for the reserves away to Birmingham. No doubt he would rather have been indoors watching Rangers lose one-nil to Manchester United in the Champions League though.

Friday 24th October 2003

Wayne Rooney is eighteen today. He can no longer be referred to as 'the boy' or 'the kid'.

Some eyebrows have been raised about the party he's got planned next week. It's apparently going to be a 'star-studded' affair. That normally means Claire Sweeney, Atomic Kitten and a load of people from Hollyoaks will be attending. Oh, and Jennifer Ellison wearing next to nothing of course.

Saturday 25th October 2003

Everton versus Aston Villa, at either Goodison or Villa Park, is traditionally one of the dullest fixtures in the top flight calendar, so we don't expect too much as we set off for Birmingham at the ridiculously early hour of 10.30 am. It's Ray McKay's thirty-first birthday so it's been decided that we'll get to the Ruskin Hall, a *Phoenix Nights*-type social club near the ground, nice and handy for a good drink. Any excuse.

On the surface, Villa Park is a cracking ground, but the facilities for the away supporters are woefully inadequate. Every time we visit, there are potentially dangerous crushes around the toilets and the one entrance. And they don't serve ale either, which is probably a good thing in this instance.

The grim autumn weather is matched by the miserable fare on the pitch as two desperately mediocre teams struggle to find any inspiration whatsoever. Even the anticipated showdown between Alpay and Wayne Rooney doesn't materialise as the Turkish defender has shamefully milked the tabloid hysteria enough to persuade Villa to cancel his contract, leaving him a free agent.

WHAT'S OUR NAME? EVERTON!

Dion Dublin, for so many years a goalscoring nemesis of ours, has to fill in at centre-half in Alpay's place. You have to give him his due though; he hardly gives Rooney a kick.

Kevin Campbell has Everton's best chance of the first half, connecting with a Gravesen corner only to see the keeper, Thomas Sorensen, tip his header on to the woodwork. At the other end, where Joseph Yobo and David Weir look untroubled by Darius Vassell and the comically bad Juan Pablo Angel, young winger Peter Whittingham looks Villa's biggest threat, especially when he beats Tony Hibbert and lashes a low shot against the foot of Nigel Martyn's far post. Luckily it rebounds to safety and the half ends goalless.

The second period produces more of the same: neither side seems capable of stringing a few passes together and slowing the game down - it's all aimless balls into the corners or hopeful high balls that the keepers deal with comfortably. Everton have probably the best chance to snatch a winner when the hardworking but unspectacular Kilbane finds space on the left and whips a low ball into the Villa penalty area. Rooney's in quickest, sliding at full stretch, but the minimal contact his toe makes with the ball only manages to divert it wide of the far post.

Duncan Ferguson is introduced for the final twenty minutes but he's unable to make any impact as the referee, Andy D'Urso, simply blows his whistle any time the ball goes near him in the air. If he threw himself to the ground like a lot of Premiership strikers he would probably get protection from the referees, but because he stands up and tries to win the ball while being pushed, pulled and obstructed by defenders he gets punished. It's never been any different - if ever a player suffered because of his reputation, it's Ferguson.

When Alan Stubbs, a central defender, replaces Li Tie in midfield for the last ten minutes, it's obvious that even Moyes has settled for a draw.

Despite the inclement weather we see a group of Asian kids playing cricket on a tennis court as we walk back towards the Ruskin Hall, and the scene reminds Redmond of his school days. He tells us about a lad in his year who was from Yorkshire and a really good cricket player. In fact, he actually describes him as a 'ponce', his catch-all label for anyone who doesn't like football. Anyway, this ponce was in the cricket nets one day, practising a few strokes off the PE teacher's bowling while Redmond looked on, bored.

Now every Liverpool school in the eighties had a young PE teacher with a Harry Enfield muzzy and perm combo - an absolute macho prick who thought that the girls all loved him as he strutted about in his Mizuno tracky bottoms and Patrick kagoul. Redmond's school, Saint Francis Xaviers, was no different, and on the occasion in question, their big hairy stud was getting increasingly wound up as the Yorkie ponce kept nonchalantly taking the sting out of his fiercest deliveries and shouting sarcastic encouragement with every flick of his straight bat.

Clunk.

"Nice try sir."

Thwack.

"Come on, try harder."

Snick.

"Is that all you've got sir?"

Crunch.

Redmond looked up as a furious full toss caught the junior Geoff Boycott flush in the kipper, scattering his teeth through silly-mid-on. As he rolled around with blood gushing from his gaping maw, the teacher's first instinct wasn't to race to his aid but over to Redmond, the sole witness, instead.

"Redmond, you saw it, it was an accident."

"What happened?" we ask, enthralled.

"I agreed with him," he replies. "I said I thought it was an accident. I didn't like the little tit anyway. He could have finished him off with a cricket stump and I wouldn't have grassed."

Sunday 26th October 2003

Charlton, our midweek Carling Cup opponents, draw 1-1 with Arsenal on the telly. They don't look bad at all - we'll need to improve a lot if we're to stay in that particular competition. If we go out and then lose at home to Chelsea on the Saturday -

which is feasible - we'll be entering the realms of 'crisis club'. I'm not worried, as like most Evertonians I have complete faith in David Moyes and I think we'll start winning games soon, but I must confess that I've started looking at the teams in the bottom three for the first time this season. We're on ten points after ten games while the teams in eighteenth and nineteenth position are on eight. It only takes another couple of bad weekends for us to slip into that relegation zone, although by the same token a couple of good ones will have us talking about the UEFA Cup again.

Tuesday 28th October 2003
Assistant manager Alan Irvine reckons that Alex Nyarko could be in contention for tomorrow's Carling Cup tie on the back of his recent good form for the reserves.

Wednesday 29th October 2003
Nyarko does indeed play, taking Li Tie's place in the starting line-up. What's more, he receives the biggest cheer of any of the Everton players when his name is read out over the tannoy. It's testament to David Moyes that he will pick the players he thinks are best regardless of their age or their past history, and Nyarko doesn't let him down. Granted, he's not the new Vieira when it comes to tackling back and getting stuck in, but he's comfortable on the ball and the other players pass to him confident that he's not going to give it away cheaply.

As expected, it's an entertaining match, with both sides trying to play good football. Everton have the better possession in the first half, although the visitors have the first clear chance to break the deadlock when a suspiciously offside-looking Jason Euell, our scourge up at The Valley, finds himself unmarked with only Nigel Martyn to beat. Luckily the man who must long for someone to refer to him just once as something other than the big, or amiable, Cornishman, saves the shot with his legs.

Of all the transfer deadline signings, Martyn has been the biggest success story so far. James McFadden looked the superstar in his first two outings but since then, and indeed tonight is a prime example, he has been guilty of dreadful over-elaboration, setting off on crazy dribbles every time he receives the ball. Martyn seems like he's been with us forever; I don't think we've ever felt so reassured by a keeper's presence since the legendary Neville Southall left Goodison.

Up at the other end, the Blues take the lead just before half-time thanks to a most unlikely source: Tobias Linderoth. The Swedish central midfielder is the quiet man of Goodison and something of an enigma. In many ways he's the anti-Gravesen in that there's no questioning his work rate and application when we're defending, but for an international footballer he offers surprisingly little creatively. Sometimes he sits so deep that the central defenders overtake him when they're bringing the ball out, so it's a shock when he's first on hand to head the ball home after Wayne Rooney's volley comes back off the underside of the bar. He can hardly believe it himself and a smile even cracks across his usually deadly serious face as he's given a bear hug by Duncan Ferguson.

The second half opens up even further as the Addicks search for an equaliser, with Euell and Herman Hreidarsson both wasting good opportunities. This leaves them open to the counterattack though and the foot of the post denies Rooney after he plays a clever one-two with Gravesen on the edge of the box.

In the 90th minute Nyarko is replaced by Alan Stubbs, and the Goodison crowd - famed for their harsh cruelty - rise as one to give an ovation to a player who only months ago was looking for a club in China.

There hasn't been a more surprising comeback than this since Pamela Ewing opened that shower door.

We hang on through four minutes of injury time and the punters packed into the Spellow afterwards seem uplifted by the performance as they gather in front of the televisions and await the draw for the last sixteen.

We're last out of the hat: Middlesbrough away.

If ever a draw had no redeeming features it's that one, so I can't say I'm disappointed when Alan Welsh points out that there's every chance we could be in Amsterdam watching Echo and the Bunnymen when it's played.

Thursday 30th October 2003

Everton hold their AGM, where David Moyes reiterates there are no plans to sell Wayne Rooney. Less reassuring is the intimation that we're going to have to sell before we can buy, especially as we were led to believe that Bill Kenwright had the money for Sean Davis safely stashed away in one of them cunning fake tins of soup with the lockable lid. There will be some awkward questions asked if that deal doesn't get resurrected in January.

Sir Philip Carter also reveals that some preliminary talks have been held with Liverpool regarding the proposal of a ground share and that more are to come. The gist of the talks seem to be that they would be interested if the council were to basically pay for the stadium as part of the whole City of Culture thing. That doesn't seem that likely.

When asked about Nyarko, Moyes says that his recent improved performances had merited his inclusion in yesterday's side, but that he still has some way to go before he becomes a first team regular.

Friday 31st October 2003

AFK Gothenburg want to take Niclas Alexandersson off our hands in January. I don't think anybody at Everton is going to try and stand in his way.

November

The Man Who Sold The World

Saturday 1st November 2003

Chelsea at home, and time to see just what you get for £110 million. The West Londoners are second in the league, just behind Arsenal, but for all Roman Abramovich's big spending it's the likes of John Terry, Frank Lampard and Carlo Cudicini, the players who were already there when the Russian arrived, who have been their best and most regular performers so far.

Twice last season we were humiliated 4-1 at Stamford Bridge, in both the league and whatever the league cup was called then, and despite pummelling Chelsea for most of the game at Goodison we still managed to dip 3-1 in a bad-tempered clash. So the portents aren't great, or we're due a result, depending on what mood you're in.

WSAG 104 is on sale today so it's big coats and thermal vests for us hardy souls who stand around the ground hawking our wares while most sensible people are ensconced in the pub. The first thing we do when we've unloaded our boxes of issues is get a cup of tea from the little fast food stand at the corner of Goodison Road and Gwladys Street and catch up on Walton's primitive internet, the graffiti down the side of the Stanley Racing. It's always good to know who this week's most reviled police informer is, and in this instance the accolade goes to a Mr Khan.

We stand outside the ground for over two hours, despite the knowledge that the majority of issues always get sold in the five minutes before kick-off, invariably to impatient drunken men with twenty pound notes. They should learn from the fairer sex, as women invariably have the exact money and buy their copy with plenty of time to spare.

As a result of the late surge we never get to our seats in the Park End before kick-off, to the displeasure of a woman at the end of our row who, for two seasons now, has been rolling her eyes and tutting as five of us do that weak half-smile thing and try to squeeze past her. Little does she know that on occasion we deliberately stagger our entrance so she has to get up five times. We're just mad us.

With the game only thirty seconds old I am just in the process of getting to my seat, and blocking Misery Arse's view, when Thomas Gravesen slides a curling ball into the path of Tomasz Radzinski. John Terry, normally so reliable, misjudges his tackle and leaves the little striker through with only Cudicini to beat. The Italian keeper commits himself and Radzinski could easily take the ball around him, but he elects to shoot for the bottom corner instead.

It goes narrowly wide.

What a chance.

After Wednesday's improved performance against Charlton, Moyes has made only a couple of changes: Kevin Kilbane has replaced the inconsistent James McFadden while Radzinski takes Duncan Ferguson's place alongside Wayne Rooney. Most notably, despite the manager's reservations at the AGM, Alex Nyarko keeps his place in central midfield.

Buoyed by that early opportunity, Everton keep pouring forward, with Chelsea looking anything but title contenders. Kilbane, who seems to have improved immeasurably and is superb throughout, heads over from a Thomas Gravesen free-kick before Rooney has an opportunity to lob a poor Cudicini clearance back towards an unguarded net. Unfortunately, the England number nine can't imitate Steve Watson's effort against Leeds and the ball drifts harmlessly onto the roof of the net.

Nyarko is even better than he was against Charlton, prompting and probing and making the likes of Joe Cole and Claude

Makelele look positively pedestrian. At the midway point he receives a short pass from Rooney thirty yards out, nonchalantly moves it to his right and lets rip with a shot more powerful than the industrial fireworks that the local ninjas use to blow up cars and postboxes at this time of year. Cudicini doesn't even appear to see the ball as it weaves through the air like a toe-bunged Wembley Trophy. In keeping with our luck so far though it smashes against the underside of the crossbar, leaving it shuddering like a tuning fork, and away to safety.

At half-time the Chelsea players look ashen-faced as they head down the tunnel with the game somehow still scoreless.

The second period starts in almost identical fashion to the first, with Gravesen, who is still getting unmerciful abuse from sections of the crowd, slipping another cunning ball through a defender's legs and into the path of Radzinski. Again he's unmarked in the box, but his powerful shot on the turn is close to Cudicini, allowing him to snake out an arm and push it away. It's a great save, but a bit more composure from Radzinski would have left him with no chance.

Less than five minutes later Chelsea take the lead.

Terry is again pressured into hoofing an aimless clearance upfield, but Joseph Yobo and Alan Stubbs, a replacement for the injured David Weir, stand off the strikers, allowing Adrian Mutu to bring the ball down and knock it out wide for Geremi. The ex-Middlesbrough man whips an evil low cross into the six yard box where Tony Hibbert is found ball-watching at the far post. Mutu takes advantage and dives in front of him to score with a combination of his arm and his head. The home crowd and the players appeal but the bright orange Jeff Winter is having none of it.

This is cruel. Mutu and Jimmy Floyd Hasselbaink have had hardly a sniff all game and one moment of carelessness has gifted them a decidedly iffy goal.

Unsurprisingly, the visitors regain a measure of composure now they're in front and start to carve out a few more chances. Moyes throws McFadden and Francis Jeffers on for the last twenty-five minutes to try and salvage something from a game we should be winning comfortably, and in the closing stages the on-loan striker gets the chance he's been begging for since his return. Gary Naysmith, who is playing the best football of his career at the moment, bursts into the Chelsea box and chips a delightful cross to Jeffers, unmarked at the far post.

We're up out of our seats ready to rejoice when the fox in the box, under no pressure whatsoever and only a couple of feet out, somehow glances his header wide of the post.

Colour Me Badd! Why did he have to try and be clever? If he had just let it hit him on the forehead it would have gone in.

There's still time for Gravesen to chase down a long ball, weave into the box and force a full length save from Cudicini, but it's become quite apparent that we are just not destined to get anything today.

At the final whistle the Everton players get a standing ovation from the home crowd. Anything less would be churlish; the players couldn't have given any more against a club who spent more on Wayne Bridge than we spent on total transfers this year.

The Chelsea fans - the ones who bothered to turn up - no longer content with hilariously waving cash at the television cameras, actually start singing 'Roman Abramovich'. They've always attracted more than their fair share of nouveau-footy planks - Damon Albarn and David Baddiel for instance - but this is getting ridiculous. Blackburn Rovers' fans used to make everyone cringe when they sang their chairman's name, but you kind of expect it from them - Chelsea are supposed to have a bit more about them though, being the big city sophisticates and all that.

Sunday 2nd November 2003

Blackburn Rovers lose two-nil at Leicester City. That's five Premiership defeats in a row for Graeme Souness' side. And guess who they play next? That's right, Everton, a week on Monday at Ewood Park.

It's a well-known fact that any club on a losing streak or striker enduring a goal drought will produce the goods or find the back of the net against us.

A good example of the sort of luck we have is the case of Derby County striker Esteban Fuertes, who was kicked out of the country when it was discovered that his passport was fashioned from a library card and a packet of Frosties. While he was here though he netted once, in a one-nil win. Need I go on?

Monday 3rd November 2003

Bill Kenwright, speaking to the official website, wants to assure folks that just because money's tight it doesn't mean we won't see any new signings.

"These days you don't have to sell a £5million player to buy a £5million player," he says. "All you have to do is, in going out and getting that player, make sure you've got enough this year and the next year and the year after - and that you don't one year build up so much future hope that you come a cropper, like Leeds."

It's significant that he uses that figure, as it just about equates to one Sean Davis. The Fulham midfielder better be a combination of Michel Platini and Bryan Robson if he does come, as the expectation is building with every poor result we endure. It would be interesting to know who Moyes plans to play alongside him though. I suspect he sees him as a partner for Gravesen. Or maybe even Nyarko, although if he continues the way he's playing at the moment we might struggle to keep hold of him!

Tuesday 4th November 2003

Unsurprisingly, David Unsworth has rejected a one-year extension to his contract. They were always going to offer him buttons, as he is pretty much surplus to requirements, but there was no need for Everton's Chief Executive, Michael Dunford, to rub the player's nose in it. His statement said: "We have made David a fair offer which he has rejected for now. There will not be another offer from Everton.

"It does entail a pay cut, but that policy is pretty general throughout football now.

"More realism is coming into the game and unless you are a megastar, and with all due respect to David he is not in that category, that's the way the game has to go."

That's all true, but it's very humiliating for a player who has never been shy about expressing his affection for the club. As stated earlier though, it seems to be the Everton way now: everyone leaves with a bitter taste in the mouth.

Wednesday 5th November 2003

"Fucking hell, have you seen it?"

"Not yet, is it that bad?"

"Worse. I can't do it justice, go and get yourself a copy."

That was a short exchange I had with Graham Ennis this morning. He was referring to the latest issue of the celebrity gossip sheet, *OK!*, the one with the big spread covering Wayne Rooney's eighteenth birthday party.

Now, to be fair, there are quite a few photos in it that are typical of any eighteenth, the ones with his family and his fiancé for instance, in which he looks like he's having a perfectly swell time in his Versace suit from Norton Barrie in Wilmslow. However, someone, his agent, publicist or whoever, has seen fit to bus in a load of 'rent-a-celeb' herberts off *Eastenders*, and Rooney's quite clearly never met any of them before in his life.

There's obviously the mandatory no-marks from *Hollyoaks* as well, but the weirdest photo, and the one in which Rooney looks the most embarrassed, is with ex-Bros singer Matt Goss. Imagine if the singer of such hits as *Drop the Boy* and *I Owe You Nothing* turned up at your party and started helping himself to the chicken wings and your Scania Green - you'd go mad.

The only big surprise is that Lesley Joseph, Dorien from television's *Birds of a Feather*, didn't turn up.

The photo that gets the most scrutiny is a big team affair with virtually all the Everton squad in it. It's always good to see where your season ticket money's being spent, and in this case a fair amount of it seems to have gone on obscenely chunky wristwatches and shirts with big, big collars. Special mention must go to Niclas Alexandersson's boy band ensemble, complete with open-necked shirt and big crucifix, while Steve Watson is resplendent in a sports jacket and jeans combo, a look that's commonly referred to as 'the Seinfeld'.

I've not laughed so much in ages.

Thursday 6th November 2003

It's revealed that Duncan Ferguson's chest infection was a little more serious than first imagined. In fact, when it was announced on Saturday morning that he had to return home from Bellefield, the rumour mill started grinding out all sorts of 'stormed off when he realised he was only on the bench' stories. It seems they were a little wide of the mark, as he was taken to hospital on the Monday after coughing up blood. He was discharged the next day, but it seems unlikely that he'll play any part in Monday's bottom of the table clash at Ewood Park.

We could do with him as well. While I think we'll eventually end up well clear of the relegation zone, we need to start getting points on the board quickly before the pressure really starts to mount. The stark fact is that if we lose on Monday and Wolves, Leicester or Leeds win at the weekend we will be in the bottom three.

Better news is that Bill Kenwright has said that the board are discussing plans to increase the capacity of Goodison Park. How times change. That idea was dismissed as an utter impossibility when they wanted to push the Kings Dock through.

Friday 7th November 2003

Sean bleedin' Davis has withdrawn his transfer request and says he wants to negotiate a new deal with Fulham. He gives it a load of 'I've been at Fulham since I was sixteen' but it's clear he's either been tipped that Everton can't afford him or else he's just trying to screw more money out of us. With Fulham flying at the moment - they won 3-1 at Old Trafford the other week - it's hardly going to crucify him if he has to stay down there.

You can't blame him for looking after his own interests, but there's going to be an awful lot of wailing and gnashing of teeth up here.

Saturday 8th November 2003

Sean Davis is back in the Fulham team, and even scores their consolation goal at the end of a 3-1 reverse at Charlton, for whom Scott Parker again looks superb. Incredibly, people are still suggesting that we push the boat out for the freckled midfield general. They choose to completely ignore the fact that we can't afford him and that he will surely be on his way to somewhere like Arsenal or Manchester United soon. Even if he isn't, Charlton, who are up in fourth, are a much better proposition than us at the moment. That's simply the harsh truth.

Wolves draw with Birmingham City while Leeds get hammered 6-1 at Portsmouth. Leicester shouldn't get much at Manchester City tomorrow so it would appear that we'll stay out of the drop zone come what may on Monday night.

Sunday 9th November 2003

Bunch of useless alcoholics.

Try as I might to round up a few people to go to the pub to watch the Sunday lunchtime game, Liverpool versus Manchester United, all I get down the phone is a series of moans and croaky apologies from people who have been up until all hours. In the end it's just the clean-living Ray McKay and myself who go and watch United triumph 2-1. Neither side looks particularly impressive, and Emile Heskey's hilariously scuffed attempt at an equaliser is the highlight of a dull match.

Unfortunately for us, while the reds of Manchester are doing the business, the blues, Manchester City, are going down 3-0 at home to Leicester, a result that lifts the Foxes a point above us.

Monday 10th November 2003

It starts badly and gets worse.

I'm excited and expectant all day, as Blackburn is one of the better aways of the season. It's only a short jaunt up the motorway and there are plenty of decent pubs if you get away from the immediate vicinity of the ground. As a result, it's one of the more popular away matches. Bolton's similar, although the locals are nowhere near as pleasant there.

Seeing as there are about fifteen of us going from the Butchers Arms, a big white van has been procured from somewhere. Luckily for me though, I'm going in Gid's new Audi A3 - a vast improvement on his clapped-out Peugeot - as the thought of being packed in the back of the distinctly manky-looking works transit with ten or twelve bevvied and flatulent ne'er-do-wells holds little appeal.

Before we set off, Alan Welsh gives us some worrying news that seems to confirm one or two rumours that have been circulating for a while. Two of the lads in his band are related to one of Everton's young reserves, and he's told them that a lot of the senior players are pissed off with Moyes. They feel that he's always criticising them and that the training is too hard. He also says that the Radzinski to Blackburn stories are true.

I don't know how anyone could have the gall to question the manager given the impact he has made on this club since his arrival. And certainly the last people who are in any position to knock him are our extremely highly-paid players. Get to the top of the league and then perhaps it will be time for lavish praise and a few afternoons off. Cheeky bastards.

Gid, Redmond and myself are still debating these revelations in a pub called the Wellington, up the hill from Ewood Park, when the occupants of the Butchers Arms happybus spill through the doors looking like the ghosts of Christmas past, present and future. Unbeknownst to them, the van they came up in is usually full of bags of cement, so they're all covered from head to toe in grey dust. Apparently there's no light in the back of the vehicle either, so several of the occupants, unable to control their bladders, had to aim into a bucket using only 'the force' to guide them.

After travelling in such inhuman conditions they are all demanding a good performance from the Blues. Unfortunately they are sorely disappointed.

I wouldn't have thought it possible if I hadn't seen it with my own eyes, but Everton's first half performance here is even worse than at Tottenham.

WHAT'S OUR NAME? EVERTON!

There are some mitigating circumstances, Alan Stubbs and Wayne Rooney are missing with flu, so young Peter Clarke gets called up to play centre-half, and a patently unfit Kevin Campbell partners Radzinski up front, but that doesn't excuse a shameful performance.

After only six minutes, Clarke, whose strengths are meant to be his aerial ability and old-fashioned ruggedness, misjudges a headed clearance, flicking the ball across the face of the goal for ex-Liverpool defender Markus Babbel to nod home from close range.

Maybe the stories about player unrest are playing on my mind but it does seem as if some of them really aren't trying. I can accept when they play badly because of a lack of ability, but a lack of effort and commitment is unacceptable, and some of these seem to be just going through the motions. No one wins a fifty-fifty challenge or closes down the opposition with any belief, and when we do get the ball there's no movement up front whatsoever. They're simply not doing the things that they're good at, and consequently they just look like a bunch of extremely limited individuals.

It comes as little surprise when, on thirteen minutes, Vratislav Gresko crosses from the right, with Everton all over the place, and Dwight Yorke leads the queue of Blackburn players steaming in to head them into a two-goal lead.

At this rate it could end up five or six nil. There are few worse feelings than going two down early on away from home, with very little prospect of making even a semblance of a comeback.

Thanks to Nigel Martyn and some poor Blackburn finishing, the score remains at two-nil until half-time.

Kevin Kilbane, who was by no means the worst offender in the first half, and Alex Nyarko, whose recent renaissance seems to have shuddered to a halt, are replaced by James McFadden and David Unsworth for the second period.

It's not clear whether it's the substitutions or what Moyes said to the players at half-time, but they certainly have a lot more purpose and drive about them when they re-emerge. After only four minutes, McFadden shows a flash of the skill that thrilled us

102

in his first two games, skinning Gresko and clipping a perfect cross over the towering Brad Friedel. Radzinski, who was appalling in the first half, is first on hand to bury the third close-range header of the evening.

The travelling supporters have had nothing to cheer all night, but with the Toffees at least now making a game of it, the players couldn't ask for more vocal backing. We're famous for not really singing, and quite frankly the contrived songs that the likes of Manchester United pride themselves on are just embarrassing, but when Everton are having a go in the face of adversity we're as loud and as animated as anyone. Opposing fans often comment on our limited repertoire of songs, but quite frankly the whole scene that encompasses brass bands, inflatables and stupid flags just isn't for us. Similarly we don't take our shirts off at games and ape for the cameras, nor do we turn up in fancy dress or have zany characters like Sheffield Wednesday's Tango Man, Liverpool's Doctor Fun or that tattooed meff you see at Fratton Park. Fans of other clubs can never work us out; they think we're curmudgeonly and contrary. They're right of course, and we like it that way. This means that Richard Keys will probably never say, in that condescending manner of his, "Great fans aren't they?" - but I feel that's a small price to pay.

Obviously we'd be feeling somewhat less curmudgeonly if we could grab an equaliser here, but despite the fact that we're taking the game to Rovers, with Gravesen driving us forward from the middle, Graeme Souness' side are defending with grim resolve.

With only minutes remaining, a corner is flicked across the six-yard box, leaving Joseph Yobo with a free header at the far post. Unbelievably, the Nigerian misses the target and although Unsworth manages to lunge at the loose ball, he can only shin it over the bar. You just can't spurn chances like that at this level, especially if you're playing like we are and not creating much. If you do, then you find yourself in the bottom three, which is exactly where we are as the final whistle blows.

They were certainly better in the second half, but that doesn't excuse the disgraceful performance in the first. Back at the Wellington, the atmosphere starts to get a bit fractious as we try and pinpoint just what is going wrong in a season that began with high hopes. Some still see Gravesen as the root of all evil, while others end up trying to defend his corner, going over the same old familiar ground - basically, who is going to do a better job than him?

At the end of a grim night, my only consolation is that I'm not going home in the back of a piss-soaked cement mixer.

Tuesday 11th November 2003

That's what you get for arguing with me. Apparently the van got pulled over by a policeman last night for having a dodgy tail-light. Imagine the constable's horror when he saw the eight or nine dusty scruffs sprawled in the back. He probably thought he'd cracked some sort of illegal immigrant smuggling ring, especially as most of them were so bladdered they were already talking Albanian when we left them.

John, the driver, has to produce his documents at the police station at some point and no one is sure whether he was actually insured to drive the van in the first place.

No such problems for the Everton team though - they've flown out to Tenerife for a break seeing as there's internationals at the weekend. Nice work if you can get it.

Wednesday 12th November 2003

Wayne Rooney is still suffering with the flu and is 'touch and go' for England's friendly against Denmark on Sunday.

I try not to read the *Echo* letters page, but I let my guard down today and found myself predictably appalled by the nonsense that people send in. Ignoring the ones that are obviously from mischievous Liverpudlians - hey, we've all done it - there are still plenty criticising David Moyes and dismissing last season's achievements as a flash in the pan. There are several articles on the internet along the same lines.

Obviously nobody is happy at being in the bottom three, but the manager surely deserves a bit more respect than this. Last season was his first full one with Everton, and we were fitter, more organised and played better football than we have done for almost ten years. That was without spending any money and just utilising the players that the previous manager, Walter Smith, had dismissed as simply not good enough.

Things haven't gone as smoothly this time around - injuries and illness have played a big part in that - but that's no reason to start panicking.

Thursday 13th November 2003

Rooney's getting over his flu and will play on Sunday.

Friday 14th November 2003

I forgot to mention Peter Reid got the bullet from Leeds on Monday. So much for 'We'll keep him as it's what the fans want.'

Saturday November 15th 2003

Scotland versus Holland at Hampden Park in the first leg of their play-off for Euro 2004.

Ricky Ross, ex-lead singer of Deacon Blue, sings *Flower of Scotland* in what can only be described as the pub singer stylee. Years ago, Dave Wiggins, *When Skies Are Grey*'s resident warped genius, was at a works Christmas function where, for some reason, Everton's evil ex-Chairman Peter Johnson was also in attendance. Unlike most Evertonians, the Wig's enduring image of the Stavros Blofeld of Park Foods wasn't of him being hounded out of Goodison with some little scally hanging on to the boot of his car, but of him waving his arms in the air, bow-tie at a rakish angle, cutting a rug to Deacon Blue's *Real Gone Kid*. He moved pretty well for an older fella as well, or so we're told.

But I digress. The Scot's bad hair day nomination goes to Stephen Pressley for this game. He looks a lot like Rick Wakeman.

Gary Naysmith and James McFadden are both in the side and it's our mercurial winger - playing up front in this instance - who scores the game's only goal.

Despite a number of close calls, especially in the second half as they tire, the Scots hang on to take a one goal advantage to the

Amsterdam Arena on Wednesday night. It's a brilliant effort, but I get the feeling that they've just built themselves up for a massive disappointment.

Sunday 16th November 2003

Wayne Rooney starts up front alongside the much-maligned Emile Heskey in an England line-up that would be best described as 'experimental'.

Michael Owen isn't playing, so he does a stint as one of Sky's experts. Not only does he wear a suit that is hideous even by footballers' standards, but he also comes across as a right snidey little twat - all his compliments for Rooney are decidedly backhanded. Even when asked whether playing alongside Heskey at Liverpool helps him score goals, he refuses to take the opportunity to back him up for fear, it seems, of detracting from his own brilliance. It's strange to see someone as exceptionally talented as Owen looking so insecure.

I can't help but imagine him seething after only five minutes of the game, when Rooney capitalises on a Gravesen error to surge into the Danish half, get a lucky break off a defender and then hammer an unstoppable shot in off the underside of the bar. He's not exactly struggling to make the step up to international football.

The Danes are no mugs though and quickly equalise, only for Joe Cole to score thanks to a clever Rooney pass, straight from the kick-off. It's a mad game, and the visitors go in level at half-time thanks to some comedy defending from the hopelessly overrated Matthew Upson.

Rooney, along with David Beckham, is substituted after fifteen minutes of the second half, but not before he almost snaps Thomas Sorenson's right-hand post with a ferocious angled shot on the turn. From that point on, the Danes, expertly prompted by none other than Mr T. Gravesen of Everton, dominate possession and begin to carve out a succession of chances. It comes as no surprise to anyone when Jon Dahl Tomasson scores the winner in the last ten minutes.

Monday 17th November 2003

Everyone's raving about McFadden, Rooney and Gravesen.

"If they're so good, how come your team are useless?" seems to be the general line of enquiry from most people. Hopefully they will repeat their international performances against Wolverhampton Wanderers at Goodison on Saturday.

Ahead of Wednesday's game in Amsterdam, James McFadden has set himself up for a bit of a fall, not only accusing the Dutch of underestimating Scotland but also of being 'an arrogant nation'. Well done Kofi Annan.

Tuesday 18th November 2003

The groundshare finally looks dead in the water. The city council have, not unreasonably, said that they're not willing to use eighty million pounds of taxpayers' money to build a stadium for the use of the two football clubs. The only other option available was apparently for Liverpool to pay for the whole stadium and Everton to pay half back to the Reds over time. Again, unsurprisingly, Liverpool's reaction has been more or less: 'Why should we, what's in it for us?'

So that would appear to be the end of that, for this year at least.

Wednesday 19th November 2003

The breaking news is that Duncan Ferguson and David Moyes had a massive argument at Bellefield on Monday, resulting in the player being ordered home.

Great, that's just what we need while we're in the bottom three and facing a run of five games against some of the division's lesser lights i.e. the teams we really have to beat if we're to get out of trouble.

Over the years, Ferguson has often come up with the goods in the crucial battles against relegation rivals; he seems to thrive on the impassioned atmosphere that those sort of games produce. For the time being at least though, it looks like we're going to have to get by without him unless there's some sort of conciliation in the near future.

In the evening, Scotland and Wales play the second legs of their Euro 2004 qualifiers, away to Holland and at home to Russia respectively. Both had such high hopes after positive first leg results, but neither has the requisite class to finish the job. The Dutch, wounded by the criticism following the game at Hampden, hammer six without reply against Berti Vogts' side. Arch phoney Patrick Kluivert - has anyone ever seen him look anything like a world-class player? - is dropped, and despite a hat-trick from Ruud van Nistelrooy, Ajax's young midfielder Wesley Sneijder steals the show. To add injury to insult, Gary Naysmith picks up a knock and doesn't reappear for the second half.

At the Millennium Stadium, Wales are expected to steamroller over the Russians but it doesn't quite pan out that way. Marshalled by the ancient and wily Victor Onopko, the men from behind the old Iron Curtain realise that as long as they deal with the aerial threat of John Hartson, the Welsh have little else to offer. Midway through the first half, Mark Hughes' side are let down by their second division full-back, Darren Barnard, who concedes a needless free-kick from which the Russians grab a vital away goal. After that the home side are treated to a masterclass in professionalism as the Russians keep possession and strangle the game. Robbie Savage once again looks shite, although the rumour is that David Moyes is at the game to watch his midfield counterpart, Jason Koumas, who isn't much better on this showing.

Thursday 20th November 2003

David Prentice, the *Echo*'s chief sports writer, writes that Duncan Ferguson is still being told to stay away from Bellefield. The falling out, he believes, is because Moyes has finally had enough of the player and has come right out and questioned his attitude.

There are few people who would side with Ferguson, or any of the players, against Moyes.

The problem now is, what do we do with the player? If he's been sent home then he's still entitled to his wages, and he's still got eighteen months to go on his contract. No club in their right minds would take him off our hands, so are we going to just swallow the loss and pay him almost forty grand a week to stay away? His influence on the dressing room must be malign to say the least, if they would prefer to do that than have him around the place at all.

Saturday 22nd November 2003

In the morning, England's public school eye-gougers win the Rugby World Cup. Obviously that's of far less consequence than Everton's home game against Wolverhampton Wanderers.

It's a sell-out crowd, although I'm sure the capacity of the ground must be reduced by a couple of thousand to accommodate the number of big coats worn by the fans on freezing days like today. Our row alone looks like a scene from *The Man Who Would Be King*, the amount of fur hoods and woolly hats that are on display. Where other sets of fans, most notably the Neanderthals of the North East, pride themselves on wearing nothing but replica shirts in subzero temperatures, Scousers have gone the opposite way and compete for the most overstuffed and elaborate jacket and headwear combos. At Stoke in the Cup a few years ago, I remember seeing one lad in a full deepfreeze suit, complete with insulated mittens, big fuck off boots and a furry Russian hat.

Mark my words, one of these days some Evertonian is going to collapse with heatstroke in mid-January.

With Kevin Campbell injured and Duncan Ferguson in exile, David Moyes has plumped for the small but extremely mobile front pairing of Rooney and Radzinski, aided by both his wingers, McFadden and Kilbane. If we're going to get anything out of this game we're going to have to play a bit of football 'on the carpet'.

Only goal difference separates the two sides in the league, but from the first whistle it becomes apparent that there is a big gulf in class on the pitch. Wolves' manager, Dave Jones, has shown a large degree of loyalty to the players who won his side promotion - experienced pros like Paul Ince, Alex Rae and Denis Irwin - but they've got so little pace it's almost embarrassing at times.

WHAT'S OUR NAME? EVERTON!

When, in the opening minutes, Radzinski tears past Irwin down the left and crosses for Rooney, the visitors seem to get the idea that it could be a long afternoon. Unfortunately, on this occasion the young striker heads straight at Michael Oakes, but we're not kept waiting too long for the opener. Tobias Linderoth pounces on a slack pass in midfield and immediately feeds the ball into Radzinski, who turns as the Wolves defenders back off towards their own penalty area. The Canadian, so prone to ugly misses from close range, takes a touch and hammers home a low, swerving drive that takes Oakes and most of Goodison completely by surprise. In fact Radzinski himself looks somewhat taken aback as the side netting ripples and referee Mike Riley points to the centre circle.

The relief from the Evertonians is palpable, and things get even better three minutes later when we double our lead. Rooney collects a ball out on the right, turns, and then floats what appears to be a long, aimless-looking ball over towards the Wolves' penalty spot. What the youngster with eyes in the back of his head has noticed before anyone else is a surging, Steve Watson-esque run from Kilbane, who easily out-jumps the tormented Irwin to loop a header over Oakes and into the top corner.

The big travelling support from Wolverhampton is suddenly less inclined to give us another verse of their hilarious and original 'Only sing when you're robbing', now that their team is all over the place.

Everton should really score more, but if anything, it's too easy and numerous chances go begging as the likes of McFadden and Thomas Gravesen try to walk the ball into the net. Some of the movement and the passing is excellent though, and it's obvious that the players are enjoying putting the Blackburn game and the subsequent criticism behind them.

The second half is less exciting than the first, as Everton are happy to keep possession while Wolves look completely incapable of producing any sort of meaningful fightback. The one occasion when one of their strikers breaks free of the attentions of the Everton defence sees substitute Nathan Blake head a deep cross straight at the legs of the criminally underworked Nigel Martyn.

For good measure, Moyes even gives Neon Leon Osman a ten minute run out at the end.

Fair enough, it's only Wolves, who are truly abysmal, but if you're not focused and on top of your game then these sort of games can prove your undoing. There certainly didn't look too much wrong with the players' morale or commitment either - perhaps Moyes should banish a few more from training before next week's game against Bolton, if it's going to provoke this sort of reaction from the rest.

Sunday 23rd November 2003

Amidst all the rugby guff in the Sunday papers there's a story in the *Mirror* that reckons that Tottenham are 'eyeing up' David Moyes for the vacant manager's post at White Hart Lane. I would be extremely surprised if he even considered going there - he would have nothing to gain by what is, at the very best, a step sideways. It's if the Celtic job becomes available that I will get worried, and there are rumours that Martin O'Neill could be on his way to Anfield in the summer. In fairness, there are always rumours of O'Neill moving, but he's been up there for a while now and taken them as far as he could really hope to.

Would Moyes go there though? In all honesty, I think he would. Obviously the Scottish Premiership is a step down from the English one, but it's still a very high profile job, especially given the fact that you're more or less guaranteed Champions League football every year. If he was to go there and do reasonably well, especially in Europe, then he could put himself in contention for the manager's job at Manchester United. He's already admired at Old Trafford - Alex Ferguson wanted him as his assistant when he was still at Preston - but the board of their plc are unlikely to take a risk on him now while he has no experience of those all-important European competitions.

I really hope we don't have to think about all this for some time though, as I'm not sure how Everton would cope without him.

WHAT'S OUR NAME? EVERTON!

Monday 24th November 2003

We haven't been linked to any new players for ages. So when Monaco defender Jose Karl Pierre Fanfan says Everton have been in touch with him, it's almost exciting. Well, it makes a welcome change from 'Everton still interested in Davis/Savage/Koumas' anyway. I've no idea if he's any good, or whether Everton have even heard of him, never mind been in touch, but what a great name Fanfan is. He sounds like one of them miserable pandas that *John Craven's Newsround* used to show wallowing in a grubby Chinese zoo, chewing bamboo and steadfastly refusing to have sex with Woof Woof or Bling Bling, the saucy she-panda sprawled on the straw in the corner.

Speaking of Sean Davis, and we were before we got distracted, he plays in Fulham's televised defeat of Portsmouth. He doesn't look a patch on Steed Malbranque or even Lee Clark, although in his defence he has hardly played since the injury. Still, for £5 million I'd want to see a lot more than the ability to run around and mis-kick the ball for ninety minutes.

Wednesday 26th November 2003

Duncan Ferguson's been allowed back to training, and in a terse statement David Moyes has declared that that's the end of the matter and he'll be treated like any other player. It's difficult to see how that can be the case though given that the *Echo* have done a couple of editorial pieces that have torn into Ferguson. One in particular claims that after our defeat away to Newcastle last year, which he unsurprisingly missed through injury, he turned up for training on the Monday asking, "How did we get on then?" You don't leak stuff like that to the press if you're desperate to resolve an issue with someone.

It wouldn't surprise me at all if the story is true, but if Everton have been so appalled with his attitude how come they've never done anything until now? The fact is that very few modern players could care less, especially when they're not playing. People really need to start accepting that players are not like supporters in the least, and when they talk about loyalty and loving the fans, etc. it's all a load of rubbish. All we can really ask is that when they go out on the pitch they show some professional pride - all this 'die for the shirt' stuff you hear is bollocks.

If Duncan Ferguson isn't showing the requisite degree of professionalism then the manager is well within his rights to take decisive action - no one would dispute that - but all this mud slinging through the press makes the club look a little cheap and undignified.

Talking of cheap, according to Everton chief executive, Michael Dunford, in Saturday's programme, the club's caterers won't accept twenty-pound notes any more after over a thousand quid's worth of forgeries were taken at one recent home game.

We occasionally get people trying to palm forgeries off on us when we're selling the mag. The printing's a lot more convincing these days - the Queen no longer looks like Karl Malden - but the paper they're on still usually feels like a Sunblest bag.

Thursday 27th November 2003

The reserves won 2-1 at Wolves last night thanks to two goals from Leon Osman. They're doing quite well at the moment - they're up to third in the league - but it remains to be seen how they will cope without their other mainstay, Nick Chadwick. Despite the Ferguson situation and Kevin Campbell's fitness problems the club have still allowed the burly striker to go on loan to Millwall for a month. He's quite popular with the crowd because he always looks willing, but when people describe him as 'a bit raw' they actually mean 'not that good'. I don't like criticising young players, but there's no point pretending they're better than they are.

Friday 28th November 2003

Some fella's been arrested with explosives in Gloucester and the *Daily Mail* have somehow deduced that he was planning a suicide attack on a football ground. Some copper on the radio described this as pure speculation and very unhelpful. He's not wrong, it's especially unhelpful if you're an Asian football fan this weekend.

Meanwhile, turning away from the international war on terrorism for just a moment, David Moyes has voiced displeasure at Wayne Rooney travelling over to Madrid earlier in the week to do some promotion for Coca Cola. The manager has stated that he would prefer players to rest on their day off, not go jetting around Europe. He's probably echoing what most Evertonians fear most, that the young star gets too distracted by the trappings of his fame and starts to neglect what's most important - his football.

Saturday 29th November 2003
Bawlton Wanderers away.

Like Blackburn, Bolton's only a short jaunt away and therefore good for a hearty drink, but make no mistake, there's plenty of history behind this tie. In short, they fucking hate us.

Much of the antipathy stems back to one particular incident in 1997, although there's also the general dislike of Scousers that's common amongst slow-witted yokels nationwide. To them, Evertonians are all belligerent cut-throats in shellsuits, while to us, Bolton fans seem to be characterised by fatties with George Michael earrings and tomato sauce down the front of their replica shirts. Considering how little distance there is between Bolton and Merseyside, it really is like entering another country.

Anyway, the incident in question that still rankles so much with our Lancashire cousins occurred live on the telly during the first ever match at their brand spanking new Reebok Stadium. The top and bottom of it is that early in the second half of a game that finished goalless, Nathan Blake had a header that hit the bar and bounced about a foot over the line before getting hacked clear by the Everton defender, Terry Phelan.

That was only the fourth game of the season. Nine months later both sides finished the campaign level on points, but where Bolton were relegated thanks to their inferior goal difference, we stayed up by the skin of our teeth.

Even if we ignore the fact that Blake quite clearly fouled Neville Southall as he went up for the header, Bolton were still ahead of us going into the last game of the season. Given that we only managed a horrible, nerve-shredding draw against Coventry at Goodison that day, the Trotters only needed the same at Stamford Bridge, against a Chelsea side with nothing to play for and with one eye on the European Cup Winners' Cup final. This is before we even consider any of the other 36 games that took place that season. No, Bolton went down that season because we're a bunch of jammy Scouse cheats, and if you ever meet one of their fans be sure to ask him to tell you about the one that: "Crossed bloody larn agernst Scoosers!"

Back to the present day, and we get up to the Greenwood - a pub near the ground that's run by a couple we know - to quench our thirst while watching Wolves and Newcastle draw 1-1 in the early, televised game. Coincidentally, it's none other than Nathan Blake who nets for Wolves before Alan Shearer - or 'the evergreen Alan Shearer' as he's now officially known - equalises.

As ever, we get to our seats in the rather boringly named Upper South Stand just as the game kicks off. Quite frankly, we need to get an away win under our belts soon, and if ever a side are beatable on their own ground it's Bolton Wanderers. They're yet to defeat us in the Premiership and we absolutely battered them here last season.

Rooney and Radzinski start up front again; there's still no sign of Duncan Ferguson. I think it seems safe to assume he's had the Fredo Corleone treatment:

"You're nothing to me now. You're not a brother, you're not a friend. I don't want to know you or what you do. I don't want to see you at the hotels, I don't want you near my house. When you see our mother, I want to know a day in advance, so I won't be there. You understand?"

The rumour from Alan Welsh's man on the inside is that the whole bust-up with Moyes came after Ferguson made an official complaint to the PFA concerning the amount of training Everton players are now expected to do. As you can imagine, few of us are very sympathetic to the players' cause. The flip side of that however, is that few of the players appear particularly sympathetic to the fact that we've paid nearly thirty quid to watch them here, as they start in a manner horribly reminiscent of the Blackburn game.

There's just nothing there from Everton. They're second to every loose ball, their passing is careless and the movement off the ball is, once again, totally non-existent. Their attitude is summed up in the opening seconds when Gravesen plays a straightforward pass up to Rooney. The England star just stands looking at the ball, waiting for it to arrive, as a defender nonchalantly steps in front of him and sets Bolton going forward. Normally he would have got his body in between the player and the ball in a situation like that, and if he did still lose possession he would chase back furiously, but here he just glares at Gravesen as if to say, 'What do you want me to do with that, dickhead?'

With pretty much the whole side showing a similar lack of desire, it comes as little surprise when Wanderers take the lead midway through the first half. In fact, it's amazing that we hold out that long.

Against Blackburn we struggled to deal with crosses and it's much the same again here as a loose ball bounces around the penalty area until eventually the normally dependable Nigel Martyn attempts to punch away Ivan Campo's harmless looking header. Unfortunately, the keeper fails to get a clean contact and the ball cannons on to the head of Per Frandsen and straight back into the Everton net.

I know I shouldn't keep harking back to last season, but it's hard not to in the face of performances like this, and quite frankly twelve months ago these players would have taken a Bolton goal as an insult. One of our biggest strengths was our resilience, in fact we often had to ask just why it was that we didn't play our best football until we'd gone a goal down. Just where's that fighting spirit gone now though? We offer nothing in reply here and it's a miracle that we go in at half-time just the one goal down.

One good thing about the Reebok is that they serve ale, so I spend half-time having a pint with a few lads who play seven-a-side with us on a Friday. They've got a minibus going back to

Liverpool after the game as one of their number, Paul, is celebrating his birthday in town. While they're deciding which of Liverpool's many lapdancing clubs is the best for, and I quote, 'a really good, hard grind' a young lad comes down the stairs shaking his head and saying that Bolton have scored again. We look at him as if he's mad, the second half can't have kicked off yet.

Lo and behold though, the young tyke isn't having us on. Seconds after the kick-off, according to an ashen-faced Redmond who rarely bothers with a half time scoop, Youri Djorkaeff got on the end of a poor Everton clearance and struck a volley that deflected past Martyn.

And as if things couldn't get any worse, David Moyes signals that he wants to bring Francis Jeffers on less than ten minutes into the half. At first we assume that he's going to go for broke, withdraw a midfielder and play with three up front, but it quickly becomes apparent that he's replacing Rooney. As he comes off, he shakes hands with Jeffers but refuses to acknowledge the manager, brushing past him and petulantly ignoring a tracksuit top thrown to him by the kit man as he skulks to the bench.

Maybe if he had shown a fraction of that intensity during the game he wouldn't have been yanked off. Acting like a brat in public is downright unprofessional, it attracts media attention and spawns stories and rumours about a 'club in crisis'. That in turn adds to the pressure on the manager and the other players, and that's the last thing we need right now. And while Rooney is the one in the wrong, Moyes might have been avoided this if he'd made the change at half-time and had a word with him in private rather than making a statement by withdrawing him so soon after the break.

No one is covered in glory this afternoon.

It gets no better, Everton fail to get a shot on target and Bolton cruise to their easiest win of the season so far. There's going to be some backlash after this, and quite frankly I'm glad I'll miss it while I'm in Amsterdam.

December

Ocean Rain

Monday 1st December 2003

I'm off to Amsterdam this afternoon. I just check the news headlines first though, and David Moyes has moved quickly to diffuse any talk of tension between him and Wayne Rooney. Instead of mentioning the spat on Saturday he says that perhaps we are forgetting how young the player is and that we sometimes expect too much from him week in, week out.

It's true. We don't just expect him to hold his own; we're speculating about something being amiss if he doesn't play like Maradona for ninety minutes of every match.

Tuesday 2nd December 2003

The Bunnymen at the Paradiso - there are more Scousers in the audience than Dutch.

Famous last words: "These aren't very strong are they, let's have another one."

Wednesday 3rd December 2003

We get back into John Lennon airport just before five o'clock. A mate is waiting to drive a glassy-eyed Weavers up to Middlesbrough for the Carling Cup game. I just can't face it. I'm the colour of boiled shite and I really need to lie down before I fall over. The thought of travelling up there and it going to extra time is too horrible to imagine.

At eight o'clock I curl up in bed and switch on Radio Merseyside in time to catch the team news. Moyes has made a number of changes to the side that was so poor at Bolton, with Li

Tie, James McFadden and Francis Jeffers all starting. Wayne Rooney's in the side as well, so perhaps things aren't too bad between him and the manager after all.

I can't remember the last time I heard a game on the radio - it reminds me of being a kid, when I used to be a bag of nerves every time the opponents crossed the halfway line. It's only as you get older that you learn to listen to the noise from the crowd to get a realistic appreciation of how dangerous any given situation is, and for the opening twenty minutes of this match the Boro crowd sound extremely vociferous as their team rip into the Blues. Luckily though, Everton weather the initial storm, thanks in particular to a couple of great saves from Nigel Martyn, and by half-time they're matching the home side in all departments and carving out chances of their own. Unfortunately our finishing is poor, with Jeffers and Lee Carsley in particular spurning the best of the openings.

The second half seems pretty even too, although Boro, with Mendieta playing well, have the more clear-cut chances. However, Everton defend well and take the game to extra time. I'd like to say that I feel guilty not being there as I hear the travelling Evertonians singing, but in all honesty it takes all my effort to keep my eyes open and force down another chocolate Digestive as the game moves inexorably towards a penalty shoot-out.

Mike Hughes, Merseyside's commentator, who forms a superb partnership with Ronnie Goodlass, tells us that the winner will play Tottenham away. The prospect of the inevitable defeat at White Hart Lane dulls the excitement somewhat as Everton win the toss and elect to take the first kick.

Thomas Gravesen steps up. He'll get slaughtered if he misses. But he doesn't, sticking it in the bottom corner.

Michael Ricketts immediately levels the score.

David Unsworth, officially our 'penalty king', hammers his high into the net.

Boudewijn Zenden is next for Boro. He's another of these big names who rarely justify their reputation, but no one expects him to do anything but score here. And he does. Two-two.

Next up, surprisingly, is Leon Osman, who only entered the game as replacement for Jeffers with less than ten minutes to go. His kick is weak and straight down the middle. Although Mark Schwarzer dives to his right, the ball hits his legs and stays out. No doubt there will be questions asked about whether such an inexperienced player should have taken a penalty, but isn't that the beauty of hindsight? Wayne Rooney, when still only seventeen, scored in a shoot-out at St. James's Park last season, and funnily enough no one batted an eyelid.

The obnoxious Danny Mills gives the home side the advantage.

McFadden brings us back level but Martyn needs to save one of the last two kicks just to keep us alive. He doesn't get near Massimo Maccarone's - if Alan Stubbs misses this next one it's all over.

Stubbs slots, so it's all down to Martyn and Mendieta.

I've got to hold my hands up and say that Mendieta looks a better player than I gave him credit for when he arrived over here. For a 'big name' he's certainly not scared of hard work, and it's only been Martyn's acrobatics in the Everton goal that have kept him off the scoresheet tonight. Unfortunately for us, the Spaniard has the final say in their particular duel, converting his penalty and dumping us out of this competition for yet another year.

I'm asleep before Weavers gets out of the stadium.

Thursday 4th December 2003

David Moyes is upbeat in the papers following last night's performance. He repeats something he's said on several occasions: that he doesn't ask the players for results, but for a certain level of performance. His theory is that if they give that level of performance regularly enough then the results will follow. Last night's was the most pleasing performance of the season, he continued, despite the disappointing outcome.

Francis Jeffers also adds that stories about dissent and unrest in the dressing room are well wide of the mark. Let's hope that's true, as we play Manchester City on Sunday, and if the players perform like they did at Bolton or Blackburn there will be hell to pay.

Friday 5th December 2003

Victor Onopko, the emaciated star of the Russian national side, is training with Everton. The thirty-four-year-old is currently a free agent and Everton are looking at taking him on until the end of the season.

The main reason we are considering this is because we are going to be in dire need of cover in central defence when Joseph Yobo goes to play in the African Cup of Nations in January. Depending on how long Nigeria stay in the competition, our best defender could be away for up to six weeks.

Sunday 7th December 2003

Manchester City have some of the most irritating supporters in the country - they're probably neck and neck with Newcastle in the self-aggrandisement stakes. All you ever hear from their fans is how great they are because they get decent gates while living in the shadow of Manchester United.

There's nothing worse than a bunch of martyrs who think they deserve a round of applause for turning up when things aren't going well. Evertonians share a city with Liverpool, the most successful club side in England by some distance, yet we don't want anyone's sympathy - we're proud of what we've achieved in our own right. Admittedly, we have some fans who have a bit of unhealthy interest in all things Kopite, who celebrate the Reds' undoing almost as much as an Everton win, but that's not the norm. City though, seem to define themselves by the fact that they hate United.

They're also obsessed with proving that, despite never really winning that much and spending long periods outside the top division, they are 'a really big club'. Again, like Newcastle, it really riles them that Everton, whom they see as somehow inferior, actually have a history of winning things and not getting relegated.

For most of the last fifteen years, Everton have been genuinely awful, the club has lurched from crisis to crisis and we've come hideously close to going down at times. In fact, it's probably fair

121

to say it's been just about the most desperate period in our history, yet, despite all that, in 1995 we still won the FA Cup.

After having my ear twisted by Ste Connor's little nephew, Liam, in the pub, I'm glad to get to the match for a bit of peace. Ste's brother, Peter, brings Liam to every game, and he's a lovely little lad - Everton mad - but I'm sure he's had too many preservatives in his breakfast today. We, the 'grown ups', are talking about the Gil Scott Heron documentary that was on the telly on Friday when Liam's freckled face pops up and he starts his Raymond Babbit stream-of-consciousness monologue.

"Did you see the Barcelona versus Madrid game on telly last night my dad let me stay up 'til half ten to watch it I thought Barcelona would win 2-1 but it was the other way around Roberto Carlos scored and so did Ronaldo but they were both deflected and Kluivert got one back do you think you should be allowed to have a player-manager I don't I think you should just be either a manager or a player what's your favourite flavour of milkshake?"

"What?"

"Mine's chocolate."

At least the hyperactive nipper makes more sense than David Moyes' team selection. I'm loathe to question the manager normally, as most of the time his decisions seem simple and sensible. Today though it looks like he's lost the courage of his own convictions, abandoning our familiar 4-4-2 system and playing Radzinski and Jeffers up front with Wayne Rooney 'in the hole'. Just the phrase 'in the hole' is enough to get me wound up, it's a mythical position that was invented for players who are too slow to play up front or too lazy and weak for midfield.

There is a school of thought that says that because Rooney is good at dropping deep and using the ball intelligently then he should indeed be employed 'behind the front two'. However, this school of thought is wrong. He's a striker, lightning quick and strong as an ox. Last season he was playing up on the shoulder of the last defender and causing panic and terror whenever he picked the ball up. He'd spin in behind the opponents' defence and leave experienced players trailing in his wake, desperately trying to haul him back. Asking him to play deep though - something that started for England - just means he gets bogged down in midfield. What's even worse than what it does to Rooney's game though is the effect it has on the overall shape of the team, and that's all too clear against City.

When teams are playing well, they pass and move instinctively as the hours of drills and training make them look almost telepathic - in any given situation the players know where they should be and where their nearest teammate is. Start messing about with the formation though, and all of a sudden players aren't so certain; they need that extra touch and a look around to locate the best pass. At the top level that extra fraction of a second in possession makes all the difference - play loses its fluency and the players become uncertain of what exactly their roles are.

I'm really surprised that Moyes has chosen to abandon his tried and trusted method to experiment in a game as crucial as this. The only consolation is that City aren't good enough to punish our stilted performance.

The viewers at home must be going mad that they've paid Sky good money to watch this. A Gary Naysmith free-kick and a stupid shot from Jeffers that finds the side-netting are Everton's best efforts of the first half. City, on the other hand, have a late rally and it takes desperate defending from the Toffees to deny Richard Dunne, Trevor Sinclair and the somewhat lacklustre Robbie Fowler.

At least Moyes acknowledges that playing with the three strikers isn't working, and makes a double substitution at half-time. Off come Rooney and Tony Hibbert, replaced by James McFadden and Kevin Kilbane.

We should take the lead immediately but when a low cross finds Lee Carsley unmarked at the far post, the Harry Hill lookalike smashes his shot over the bar from close range. We're giving it a better go than City, but still everything looks disjointed and unconvincing. Kevin Campbell replaces Jeffers with twenty-five minutes remaining and his physical presence at least gives us something to aim for as we hump the ball forward and hope for a City mistake.

123

In the dying minutes, with both teams stretched all over the place, Campbell picks up a loose ball and feeds Radzinski out on the right, just inside the City half. With little support, the Canadian opts to break down the wing and, spotting a late run by Gravesen, picks the Dane out with a cut-back to the penalty spot. Unlike Carsley, Gravesen keeps his cool and side-foots his shot past substitute keeper Kevin Ellegaard, only for the ball to strike the foot of the post and rebound to safety, stifling the cries of jubilation in the throats of thirty-five thousand Evertonians.

There's still time for a David Unsworth header straight at Ellegaard but almost inevitably this miserable encounter finishes goalless.

I'm still fuming in the pub afterwards - why did we give up the initiative by trying that daft formation? Despite our poor form this season we've still got one of the best home records in the Premiership, we should have just played our normal game, especially against as poor a side as City.

Portsmouth away is hardly going to be a cakewalk next Saturday, and if we lose that then the next home game against Leicester starts to look a bit iffy. That's before we even contemplate Old Trafford on Boxing Day and the visits of Arsenal and high-flying Birmingham.

The news that we've drawn Norwich at home in the third round of the FA Cup and that Robbie Savage is, and I quote, 'a done deal for January', hardly lifts the spirits.

Monday 8th December 2003

Tony Cascarino is in the paper and on the radio telling everyone that Wayne Rooney and Everton would be better off if he was sold to someone like Chelsea. The same beauts who say stuff like this often complain that the Premiership isn't competitive enough because the top three have all the best players.

Wednesday 10th December 2003

Apparently Victor Onopko returned to Russia after only one training session. I have visions of him being comically bad, like that fat lad on the Carlsberg advert, the one with Alan

Hansen as his butler, and Everton's management team all looking at each other in horror like the judges at the Phoenix Club's auditions.

Friday 12th December 2003

Belle and Sebastian at the Royal Court, now that's what I call a gig. The fey Glaswegian pop combo are excellent as ever, and so are their support band, Franz Ferdinand. The only down side is I don't get home until after one o'clock, slightly merry, and we're leaving for Portsmouth at 8.30 in the morning.

Saturday 13th December 2003

Sonny Von Bulow would be easier to wake up than me this morning, but somehow I manage to arise just in time to pour myself into the passenger seat of Gid's car for the start of a five hundred mile round trip.

The weather report says that the rain isn't as bad down South, but in truth the whole country is covered by one single, slate-grey cloud and the downpour is simply relentless. This wouldn't normally be of particular concern, it is December after all, but the away end at Fratton Park has no roof on it. In this day and age that is simply shocking, and what's worse is that they still have the brass cojones to charge a whole twenty-nine pounds per seat.

And who can sit down? By the time we get into the ground the rain's moved up a gear from 'downpour' to 'monsoon' and the seats are absolutely soaking. Before the teams can even take to the field there's water dripping off the ends of noses, down the backs of necks and down sleeves to slowly fill up pockets. It's like a scene from Moby Dick, but that still doesn't stop the determined spliff builders in our party. Teamwork worthy of one of those outward bound courses that companies send junior managers on - you know, where they have to get a stretcher across a crocodile-infested river in Cumbria using only pipe cleaners and a traffic cone - ensures that the potheads fashion something resembling a reefer despite the inclement conditions. With that sort of determination and ingenuity it's no wonder the sun never set on the British Empire.

WHAT'S OUR NAME? EVERTON!

The potheads, or 'fucking hippies' as Gaz calls them, aren't the only ones showing a bit of defiance, as Everton start the game in a positive fashion, forcing a number of corners in the early stages. However, we fail to capitalise and after a quarter of an hour Portsmouth take the lead against the run of play. Thomas Gravesen mis-controls a short pass from Steve Watson and before we know it Teddy Sheringham has put Jason Roberts through on goal. The skilful yet erratic ex-West Brom striker shows uncharacteristic composure to draw Nigel Martyn before slipping the ball underneath him and into the net.

The wet, the cold, the hangover and the feelings of dread at the prospect of the journey home suddenly feel ten times worse.

The home side are obviously buoyed by taking the lead, but Everton don't look ready to collapse just yet. Kevin Campbell's back up front and looks fitter than when he appeared earlier in the season - he's holding the ball up well despite the conditions and causing the Pompey defence problems.

Watson pulls up after twenty-five minutes and is replaced by Wayne Rooney, who takes up an unfamiliar position on the right wing, and a minute later we're level.

Pompey are playing with Sheringham 'behind the front two', and our equaliser should be shown in coaching manuals as an example of that tactic's deficiencies. With their midfield so narrow, the Portsmouth right-back, Boris Zivkovic, has no cover whatsoever when Kevin Kilbane picks a ball up and slides a pass into the corner for the overlapping Gary Naysmith. The Scottish full-back has time and space to pick out Lee Carsley with a cut-back and the ex-Derby midfielder atones for his miss against Manchester City by steering home a low shot from twelve yards.

This is more like it.

Portsmouth are getting bogged down trying to play through the centre, while Everton are getting the ball out wide where Rooney and Pistone look threatening on the right and Kilbane and Naysmith continue to combine well on the left. With a few minutes to go before half-time it's Naysmith again who is instrumental in us taking the lead. This time he hangs a high cross up to the far post, panicking Pavel Srnicek into punching the ball into the path of Rooney. The 'fat bastard', as the Portsmouth fans refer to him throughout, shows great technique to strike an awkward left-footed volley that takes a slight deflection en route to the bottom corner.

That rain now feels positively refreshing.

At half-time hundreds of Blues try to find some shelter underneath a television gantry, completely blocking the gangway and preventing any serious attempt to get to the toilets. When we played Shrewsbury in last season's FA Cup they had better facilities than this.

Everton, so often a Jekyll and Hyde team from one half to the next, start the second half in similar vein to the first, with Rooney bursting down the right and slipping a clever pass along the edge of the box for Kilbane. His shot, although fiercely struck, is straight into Srnicek's chest.

I always have this feeling when I go to the toilet while the game's in progress that the opposition will score, but I'm bursting thanks to several pints before kick-off. Just as I reach the now deserted gangway behind the stand, there's a huge cheer from the Pompey fans that makes me think that they have indeed equalised. However, a copper at the top of the stairs informs me that Rooney's been sent off.

I complete my ablutions in toilets resembling those in the betting shop in *Trainspotting*, before returning to my seat, fuming.

"What's he gone off for?" I ask Alan Welsh.

"It was mad," he replies. "Steve Stone fouled him and the ref waved play on. Rooney went mad, pushed Stone over and started towards the tunnel straight away. He got all the way there before the ref called him back and showed him a yellow card."

And indeed he was still on the pitch.

It's an old cliché, but I subscribe to the theory that 'things even themselves out over time', and so as far as the karmic scales go, this incident probably cancels out the undeserved sending off Rooney received at Birmingham last season.

Portsmouth are working hard to try and force an opening, but they're struggling against a resolute Everton side who look a lot more like the team of last season. Alan Stubbs and David Unsworth defend magnificently as the hosts get desperate, launching high balls into the box in the hope of a slip or a lucky break, and on more than one occasion we catch them with swift counter-attacks, only to be let down by some tentative finishing.

There's an agonising four minutes of injury time but eventually Uriah Rennie blows his whistle and we've done it, we've taken three points away from home for the first time this season. It feels like forever since we've enjoyed the journey home from an away game, and this one is made doubly pleasurable by the fact that Liverpool have lost at home to Southampton. The Radio Five phone-in has us rapt, listening to the assorted accents of people ringing in to demand Gerard Houllier's head.

Even after a couple of pints in Banbury, one of the most evil-smelling places in the country, we're still home just after ten o'clock, right in time for *The Premiership* on ITV.

Tres bon, as the French say.

Sunday 14th December 2003

There's an interesting interview with Arsene Wenger on the radio. The pasty-faced Frenchman, when asked would he accept fifty million pounds - the sum that Chelsea are apparently ready to offer - for Thierry Henry, said he wouldn't. He reasoned that it's better to have great players on the pitch than money in the bank, and also added that supporters can accept when a club hasn't got the cash to go and buy star names, but they will not accept seeing their best players sold.

Spot on, Arsene, and hopefully Everton feel the same way about Wayne Rooney.

Monday 15th December 2003

We've apparently been linked with a move for Manchester United's Nicky Butt. David Moyes laughs it off though, stating the obvious: we simply couldn't afford him.

The deal for Onopko might not be dead in the water though. The problem wasn't with his performance in training, rather the length of the contract that Everton offered him. He wanted something longer than just until the end of the season, but at thirty-four years of age he's got no chance; we've been down that road too many times before. It's reported, however, that he's still considering our initial offer.

Saturday 20th December 2003

There's been hardly a drop of rain all week since the soaking at Portsmouth, but cue soft ollies and his compadres having a new magazine to sell and the heavens open for another downpour of near biblical proportions. Which reminds me of my Uncle John.

Whenever Jehovha's Witnesses or other sundry religious pests knock on my Uncle John's door he has something of a unique way of dealing with them. Rather than throwing a bedpan over them and slamming the door, like normal people do, he engages them in a discourse, almost like Peter Falk in *Columbo*.

He usually starts with something along the lines of: "We're not meant to take the bible literally are we? They're just parables, correct?"

The immaculately dressed messengers of God are invariably overjoyed that someone has deigned to interact with them. "No sir, the good book is the word of God."

"Really? It's just the ark you see. I mean I have no problem with the whole resurrection bit or even the water into wine, but that ark…"

"What exactly is it in the story of Noah that troubles you sir?"

"Well it's a couple of things really. Polar bears for a start."

"Polar bears?"

"Yes, polar bears. I mean, even if they set off at the first sign of rain, did the two of them really have enough time to make it all the way to the Middle East? Or do you think it's more likely that they just tread water and Noah picked them up?"

"I've never really though about that, sir. They may have stood on a big piece of ice rather than tread water."

"That's possible, good point."

He's got them now.

"It gives the dimensions of the ark as well. It's a fair size, I admit, but it's not the USS Nimitz by any stretch of the imagination. How do you think they got all those animals on board?"

"With great difficulty and no small amount of patience we imagine," they offer in jest as the first hairline cracks began to breach their faith.

"And even if it was possible to get them all on board without them eating each other, where did they keep all the food?"

The last time he had this conversation it ended with the shaken zealots drawing him a sketch of a series of 'sub-arks' being towed behind the principal ark while a couple of polar bears floated past on a small glacier.

So anyway, it's wet while we're selling the mag and by three o'clock I want to stab the next person who says "Make sure my copy's a dry one" as they hand over their high denomination note. It really is grim selling in the rain, especially when all you have to look forward to is a game against Leicester City, traditionally one of the most dull and uninspiring contests on the football calendar. It's pleasantly surprising then that Everton, obviously buoyed by the win at Portsmouth, come out firing on all cylinders.

Alan Stubbs and Thomas Gravesen both have decent chances in the opening period as Micky Adams' burly but limited side struggle to get out of their own half.

Incredibly, on half an hour, Alessandro Pistone, who has only just returned to the side, goes up for a header and lands awkwardly, injuring his shoulder. Honestly, I've had CD cases that were more robust than the dashing Italian. The physio helps him off the pitch, obviously in some pain, and he's replaced by Tony Hibbert. And then Everton take the lead.

A straightforward ball down the middle is mis-controlled by Muzzy Izzet, allowing Lee Carsley to bundle through and force it home with the help of a couple of ricochets off Ian Walker and Steve Howey. That should be the cue for Everton to pour forward and crush a desperate looking Leicester, but the goal appears to galvanise the Foxes, if anything. As the game heads towards half-time the visitors' strikers, Marcus Bent and the thirty-seven-year-old Les Ferdinand, start to get hold of the ball and give problems to Everton's central defenders.

Deep into injury time the referee, Mr Dowd, awards a free-kick to Leicester for an innocuous challenge on Bent midway into the Everton half. Alan Stubbs is understandably furious but makes the mistake of throwing the ball away in disgust. As is his right, the official marches the kick ten yards forward to the very edge of the Everton penalty area.

"Les Ferdinand's going to score from this," announces Ste Connor.

"Ye of little f...ucking hell." Ferdinand scores his sixteenth league goal against us, almost bursting the net with a shot into the top corner. Luckily he's retiring at the end of this season, although no doubt he'll net at the Walkers Stadium as well.

Despite the disappointment of conceding an equaliser on the stroke of half-time, we make no changes for the second period and we're almost immediately back in front when Kevin Campbell glances a Gary Naysmith corner onto the Leicester crossbar.

Horror of horrors though, the Foxes spoil the best laid plans of mouse and Moyes by scoring again fifteen minutes in. Since replacing Pistone, Hibbert's had an absolute nightmare; his distribution's been appalling and his confidence seems shot to pieces. Once again he's standing in no man's land as Jordan Stewart breaks down the Leicester left and sends a deep cross over to Nigel Martyn's far post. The ball clears the scrum of players in the six-yard box but James Scowcroft, making a run from the right wing, stoops low to power a header into the bottom corner of the net.

Most of Goodison is stunned as a handful of wacky Leicester supporters dressed in Santa outfits go mad.

Moyes' reaction to this setback is to send Rooney on in place of the extremely disappointing James McFadden. Who would have thought after their first two games that McFadden would fade out like he has while Kevin Kilbane has gone from strength to strength? The lanky Irishman is playing out of his skin and almost puts us level with a determined run and powerful shot that Walker has to tip over at full stretch.

For the next ten minutes or so, Leicester look comfortable, but then they're outdone by a moment of class. The move starts when Radzinski finds space down the right and fires in a low cross that reaches Campbell, lurking on the edge of the visitors' six-yard box. The veteran shows his strength and cunning to hold off a defender and poke the ball back to the edge of the box for the unmarked Rooney to bladder a first-time shot into Walker's top corner. Before his teammates can mob him the England centre forward makes a forty-yard dash to celebrate in front of the Everton dugout. It's difficult to tell whether he's just overjoyed or whether he's indicating a certain amount of 'fuck you, I told you I should have started the game' as he leaps about six feet in the air in front of Moyes and the coaching staff.

This is what all the rumours of disquiet do to you; they have you psychoanalysing players' goal celebrations. Pathetic, isn't it?

The Leicester Santa Squad look slightly deflated and it only gets worse for them when, with just over ten minutes to go, Moyes makes another substitution. He withdraws Campbell to a standing ovation and introduces none other than... Duncan Ferguson. Having missed the announcement of the teams at the start of the match, I didn't even know that the big fella had been brought in from the cold.

Moyes' decision to bury the hatchet pays off in less than a minute. David Unsworth launches a free-kick from our half up to the edge of the Leicester box where Ferguson's presence panics four defenders into challenging him. Despite being corralled by this black-clad posse, the big Scot still manages to get his head onto the ball and knock it down into the path of Radzinski who steers a volley just inside the foot of Walker's left-hand post.

The police have an angry Santa in a headlock.

Sunday 21st December 2003
Without even having to try, Manchester United win 2-1 at Spurs in the televised game. It doesn't bode well for our visit to Old Trafford on Boxing Day.

Monday 22nd December 2003

Viktor Onopko's signed for the somewhat obscure Russian side Saturn REN TV. In years gone by they would have been described as a 'crack Soviet outfit'.

Wednesday 24th December 2003

Everton announce that they won't be renewing any contracts until the summer as the manager wants to fully assess the squad before committing to any new deals. This applies across the board but naturally the tabloid stories all have titles along the lines of 'Rooney Contract Freeze'.

Thursday 25th December 2003

To celebrate the birth of Jesus, every man in Great Britain receives a DVD of *Peter Kay Live at the Bolton Albert Hall*.

Friday 26th December 2003

You can't whack Boxing Day footy. It comes at the point when cabin fever is about to set in and you simply can't face another Thorntons chocolate. Manchester United away is the ideal match in that it's dead handy, but there is the obvious drawback that Everton go there almost certain to get battered.

It's pointless trying to get a drink anywhere in the vicinity of Old Trafford as the few pubs around the ground are exceptionally snidey, especially for Scousers. Instead we drive to a little posh place called Brooklands, just outside Altrincham, and go for a few pints in a pub next to the metro station.

Charlton are beating Chelsea on the telly when we get in there and the well-heeled United fans are positively cock-a-hoop. And while I've been looking forward to a day out and a good drink it must be said that the company I'm keeping is not exactly the most convivial. Gid looks as if he's got SARS, such is the potency of the flu he's suffering with, while Ray McKay has been on a bender since Christmas Eve and looks ready to spew his ring up after his first sip of lager top.

There's a nice atmosphere in this pub as it fills up with middle-aged United fans in their Next leather jackets and Marks and Spencers jumpers, while Charlton keep hammering the goals in at The Valley. However, every now and again I overhear snatches of conversation about today's game and these seemingly inoffensive pillars of the community cannot help but refer to Everton as 'these fucking Scouse bastards'. Mancunians, you see, especially those who follow United, are absolutely obsessed with all things Merseyside.

The lads who do one of United's fanzines, *United We Stand*, are dead sound, but you only have to read *Red Issue*, one of the other main publications, to get a feel for the pathological hatred towards Merseyside felt by swathes of their supporters. They follow one of the biggest clubs in the world, around which there is constant activity, yet huge portions of every issue are dedicated to the most puerile jokes and comic strips about Scouse 'Granny Stabbers' and 'Bin Dippers'. They sell a lot of magazines so there must be a big market for this lowest common denominator stuff, but ultimately it must say more about the Mancunian mindset than anything else.

Even as we're crammed on to the dangerously full tram to Old Trafford, I hear two blokes talking about Robbie Fowler in the recent Manchester derby.

"As he were goin' off he held up four fingers like, to United fans, meanin' four European Cups for Liverpool. They might have won four like, but who the fuck did they beat in the finals?"

I'm almost tempted to point out to him how desperate that sounds when I'm distracted by some little fella crushed up against me who says, "Good job there's no fuckin' Scousers on here, we'd have nothing left in our pockets."

I have no choice but to ignore him; even if I was the angry type I'd struggle to hit him given that my eyebrows are the only bit of my body I can move.

Once inside the ground it's good to see that they've still got those wanky banners, especially the big 'Republic of Mancunia' one - some of their fans try so hard it's painful. They constantly berate Scousers, calling us all the reprobate drug addicts under the sun yet simultaneously try and propagate this whole post-

Madchester 'clued-up lad' image. Part of it's a reaction to the much-maligned 'prawn sandwich brigade', and you can sympathise with that to a degree, but that doesn't make it any less hypocritical - Scouse scallies are smackhead granny-stabbers while their Manc counterparts are just a bunch of loveable 'grafters' with 'top one, nice one' accents. Weird.

The fat-necked, bulging-vein society in K Stand are still doing exaggerated syringe actions towards the Everton fans when Nicky Butt opens the scoring for United. Alex Ferguson has sent out his Worthington Cup side: the likes of David Bellion, Kleberson and Cristiano Ronaldo are playing instead of Ruud van Nistelrooy, Paul Scholes and Ryan Giggs, but they still pass it around crisply and whip a succession of great crosses into the Everton goalmouth. Alan Stubbs heads one such centre out to the edge of the box, but despite the fact that we're playing with five in midfield no one picks up Butt, who raps a low shot into Nigel Martyn's bottom left-hand corner.

We're struggling to string two passes together, although it's hardly surprising given our bizarre formation. Kevin Campbell's up front on his own as we've sacrificed a striker to allow both Tobias Linderoth and Li Tie to operate in the congested midfield. They both work hard but once we win the ball they've got almost nothing to offer in an attacking sense. Wayne Rooney's out on the right wing, but he's trying to get forward to support Campbell as much as possible; as a result he often seems caught between two stools.

It's looking really ugly, and then we equalise.

Thomas Gravesen curls a free-kick in towards Tim Howard's near post forcing Gary Neville, under pressure from Campbell and Rooney, to head into his own net. Fulham came and got a result here recently - maybe we can as well, given this bit of good luck.

And United do look a bit rattled for a couple of minutes but we simply don't take advantage and offer enough threat going forward. It looks like we're going to get to half-time all square though, until Neville atones for his own goal by whipping in yet another peach of a cross for the diminutive

Kleberson to head home from close range. The referee allowed the free-kick which started the move to be taken miles from the infringement but that's still no excuse for Everton's appalling marking.

We might as well just fuck off home at half-time. Everton look like they've come with nothing but damage limitation in mind and one eye on the much more winnable game at home to Birmingham on Sunday. That might make sense in the big scheme of things, but it's little consolation to us, standing here on Boxing Day being laughed at by this lot as we're taken to the cleaners by the likes of Quinton Fortune.

David Moyes makes no changes to his team in the second half and United continue to pour forward, particularly through Cristiano Ronaldo down the left. The Portugese winger is a despicable little ponce - he's completely anonymous in big games but likes to act like some sort of matador when United are on top at home. Unfortunately for us that's the case here and he's ripping the back out of Tony Hibbert who, out of frustration and desperation, puts in a heavy tackle down by the corner flag. Ronaldo delights the United crowd by deliberately smashing the resultant free-kick straight at Hibbert, only for Rooney to go one better moments later, almost slicing the bizarrely-coiffured winger in half with a lunging tackle.

It's got to the point now where you can see the Rooney moment of madness coming a mile off. He normally does a couple of mad dribbles first or a wild shot from distance, followed by a brief spat with the ref and then, inevitably, comes the horror tackle. No one would be surprised to see him get a straight red card here, but thankfully the referee only produces a yellow.

After that, with both Hibbert and Rooney scared to go near Ronaldo, the Portugese under-21 international tricks his way to the line and cuts the ball back for Bellion to smash United's third into the roof of the net.

Moyes immediately drags Rooney off and replaces him with James McFadden who, along with two other substitutes, Duncan

Ferguson and Francis Jeffers, at least try to attack for the final twenty minutes of the match.

Mindful of the Altamont-type crowd scenes on the metro on the way in we make our exit a few minutes before the end, and it's only when we get back to the pub that we realise that Ferguson scored a ninetieth minute header to make the final score a deceptively respectable sounding 3-2.

Maybe we should get used to going to places like Old Trafford and getting hammered, it's happened often enough after all, but we never do. Every time you secretly think that you're going to go there and put on a barnstorming performance, catch them on an off day and record a famous victory. Let's face it, much as it pains me to say so, it would be famous, as the days of Everton regularly beating United are slipping further back into the mists of time.

This time next year, hey Rodney, this time next year.

Sunday 28th December 2003

Half-time at home against Birmingham City and nothing has happened. Nothing. At all.

If proof were needed that we more or less wrote off the game against Manchester United before it even kicked off, it's in today's team selection. Tobias Linderoth and Li Tie aren't even on the bench.

Thankfully Duncan Ferguson is back in the fold as he was the brightest thing about this game in the first half, carrying on where he left off on Friday.

Birmingham have had a decent first half to the season, but they're missing David Dunn and Christophe Dugarry today and seem happy to grind out a draw. Luckily for us though, David Moyes introduces Wayne Rooney at the start of the second half and we immediately look more threatening.

The youngster's on the right again, but Tomasz Radzinski's good at coming out wide and leaving a gap for him to cut into, as he did for the second goal against Leicester. At the moment this looks like our best method of having the pair of them - our two most dangerous players - on the pitch at the same time, and they combine almost immediately to set up Kevin Kilbane, who forces a close range stop from Maik Taylor in the Birmingham goal.

For all our extra invention in the second half the breakthrough eventually comes from a very straightforward piece of play on sixty-nine minutes. Gary Naysmith swings over a corner that Taylor, under pressure from Ferguson and Stubbs, can only pat down to the edge of the six-yard box. Rooney blasts it straight back into the net. The Birmingham players and fans all expect referee Rob Styles to automatically disallow it, as is the custom whenever anyone goes near the keeper these days but quite rightly he points back to the centre-circle.

Rooney's again ecstatic and runs back to the halfway line to celebrate as he did against Leicester. Quite a few people questioned whether he was having a go at Moyes on that day, myself included, but it turns out that his family's box is right behind the dugouts and he's actually signalling to them.

That's three crucial goals in four games now for the lad who many 'experts' still think is wasting his time at Everton. More importantly it proves to be the winner and we find ourselves up to eleventh place in the league. Crisis averted for the time being then.

We are starting to look a lot more like the team of last season now, the Manchester United game apart. One of our biggest strengths last time around was the ability of the less vaunted players to come in and do a good job, and that seems to have been the case again in the last month or so. David Unsworth's excelling at centre-half still, Kevin Kilbane's been a revelation on the left wing and even Alex Nyarko returned here today and looked a lot better than his opposite number, none other than Robbie Savage. There's also the fact that we now have two fit target-men to choose from and Rooney and Radzinski are finding the back of the net regularly. Perhaps we can look forward to a better second half of the season.

Tuesday 30th December 2003

It's my birthday, which I share with 1995 FA Cup semi-final hero Daniel Amokachi. Hopefully Amo doesn't feel quite as lousy with a cold as I do on this, our special day.

Wednesday 31st December 2003

While playing so well on Sunday Alex Nyarko managed to chip a bone in his foot and will be out for several weeks. I've no idea whether this has put a dampener on his New Year celebrations but mine are decidedly low key, drinking Lemsip shandies in front of the telly and applauding the heavy rain outside.

Why should everyone else have a good time while I'm stuck in with Jools Holland and his frigging Hootenanny?

January

If You're Feeling Sinister

Friday 2nd January 2004

David Moyes says that contrary to recent reports, Everton have not improved their new contract offer to David Unsworth. He's playing well at the moment but with the purse strings being so tight at Goodison there really is little room for sentiment. It seems that the manager thinks he can get someone better, and possibly younger, for the same money.

You often hear people say that he's earned a new deal with his recent performances, but surely he's simply earning the money that he's getting from his current contract?

Saturday 3rd January 2004

You can tell it's FA Cup third round day, *Football Focus* is awash with eccentric managers, part-time players with vaguely interesting day jobs and the lesser-talented siblings of Premiership stars. I'm so excited I'm almost tempted to get some tin foil and make a ridiculously flimsy replica cup that will fold at the base when I wave it at the television cameras.

Top of the first division Norwich are the visitors to Goodison and quite a few of the pundits see this game as a potential banana skin. I must admit I wouldn't be keen on playing them at Carrow Road but as long as we don't do anything stupid, like fielding a weakened team, the gulf between the two divisions will show. You only have to look at the teams who come up from the Nationwide, like Wolves for instance, to see the difference in class is bigger than it's ever been at the moment. Rightly or wrongly the Premiership is the be all and end all - few good players are willing to stick with sides outside the top flight.

Take Norwich for instance they've had to break the bank to secure the permanent signature of a player who is apparently head and shoulders above just about everything else in that division. When you hear Norwich fans on the radio talking about him you'd think they were describing Ferenc Puskas or Johann Cruyff, not Darren Huckerby.

We haven't got our normal seats for this game; we're three rows from the front of the Park End instead. I like sitting this low now and again as it always reminds me just how fast the game is and how little time the players get on the ball. You tend to reassess the fan's favourite insult, "I could play better than him", when you're close enough to feel every tackle and hear every high-pitched shriek.

I often try to imagine what it would be like to play in a Premiership match, bearing in mind that on the occasions when some semi-pros come along to our regular Friday seven-a-side game, the likes of myself spend our hour of 'leisure time' running around after them like idiots, never touching the ball other than to go and get it when it's been volleyed out and landed by the swings. What would it be like in a top-flight game then, going up for a header with Duncan Ferguson or chasing back after Tomasz Radzinski? Like the opening scene in *Saving Private Ryan* I reckon, with bodies flying everywhere and people shouting bewildering commands at you from every angle.

With all that in mind, it makes Thomas Gravesen's first half performance here all the more of a joy to behold - the Dane seems to have hours on the ball as he dictates the play from the very start. Norwich are being spurred on by an extremely healthy following of around six thousand who have made the trip from East Anglia, but it's to little avail in the opening exchanges as Duncan Ferguson heads against the bar in the first five minutes and Everton pepper their goal with shots.

Wayne Rooney spurns an excellent chance when he pokes James McFadden's pass through Malky Mackay's legs and then hammers his shot over the bar with only Robert Green to beat, but the visitors can't hold out forever and the breakthrough comes just fifteen minutes in. Gravesen fires in a free-kick identical to the one that forced Gary Neville into an own goal at Old Trafford, but this time it's an Everton player, Kevin Kilbane, who rises to power a header into the top corner. According to Graham Ennis, someone somewhere has recently christened the Irish international 'Zinedine'.

We're all expecting a stroll and a cricket score at this point but it's not to be. All our good work is undone when a Paul McVeigh free-kick is only half cleared by David Unsworth, allowing Jim Brennan to lash a half-volley across the face of the Everton goal and in off the far post. The yellow and green half of the Bullens Road stand goes justifiably nuts.

Unfortunately for Delia's boys, who I must say sport some of the most awful boy-band haircuts ever to grace Goodison, their fightback is relatively short-lived. With less than ten minutes until half-time, Rooney heads a cross down into the Norwich six-yard box, forcing Iwan Roberts into making a crude challenge on Alan Stubbs that has the referee instantly signalling for a penalty.

Rooney looks desperate to take the kick and Unsworth, the obvious candidate, is also indicating that he wants the ball, but Ferguson is having none of it. It's clear that despite his problems behind the scenes, he can still pull rank as he ushers his teammates away and places the ball on the spot. Such is the Everton psyche, we're all convinced that any player this confident is bound to miss. But he doesn't, he sidles up instead and side-foots the ball coolly into Green's bottom left-hand corner.

Gravesen, through whom everything flowed in the first half, doesn't reappear for the second, replaced by Joseph Yobo. The Nigerian goes straight into central defence, with Alan Stubbs pushing into midfield and the difference is immediately noticeable. All of a sudden we're relying on the industrious but uninspiring Lee Carsley to get hold of the ball and do the prompting from the middle, and it just doesn't happen. Suddenly we're struggling to put even a couple of passes together and the Canaries begin to grow in confidence and play like a team who are not used to losing.

Moyes swaps Stubbs and Yobo around after only five minutes - the Nigerian has apparently played in midfield for his country before - but it makes no difference. Despite the pummelling they received in the first half, Norwich are still only one goal behind and Huckerby seems certain to level matters when a McVeigh cross lands at his feet inside the six-yard box. However, Nigel Martyn flings himself at the gormless striker's feet and smothers his shot, maintaining Everton's slender lead. It is a cliché, but it's true that it's the sign of a great keeper when he can have virtually nothing to do all game but still pull off great saves when called upon.

If Norwich had equalised there we could have easily folded, but it wasn't to be and the game is finished on seventy minutes when Roberts again fouls Stubbs, this time at a corner, and another penalty is awarded. It's Ferguson again who steps up and this time slips the ball into the right-hand corner.

Cool fucker.

In the end a potentially awkward tie proved relatively straightforward. I just hope Gravesen's injury isn't too serious as even his harshest critics must have been able to see just how important he is to us after watching today's contrasting halves.

Everyone in Orry's after the game wants Yeovil at home in the next round. Firstly, because we'd batter them, and secondly it would mean they'd beaten Liverpool, who they play tomorrow.

Sunday 4th January 2004

The *WSAG* messageboard is full of posts regarding allegations of racist chants by the Norwich fans yesterday. I certainly never heard any and over time the picture that emerges, or the consensus of opinion is at least, that some people mistook their boringly predictable chants of "You fat bastard" aimed towards Wayne Rooney for "You black bastard" following a booking for Joseph Yobo.

While subtle and insidious racism is still a problem in football, I would nevertheless be absolutely amazed to hear mass chants again from any set of fans, least of all Norwich. Therefore I can understand why some of their supporters are so offended by the allegations, although some of them overstep the mark by telling us that we've got a cheek accusing anyone of racism given our past behaviour. What's that got to do with it?

Liverpool struggle badly in the first half against Yeovil but eventually come through 2-0. Arsenal, who we play at Goodison on Wednesday night, make light of going a goal down in the first minute at Elland Road, as they eventually annihilate Leeds 4-1. I fear for the likes of Tony Hibbert and David Unsworth trying to keep up with Thierry Henry and Robert Pires.

Just as the Arsenal game is drawing to a close, I answer the phone to a journalist from the *Daily Post* who asks me about the Norwich chants. I'm honest and say straight away that I wasn't even aware of any incident until I looked at the internet this morning.

"So you can't comment then?"

"No, sorry, I never heard anything."

"Me neither to be honest, it's Everton's safety officer who has made the allegations though. What are other people saying?"

"No one I've spoken to heard anything either. All I've seen is what's on the internet and the consensus of opinion seems to be that they were chanting 'fat', not 'black.'"

"Alright then, fair enough. Bye."

"Bye."

Monday 5th January 2004
Fulham at home in the next round of the FA Cup. It's hardly the most inspiring tie; the ideal is either someone shit at home or an away trip to someone you've not played for years but who have got a decent ground so you get plenty of tickets.

We play Fulham away on Saturday as well and no one likes playing the same team in a short space of time, although we've got off lightly compared to Middlesbrough who face Arsenal, in various competitions, four times in eighteen days.

Tuesday 6th January 2004
Wayne Rooney, Duncan Ferguson, Alan Stubbs and Thomas Gravesen all have various ailments that make them doubtful for

tomorrow's big game with the Gunners. We'll need as many of our big players fit as possible, especially if we're to impress thirty-one-year-old Schalke 04 defender Tomasz Hajto. We've apparently made an offer for him, but the Polish international is being a bit cagey, saying: "I am considering the move, but Everton have not been that strong and have big games coming up. I am going to see how they get on against Arsenal on Wednesday."

No one's holding a gun to your head, Tomasz.

Despite me saying that I had no comment to make, I'm quoted in the local and national papers as saying: "I never heard anything, the consensus seems to be that they were chanting 'fat' not 'black'" I can't really complain, because they were my words, but it's disconcerting when you believe you've established with the journalist that you've no comment to make.

Nearly all of us involved with *WSAG* have been misquoted or quoted out of context at one time or another and we decided a while back that we weren't going to give out any more quotes after Graham Ennis was labelled 'fans' leader' in one paper. However, it's easier said than done as your natural tendency to be polite and not slam the phone down on people means you end up trying to explain yourself, and you sound like some right ego-maniac saying: "I'm sorry, we don't speak to the press." You half expect the person on the other end of the line to say, "Fucking hell lad, who do you think you are, JD Salinger? You only write a fanzine."

You can't win.

Wednesday 7th January 2004

I'm doing some work at the Liverpool Institute for Performing Arts at the moment, giving lessons to aspiring musicians on such diverting topics as writing CVs, press releases, biographies and putting together their own websites. I've got some sessions with the students today so I plan to finish them, have some tea at the wonderful Kimo's Café on Mount Pleasant, then head up to the match. However, my Dad's off work and gives me a bell, offering to meet me in town for a pint.

"Sound, what time?" I ask.

"I'll meet you in the Beehive at four o'clock."

He's nothing if not keen.

By the time the match kicks off at eight o'clock, I'm a tad squiffy to say the least. In fact I'm so plastered that I think most of the Park End are privy to my conversation with Ste Connor as I try to describe a vision of loveliness who was sharing a bottle of wine with her mate in Wetherspoons.

"She had them big mad furry white Yeti boots on and a denim mini skirt that kept riding up so high that her mate kept slapping her arse. I nearly never made it the match. I tell you, if I wasn't married, and maybe a bit younger, and a bit better looking as well..."

Scientists have proven that there are more drop dead stunners per head of population in Liverpool than in any other place on the planet. Well, probably not scientists exactly, but as anyone who visits the city will tell you, Liverpool women are unbelievable. Most of them are gorgeous, and the ones who aren't still make tons of effort and wear very little, no matter what the weather.

And from sexy women to sexy football, and Arsenal, amazingly, seem incapable of producing any tonight as Everton set about frustrating them and hassling all over the pitch. While I'm never a fan of changing your formation - I'm 4-4-2 and proud - Moyes has got Duncan Ferguson up the middle on his own with both Tomasz Radzinski and Wayne Rooney playing out in wide positions, and it's stopping the Arsenal full-backs from getting into the game at all. Admittedly we're not doing much in terms of passing the ball about ourselves, but we're stopping the Gunners from taking the piss, and we actually have the best chance to open the scoring when Ashley Cole has to scramble a Kevin Kilbane header off his own goal line.

For the most part though it's pretty grim stuff, with the ball spending more time in the stands than on the pitch.

Then, suddenly, on half an hour, Arsenal take the lead with a goal out of nothing.

With most of the Everton side back defending, there seems to be no danger when Freddie Ljungberg picks the ball up in midfield, but the Swede spots an angled run by Nwankwo Kanu and slips a straight pass into the space between the full-back and the centre-half. Kanu, exceptionally gifted but often over-elaborate, shrugs off David Unsworth and rounds Nigel Martyn before rolling a shot into the back of the net.

I'm obviously gutted that we've gone behind but I can't help admiring Arsenal's class - they make scoring look so simple. Luckily for us though, they don't relax and start strutting their stuff once they're in the lead; in fact they look genuinely rattled by Everton's approach and the satisfyingly hostile atmosphere that Goodison generates for big games like this.

How we don't go in on level terms at half-time will remain forever a mystery, as Wayne Rooney conjures up a miss that is possibly worse than Francis Jeffers' against Chelsea. Kilbane - he's going to end up as player of the season at the rate he's going - curls a cross to the edge of the Arsenal six-yard box, just begging for someone to nod it past Jens Lehmann. Rooney's first to it - he doesn't even have to jump - but he gets his timing horribly wrong and the ball strikes him on the neck and bounces well wide of the post. It was literally easier to score than do that.

Arsenal almost punish that miss when Henry's ridiculously ambitious free-kick clips the wall and bobbles towards the unguarded portion of the Everton goal. Martyn is left as helpless as everyone else in the ground, and he joins the home crowd in breathing a sigh of relief as the ball spins narrowly wide.

Two-nil would have been horribly unfair and nigh on impossible to recover from, even given the fact that the Gunners look a shadow of their normal selves. As it is, we're still right in the game in the second half as the Blues re-emerge with Tobias Linderoth replacing the extremely poor Li Tie. Neither player is the long-term solution to our midfield problems but the Swede, although very limited, is at least the more competent of the two.

The second period is as tight and furiously contested as the first, with chances again few and far between: Rooney's fiercely struck free-kick smacks the bewildered Lehmann and rebounds to safety, while a rare break from Henry is foiled by Stubbs' magnificent recovery tackle.

Moyes withdraws Kilbane on seventy minutes and introduces Francis Jeffers, the player still on loan to us from today's opponents, and within five minutes he creates the equaliser. Ferguson once again rises above both Pascal Cygan and Sol Campbell and flicks a long punt from Martyn towards the corner of the Arsenal box. Ashley Cole, who has struggled all game, mis-controls and allows Jeffers to barge him aside and crack a half-volley at goal. Lehmann saves at full stretch but Radzinski is first onto the loose ball and slides it home from a tight angle.

There are still fifteen minutes remaining so we're hardly about to count our chickens, but if anything we look like the side more intent on pushing for a winner. In the last ten minutes, Arsene Wenger replaces the attack-minded Ljungberg and Kanu with midfield destroyers Edu and Gilberto, leaving his side with one striker on the pitch compared to Everton's four. That says all you need to know about Everton's performance, although the extra goal never comes and the game finishes all square.

"I'm surprised at Arsenal," says Redmond, as we scald our mouths on spring rolls from one of the eight hundred chippies on County Road. "They came here and their bottles went when they had to put up with fatties hanging out of the Paddock screaming at them and Duncan Ferguson jumping all over them. You couldn't imagine it happening to Manchester United. The likes of Roy Keane and the Nevilles thrive on that."

Thursday 8th January 2004

If Evertonians are pleased with our result last night our joy is nothing compared to the Liverpudlians' reaction to a one-nil win at Stamford Bridge, especially given that the scorer was none other than Bruno Cheyrou. One minute Liverpool are the club in crisis, the next they're going to win the league. The truth is, as always, somewhere in between. They've got some excellent players - more than us - but they've got some shite as well. Chelsea, as predicted, have started to cave in at the first sign of trouble. There's talk of them buying yet more players now the transfer window is open but unless they get someone of the very highest calibre - van Nistelrooy or Ronaldo - then they're just making things worse if anything.

And speaking of signings, there's no news on whether Tomasz Hajto was suitably impressed with us last night.

Friday 9th January 2004

Thomas Gravesen is linked with a £4 million move to Germany's Schalke 04, but David Moyes insists that "We are not letting anyone go, especially not Thomas."

It's starting to dawn on a lot of people just how important Gravesen is. Unfortunately he'll be missing for the trip to Loftus Road tomorrow. Fulham aren't having the best time of it lately, especially with their star striker Louis Saha throwing his toys out of his pram after being denied his dream move to Old Trafford the other day, but anyone who thinks that they will be pushovers is in for a shock.

Saturday 10th January 2004

Men are from Mars; women are from Venus, apparently. I've already said that you notice the difference in attitudes between the sexes when you're selling the magazine - well, another time is when you're at one of those cash-points you find at petrol stations and motorway services. The top and bottom of it is, women never use them, ever. Visit one on a Saturday morning when there's a match on though, and you'll invariably find a queue of unshaven blokes waiting to be charged £1.50 or whatever to get at their own money.

For instance, I've known all week that I'm going to need to give Bob thirty quid for my ticket, Weavers another tenner or so for petrol and various Australians another thirty or forty nicker for ale. Have I been to 'the hole in the wall' in all that time though? Have I shite; the first thing I say when I'm picked up at 9.30 is, "I'm going to need to stop for money."

"Me too," chime in Alan Welsh and Eddy, another lad from the Butchers. Between us we've got about thirty-seven pence in our pockets and zero credit on our mobile phones. That could never happen to women - they invariably have at least fifty notes stuffed into their purse at any given time. Except for Thursday nights when the window man needs paying of course.

Once we've made a quick stop for funds, we're on our way and making ace time in Weavers' new company car, a far sight more comfortable than the old wreck that somehow got us to Charlton. We make such good time in fact that we're actually settled in O'Neill's in Shepherd's Bush half an hour before our London-based mates show up. Last season we all met up in the Springbok, right next to the ground, but quite frankly it was a magnet for the most annoying elements of Everton's away support. A lot of Blues seem to have learned their lesson, as O'Neill's fills up with plenty of familiar faces intent on having a peaceful pint without the need to leap up and down, throw ale everywhere and sing songs about murderers.

The ground's a bit further away than I remembered, so it's almost kick-off when we arrive, only to be confronted by a massive queue to the tiny alley that provides access to the away end. A line of stewards and coppers seem to be only allowing people through in dribs and drabs, prompting me to enquire what the problem is.

"Loads of people have got junior tickets," explains one policeman.

"You're joking?" I reply, aware that at least three of our lot fall into that category.

When we get to the mouth of the alley, we think we're being dead clever by milling around the stewards and causing a general distraction as the lads with the juniors get bundled through towards the turnstiles. In reality, the stewards are probably perfectly aware of what's going on but with the queue swelling behind us, and tickets being passed backward and forwards, they probably can't be arsed with all the hassle. And who can blame them?

We get in and take our seats in the upper tier just in time to see Kevin Kilbane shoot wide while unmarked in the box. Then, as is the norm now with Everton games, it takes a few minutes to work out exactly who is playing where. Apparently we've used more players than any other side in the division - good going considering we're meant to have such a small squad.

Initially it looks as if Kevin Campbell's up front with Francis Jeffers, with Tomasz Radzinski on the right wing, although midway through the half it looks as if they switch to more of a 4-3-3. Duncan Ferguson and Wayne Rooney are on the bench while Tobias Linderoth's been rewarded with a start after his decent second half performance on Wednesday. Despite all the chopping and changing - even the defence is different, with David Weir coming in to replace the injured Alan Stubbs - we look easily the more menacing side in the opening period. Jeffers works a couple of decent openings but fails to trouble Edwin van der Sar, while Radzinski almost scores a corker, flicking the ball over the head of Andy Melville and striking a left-footed volley that the keeper does well to save.

Inevitably the home side get their act together though and start to keep possession and manoeuvre their way upfield. They've definitely got the edge in midfield where the likes of Steed Malbranque, Lee Clark and yes, Sean Davis, all look comfortable on the ball. Davis himself almost opens the scoring with an angled volley that has Nigel Martyn scrambling across his goal to force wide. The shaven-headed Cockney then laughs good-naturedly at the somewhat churlish chants of "Who the fucking hell are you?" from the Everton fans behind the goal.

Nil-nil is looking like a fair result as half-time looms, when suddenly Gary Naysmith makes a mad lunge at Malbranque and concedes a stonewall penalty. The Frenchman threw his head back a bit dramatically, but that doesn't change the fact that Naysmith got nowhere near the ball.

Saha, who certainly isn't playing like someone in a sulk, cracks the spot-kick into the roof of the net.

The cramped and dingy concourse below the stand is not a happy place to be at half-time. I bump into a lad who I went to university with who assures me that we'll come back and win 2-1 in the second half.

He obviously learnt less than me during his four years in Leicester, as his prediction is blown out of the water within sixty seconds of the restart - Malbranque drills a low shot inside Martyn's far post to put the Cottagers two up. It's Tottenham all over again.

Less than fifteen minutes in, Moyes has seen enough and signals for a triple substitution. Campbell's number is the first to be shown, to the cheers of quite a few of our fans. What sort of way is that to treat your own players? By all means cheer the arrival of his replacement, Ferguson, but why humiliate Campbell like that? What does it achieve?

Rooney and James McFadden also replace Radzinski and Lee Carsley as we reshuffle and try to salvage something from a game that's run away from us in the space of two minutes either side of the break. The changes do produce some impetus, but nearly all of our play is reduced to long balls down the middle for Ferguson to flick on. It's exciting stuff but it all looks a bit desperate. Fulham defend well too, although van der Sar has to make one superb stop with his feet when Ferguson connects with a Jeffers cross on the edge of the six-yard box.

Then, with just less than ten minutes remaining, Kilbane picks a ball up in midfield and advances slightly, looking for a runner to try and slip in behind the defence. The Fulham defenders, mindful of the runs of McFadden and Jeffers, back off, leaving a gap through which the spindly Irishman creams the ball past van der Sar from thirty-five yards out. It's an absolute beauty, easily the best goal we've scored this season.

A point looks well within our grasp now.

The aerial bombardment continues, but to give Fulham some credit they seem to have become a lot more robust since we played them at Goodison, and the likes of the twelve-foot tall Zat Knight throw themselves at everything launched into their box. Meanwhile, Saha, up front on his own, does well to pick up the clearances and relieve the pressure on the defence.

In the final minute, we win a free-kick about eight yards in from the corner flag and every Everton player except Martyn piles into the box for the final throw of the dice. All the usual jockeying and jostling takes place as the defenders try and keep track of the big men like Ferguson and Weir - we just need Naysmith to keep the delivery away from van der Sar. The

Scottish full-back, whose mistake gifted Fulham the first goal, looks up and strikes the ball left-footed. It goes about ten yards at knee height, strikes the first defender and is easily belted to safety.

Game over.

Stupid things like that, downright poor play, are a big part of what separates the top sides from the rest. Imagine Manchester United with a free-kick like that in the last minute - they would at least make their opponents defend it and work for their victory.

On the way home I moan about that and so much more while putting a big dent in a box of Stella.

Sunday 11th January 2004

Graham Poll, the referee yesterday, has included in his report that a number of missiles were thrown onto the pitch by the Everton fans. I do remember seeing a programme getting lobbed, but it just sort of unfurled in the wind and fluttered harmlessly about a bit. According to various newspaper reports, however, a disposable cigarette lighter was also lashed and almost hit Luis Boa Morte. The Portuguese winger is a bit of a hate figure since he sparked a mass brawl between the two teams a couple of seasons ago, but that obviously doesn't excuse this.

Quite a few reports from fans on the *WSAG* website and some of the other Everton ones say that a lot of our fans were behaving badly before and during the game. Like last season, a lot of it seems to have been centred around the Springbok, although quite a few say that there were plenty of racist comments being shouted during the game itself.

Monday 12th January 2004

Despite the defeat at the weekend, and the obvious edge that Fulham had in midfield, David Moyes insists he has no regrets about not signing Sean Davis as he is so pleased with the players he got in instead. He also reiterates that there will be no transfer movement in or out of Goodison during this transfer window.

WHAT'S OUR NAME? EVERTON!

Tuesday 13th January 2004

Everton have stated that, if he's identified, they will consider banning from Goodison the individual who threw the lighter on Saturday.

Manchester United have said that they are willing to let Nicky Butt go - the speculation is that they want somewhere in the region of five million pounds for him. Inevitably the cry goes up that the board must get the money from somewhere to bring him to Goodison. No one is quite sure where 'somewhere' is though.

Wednesday 14th January 2004

The Everton Shareholders Association have apparently approached the board with a proposal for a share issue that involves creating fifteen thousand new shares, at a grand apiece, which will initially be offered to the existing shareholders and then to the fans at large.

According to Steve Allinson, vice-chairman of the association: "There are an estimated half a million Everton fans in the UK alone - never forget it is the breadth and depth of our support that marks Everton as a truly great club.

"We are a huge family, and the sooner we give all fans worldwide the opportunity to demonstrate their support through ownership, the less the burden will rest solely on our magnificently faithful attendance.

"Make no mistake, the first big football club to genuinely harness all its latent support will be able to call upon riches that put Chelsea in the shade."

A more democratic - or even quasi-socialist - ownership of the club sounds great in theory, but I'm always a bit dubious when it comes to these proposed panaceas. Where does that figure of half a million Evertonians come from for a start? And even if it's accurate, how many of them are willing to stump up a thousand pounds for little or no return?

It will be interesting to see if it ever gets off the ground and if it can really make a difference.

Thursday 15th January 2004

Niclas Alexandersson's still around. The two Swedish clubs who are interested in signing him have decided that as their season doesn't start until April, they would rather let him get paid by Everton for now and sign him in the summer.

Elsewhere, the lunacy that is the quest for derby tickets is starting to get into full swing. We play the other horrible lot at Anfield in a couple of weeks and already every conversation ends with, "Oh, by the way, if you hear of any spares for the derby…"

People assume that because you're involved with the fanzine you have some secret source of tickets, when the truth is that I just give my away stubs - you need nine to qualify for a derby ticket - to Bob the Bookie who, it is reported, has gone and lost a load of them. At this rate I don't even know if I'll get a ticket for myself, never mind anyone else.

You can tell the people who do have illicit contacts though, as they become really vague and furtive whenever the subject of the derby arises. They say stuff like, "Oh, I'm not sure what I'm doing, some fella I know through work sometimes sorts us out," which translates as, "Fuck you, it's every man for himself. I've got mine locked in a strongbox under the floorboards."

Saturday 17th January 2004

Ray McKay has chosen today to come out bedecked in a load of new clobber, a sort of country gentleman ensemble comprising of: some Timberlands, a pair of brown jeans, a cream shirt, a beige Acquascutum cardigan and a brown Paul Smith coat. There's no doubting the fact that he looks very smart, but every time someone enters the Stuart they ask him if Ted has fixed the drainage in the bottom field yet, or else they mime firing a shotgun and shout 'pull!'

It's to his credit that he doesn't get cheesed off, as it goes on for hours.

The Everton side for the day is completely different to the one that faced Fulham. Ferguson's back in and so is Stubbs. Rooney's in as well, but on the right wing, while Radzinski's on the bench with Campbell - the other striking berth has gone to Jeffers. Gravesen's back in the middle as expected, and Pistone's starting at right back, with Hibbert not even in the squad. Some of these changes are unavoidable, but up front it feels like Moyes is trying to be too clever.

Despite all the changes we open brightly, with Gravesen smashing a twenty-five yard half-volley straight down Dean Kiely's throat, and Jeffers setting Ferguson up for a low strike that is deflected just wide of the bottom corner. We're getting the ball out wide and getting crosses into the box, which is better than just humping the ball down the middle, but there still seems to be an over-emphasis on finding Ferguson's head. With Mark Fish and Herman Hreidarsson prepared to stand up and deal with the aerial threat, this feels a lot like Fulham - we're piling on the pressure but we've little to show for it.

Alan Curbishley's team, who are presently fourth in the table, are not prepared to be battered into submission, and on thirty-seven minutes, following a terrible pass by Carsley, they hit us with a classic sucker-punch. No sooner has the Irish midfielder's ball been intercepted on the edge of the Charlton box, than Paolo Di Canio is released down the right as the Everton defence backtrack desperately. The Italian's chip into the box eludes both Stubbs and Carlton Cole but cannons off the unsuspecting Pistone, allowing ex-Everton midfielder Graham Stuart an easy finish from close range.

It would be easy to say the Addicks were lucky, given that most of the game had been played in their half, but they've always looked composed, just waiting for their opportunity to pounce. And if proof were needed that they're no mugs, it comes minutes later as Stuart turns provider, curling a teasing low cross into our box that the unmarked Jason Euell thankfully pokes wide with the goal at his mercy.

We come out in the second half and again go right at the visitors, but they refuse to be cowed. Fish does brilliantly to clear a Ferguson header off the line while Radzinski, on for Jeffers for the last half hour, has a shot saved after pouncing on yet another flick-on. Why the Canadian wasn't on from the start is a mystery.

Charlton mustn't have been able to believe their luck when they saw our starting line-up: we hamstrung ourselves by leaving one of our two most dangerous players on the bench, with the other stuck out on the wing. Jeffers is trying, but he is clearly the third best contender for the position he's occupying.

Kiely makes a great low save from Carsley's long-range header while Kilbane and Stubbs have speculative strikes from distance, but Charlton, despite having not a single effort on goal in the second half, are value for their three points at the final whistle. They've done to us what we did to several sides away from home last season. With Liverpool going down 2-1 at White Hart Lane, the Addicks hold on fourth place has been reinforced as well, although they will fall away eventually - again, like us last season.

Sunday 18th January 2004

Di Canio praises the Evertonians for the great reception they gave him yesterday. A couple of seasons ago when he played for West Ham he stopped play while in our box so that our stricken keeper Paul Gerrard could receive treatment. The incident has been somewhat exaggerated over time - he still had a lot to do before he could score - but it was very sporting all the same and it's nice to see Evertonians showing their more magnanimous side, especially after all the bollocks at Fulham.

Tuesday 20th January 2004

Bob calls a summit meeting at the Butchers for all those without derby tickets. I feel a bit sorry for him; he is the one good enough to nip out of work to go the box office for everyone, but as a result he has sort of become responsible for making sure that whoever wants a ticket gets one. Give him his due though; he comes into the pub armed with a load of ready stamped envelopes, official savings sheets and a tube of Pritt Stick. What ensues is like a game of Top Trumps: "I'll swap you a Boro in the Cup for a Bolton, that leaves you with an extra Man United that you can give to him in exchange for that water-damaged Portsmouth which leaves you with nine vouchers. Laughing."

WHAT'S OUR NAME? EVERTON!

This goes on for a while but, not unlike Jesus with the loaves and the fishes, everyone who wants a ticket eventually ends up with a savings sheet with the requisite nine vouchers attached. These don't guarantee us the goods though, just entry into a lottery, although we're pretty confident that no one will miss out. And I might have a little back up in the pipeline anyway, but there's no point mentioning that to this lot right now...

Saturday 24th January 2004

Straight out of left field - whatever that means - comes a statement from Dinamo Moscow's president saying that their Russian international striker, Dmitry Bulykin, is due to have a medical at Goodison in the next few days. At about the same time, Arsene Wenger announces that Arsenal's deal with Everton would allow him to recall Francis Jeffers if the Gunners needed him.

Coincidence? Probably.

Norwich, meanwhile, have apparently contacted the FA in a bid to force Everton to apologise for the racist chant allegations. The East Anglian press refuse to let it lie, even publishing the contact details of Ian Ross, Everton's Head of Public Relations and Corporate Affairs, and urging supporters to get in touch. I spoke to him recently and he said the loveable fans of that wholesome family club have been deluging him with calls and e-mails wishing him cancer, AIDS and all manner of misfortune. It must be like that episode of Alan Partridge when he upset the farmers.

"Ross, you wan..."

Sunday 25th January 2004

Dmitry Bulykin can't sign until the summer apparently, as he hasn't enough caps to be eligible for a work permit, so he's just training with us at the moment. We're told he's very good in the air, which is a good thing for him if today's cup-tie with Fulham is anything to go by. The first half is a carbon copy of the Charlton game and the last half hour of the one at Loftus Road, with us dominating possession but continually slinging crosses into the box for Duncan Ferguson to battle for in the air. Tomasz

Radzinski, Wayne Rooney and Ferguson himself all have half-chances, but once again Edwin van der Sar and Zat Knight stand firm.

We're not in our normal seats, instead we're near the front again but over at the side of the Park End that butts up to the away section. It's the area preferred by the lads who used to sit at the back of the bus on the way home from school, but unfortunately for them there's not much taunting and goading action to be had today, as Fulham have brought very few fans. We can't really knock them though given that the Goodison 'faithful' have hardly turned out in force either. A gate of just under twenty-eight thousand is either testament to inflexible pricing or the fact that there are legions of younger fans nowadays who believe that the Premiership and the Champions League are the only competitions worth bothering with. Whatever the reasons, it's a pretty limp atmosphere despite the huff and puff of the evenly-matched sides on the park.

Early in the second half, a Fulham counter-attack sees Everton struggling to deal with a bouncing ball in the area and Carlos Bocanegra's strike for the visitors is only half blocked by Tony Hibbert. Fulham's midfielders have pushed on and the ball breaks for Sean Davis - fancy that - who tucks his shot into the bottom corner of the Park End goal.

We're going to struggle now. Fulham have absorbed everything we've thrown at them so far, and now they're a goal ahead they can bide their time even more and pick us off on the break. Our only consolation is that without Louis Saha, now a Manchester United player, their attack is not quite as potent, a fact demonstrated when Barry Hayles has a chance to put the game beyond doubt but shoots into the side-netting.

Having Ferguson in our side is such a double-edged sword. He is brilliant at what he does, and he's playing well, but the temptation, especially when we're behind, is to continually pump high balls into him. As soon as we get the ball out wide, the opposition set themselves up, ready to deal with the inevitable aerial attack. Even if they don't win the first header, they'll get another chance at the second ball, and where the Everton attacker needs to try and get it under control, the defender only has to lash it clear or poke it behind. In essence, we keep giving up good possession in favour of a lottery in the opposition's favour.

As the clock ticks down we look to have strong claims for a penalty when Knight halts a jinking Rooney run by palming the ball behind, but the referee, Dermot Gallagher, waves the appeals away. With five minutes remaining, Thomas Gravesen finds Ferguson unmarked with a clever chip into the box, but the big striker has to stretch to reach the ball and only succeeds in diverting it wide.

Francis Jeffers is then thrown into the mix as we look for any sort of opening to force a replay. Once again, as in the recent game against the Gunners, the fox in the box's late introduction proves crucial.

In the eighty-ninth minute we're awarded a corner that Gravesen drives to the back post. Ferguson in turn does what he does best, leaping above a crowd of Fulham defenders to power a header goalwards from close range. Van der Sar, who denied Ferguson with a wonder save at Loftus Road, repeats the feat again, twisting in mid-air and somehow clawing the ball off the line. This time luck's on our side though as the rebound falls for Jeffers who scuffs a weak first-time effort over the line. His first goal has been a long time coming, but somehow you always knew it was going to be crucial. Personally I was hoping it would be next week at Anfield, but this will do in the circumstances.

Naturally we're elated with a last-minute equaliser, but it's tempered somewhat by the realisation that the replay is going to be very tough. We needed to win this one today.

Adrenaline and lager have every man and his dog vowing to make the journey to West London a week on Wednesday. If they all stick to their guns then we'll need a whole fleet of minibuses, but no doubt there will be a few second thoughts in the cold light of day when people have to book time off work and they're still counting the cost of their derby day bender.

After watching Liverpool beat Newcastle on the telly yesterday I'm not particularly confident about next Saturday.

Henchoz and Hyypia hardly gave Shearer a kick - if we keep knocking in high balls for Ferguson, despite his good record in derbys down the years, we're going to play right into their hands.

Monday 26th January 2004

David Moyes says that he has made an enquiry regarding Nicky Butt. As with Barry Ferguson though there are clubs with more money than Everton who are also after him so it's difficult to envisage any deal ever happening.

Another midfielder, Leon Osman, has joined Derby County on a month's loan.

If we beat Fulham in the Cup we will play West Ham at home. I listen to the draw with a lad named Liam, who I didn't expect to see for a while. He's been working in Australia but his stay was cut short when customs found some contraband in his bags as he got off a flight from New Zealand.

His booty? Well, it was hardly raw opium or weapons grade uranium. No, he was deported and banned from entering the country for three whole years for being in possession of one-hundred-and-ninety-six fake Metallica headbands.

Tuesday 27th January 2004

Graeme Souness says in the paper that he made an offer for Tomasz Radzinski. Fortunately he was told that the player is not for sale.

Other positive news is that Bill Kenwright has offered free coach travel to Fulham a week tomorrow. We've already booked a minibus, so we won't benefit, but you can't knock our Deputy Chairman for this gesture, although some undoubtedly will. His motivation, he says, is that he wants to ensure that we've got a good following for such a crucial game.

Thursday 29th January 2004

The FA are apparently charging Luis Boa Morte with inciting the crowd by making obscene gestures during the missile-strewn league game at Loftus Road.

WHAT'S OUR NAME? EVERTON!

Friday 30th January 2004

Boa Morte is now alleging that Duncan Ferguson punched him
and racially abused him during the cup game on Sunday. A
spokesman for Ferguson has denied the allegations, while a lot of
Evertonians are obviously quite sceptical about Boa Morte's
timing.

It's pointless speculating though, only the two players involved
really know what happened. It's a sad incident, whichever one of
them is telling the truth.

The derby ticket panic is over. In fact I may end up with extras
and strangely enough find myself with new best friends
everywhere I turn.

Saturday 31st January 2004

It's only just turned 11am and there's already about thirty-
odd of us, Reds and Blues, in Fridays, the minty but cheap
boozer underneath the world-renowned Adelphi Hotel.
Somehow, we manage to get a ticket for everyone here,
although a couple of people sitting at home by their phones
end up missing out.

Alan Stubbs is featured on the back of the *Daily Post* saying that
the atmosphere at the derby needs to improve before we end up
going down the same route as the Old Firm in Glasgow, where
clashes between Celtic and Rangers are poisonous, dangerous
affairs.

Now, I can't stand Liverpool FC. I grew up in Liverpool in the
seventies and early eighties, when even the kids at school who
didn't like footy pledged allegiance to the all-conquering Reds,
so I feel I've got every right to have a healthy dislike of them.
Some of these young lads who profess an all-consuming hatred
for them though, and call each other nasty names on the internet,
really don't know they're born. They think they detest the
Liverpool of Biscan and Cheyrou; I dread to think what they
would have been like if they'd been born when the twats had the
likes of Dalglish and Souness in their side.

At the end of the day, when half your mates and a large portion
of your family support Liverpool though, there has to be a limit

to your antipathy. And while there have been the recent spates of vandalism, and there will always be the odd chinning on derby day - there always has been, mostly thanks to the amount of ale that gets drunk - there's still thankfully a long way to go before it's anything like Glasgow.

Despite our early start we still manage to just miss the kick off, with Redmond, Eddy and myself taking our seats at the very end of the Anfield Road just as the Reds start pouring forward. Dietmar Hamman has the first decent opening, striking a volley that Nigel Martyn does well to palm wide.

I normally ignore the home supporters whenever I'm sitting close to them at an away match, but the angry fatties in the Main Stand here, up and down like jack-in-the-boxes and making cut-throat gestures, are too good to be true. Apparently communication is only allowed in one direction though, as one of the many coppers stationed to my right tells me to keep my eyes on the game after I shout some undoubtedly good-natured remark. I give a look of pained innocence worthy of an Inter Milan centre-half and then turn to see Tomasz Radzinski eluding the normally assured Liverpool central defenders before attempting to score with a backheel from the edge of the box.

Thomas Gravesen then has an even better chance, skipping through a succession of challenges and bursting into the box - only to see Jerzy Dudek block his shot, much to the annoyance of the unmarked Wayne Rooney. On half an hour that anger, and that of all the Evertonians inside the ground, is turned on the referee Steve Bennett. Radzinski is set clear through the middle but as he bears down on the Liverpool penalty area Sami Hyypia runs across the back of him, catching his heels and bringing him down. It's a blatant professional foul, but rather than send off a Liverpool player in front of the Kop, Bennett bottles out and waves play on.

I'm out of my seat voicing my displeasure and vexation at this heinous decision when the gloved hand of the law lands on my shoulder.

"If I hear you say either of those two words again you're out," I'm told.

WHAT'S OUR NAME? EVERTON!

In fairness to the balding Bennett, he quickly gets a decision wrong at the other end when, as a corner is cleared from the Everton box, Duncan Ferguson blatantly wrestles Hyypia to the ground. Again, play on.

It's end to end, and Martyn has to make an incredible low save from Steven Gerrard when the England midfielder tricks his way into the box and lets fly. At the other end, Jamie Carragher escapes a strong handball claim before Dudek makes a flying one-handed save to deny an Alan Stubbs header that seems destined for the top corner.

Ferguson then glances a header just wide of the post, as a half in which Liverpool looked more composed in midfield, but Everton created more chances, draws to a close.

We all meet up at half-time and the consensus is that the game is winnable - in fact if we were anywhere but Anfield, where we never have any luck, we'd be brimming with confidence. As it is there's a gnawing feeling that we should have converted at least one chance. The other worry is that Michael Owen's not had a sniff yet either - Alessandro Pistone, covering at centre-half, has marked him well - and that can't continue for ninety minutes.

Just before I go back up to my seat I go to the toilets, where for some reason they've got the half-time announcer piped in on speakers. Now Shaun Tilley at Everton gets some stick for his over-enthusiastic style, but surely even he's preferable to the lush tones of Anfield's Smashy and Nicey clone who has the whole bog in stitches when he fades a record out and announces, dead straight: "That's great, Alannah Myles with *Black Velvet*…"

According to that particular power ballad dirge, "The way he moved, it was a sin, so sweet and true". And she could very well have been warbling about Wayne Rooney. At the very start of the second half he cuts in from the right, rides two challenges, stumbles through a third from Hyypia and finds himself with only Dudek to beat. Instead of striking it with his left foot though he tries to be too clever, uses the outside of his right instead and ends up scooping a glorious chance over the bar. Some Buster Bloodvessel in the Main Stand puffs his cheeks out and rubs his gut to indicate his belief that Rooney is the wrong side of svelte.

I get my final warning from the police.

After Rooney's chance goes begging, Everton spend much of the remainder of the game on the back foot. Gerrard drives the Reds forward but in all honesty, without the much-maligned Emile Heskey, their attack lacks focus. Liverpool no longer play the sort of football they were once renowned for. They've got plenty of pace and they work the ball out wide well, but more often than not they end up swinging in crosses and hoping for a break, a tactic that only ever has mixed results for us and we've got probably the best target man in the country. On the occasions when the Liverpool forwards do beat the Blues' defenders to the ball, they find Nigel Martyn in breathtaking form as he repels good efforts from Jamie Carragher and Harry Kewell.

It's not all one-way traffic though, as Dudek has to produce the goods at the other end to keep out another Stubbs effort, this time a fierce, low free-kick.

Martyn's undoubtedly man of the match but even he needs assistance from Tony Hibbert in the closing stages as the young defender first hacks an Antony Le Tallec header off the line and then heads a dangerous cross narrowly over his own bar in injury time to ensure the game ends scoreless.

The Reds in the Salisbury all seem to think that we were lucky to hang on but they're choosing to ignore the chances we had, especially in the first half, and the saves that Dudek had to make. Admittedly we were under the cosh for much of the second half, but no more so than, say, Charlton were at Goodison the other week. It appears that defending well is only an art form when performed by Hyypia and Henchoz; when it's Everton it's just luck.

These Loveable Reds never change, bless them.

February

Burning Down The House

Sunday 1st February 2004

David Moyes isn't happy about several decisions in the derby, namely the Hyypia foul and the Carragher handball, to which Gerard Houllier responds with some nonsense about English managers always making excuses when they get beat by Liverpool. For a start, we didn't lose, and for the crackers Frenchman to criticise other people over making excuses is, well, crackers.

Monday 2nd February 2004

It's the final day of the winter transfer window, and in the morning a rumour starts on the internet saying that we're trying to get Joe Cole on loan from Chelsea until the end of the season. The thinking is that he might be tempted as his opportunities at Stamford Bridge have been limited and the situation's only going to get worse for him seeing as Claudio Ranieri has just added Scott Parker to his squad. With the European Championships coming up in the summer, it's thought that Cole might want first team football elsewhere.

However the five o'clock deadline passes without a press conference from Goodison Park, so we'll just have to continue the rest of the season with the players we've got.

Tuesday 3rd February 2004

Luis Boa Morte still hasn't made his official complaint to the FA. The Association are said to be concerned that he's failed to do this while making serious allegations in the press.

I really want to believe that Ferguson is innocent, and I've got mates who are certain that he is, but how can you know for sure?

Racism on the pitch isn't as bad as it used to be, but I'm sure it still goes on. After all, it wasn't that long ago that big, cuddly BBC pundit Peter Schmeichel was caught bang to rights by telly cameras, racially abusing Ian Wright. On the other hand, there have been cases such as the Barmby/Boateng and the Collymore/Harkness ones where there was a strong suspicion that the allegations were groundless. Both situations are deplorable, but ultimately it seems as if the FA are going to be left with a case of one man's word against another's.

Wednesday 4th February 2004

Graham Ennis tells me this book is the diary of doom. We're just past the halfway stage in the league and we're in fourteenth place. That's a position that falls firmly into the category of 'languishing'. We're out of the Carling Cup, the final of which will be contested by Bolton and our conquerors, Middlesbrough, so our last chance of some sort of glory resides in the FA Cup, starting with tonight's replay at Fulham.

We've not taken advantage of Bill Kenwright's kind offer of free coach travel; instead we've hired a fifteen-seater minibus. With fourteen Blues on board, that works out spot on as it leaves a seat free for the crates of lager. We pass loads of official coaches on the way down to London, and to be honest they don't look as much fun as ours - that is of course if you define fun as choking on clouds of skunk smoke and singing along to *Into the Valley* and, erm, *Swords of a Thousand Men*.

We park up by O'Neill's - football fans are nothing if not creatures of habit - and just before we all climb out of the minibus there's a final reiteration of tonight's ground rules. Essentially, we're all to meet up back at O'Neill's after the game, and if anyone is arrested then they have to make their own way home - we're not hanging around, as people have to be in work tomorrow. Normally you don't have to be so strict, but there are a number of distinctly loose cannons on board today and they've been hammering the loony soup all the way down.

"Now don't forget," says Bob. "It's O'Neill's. Like the jockey, Jonjo O'Neill. Just remember that."

There is a larger than normal police presence around the ground and, almost inevitably, a great big queue to get in. I'm not surprised to find that the Everton end is absolutely chocker, but I can't believe the vast swathes of empty seats around the rest of the ground. You would have thought that the place would be rammed, given the bad feeling between the sides and the fact that this competition is as vital to Fulham as it is to us.

Once I'm settled into my seat, next to a journalist mate from London, Mike Harris, I do start to think that perhaps those who have vetoed this one might have the right idea after all, as the two sides produce little football of note for the first forty minutes. Again Fulham look strong in midfield, but Barry Hayles is no replacement for Louis Saha. On the other hand, Wayne Rooney and Tomasz Radzinski look willing runners for Everton, but the service from our midfield is dire.

Then, with three minutes to go before half-time, Alex Nyarko, who has been truly appalling, picks up a loose ball and sets Radzinski off for a run on goal. The Canadian's shot beats van der Sar but, in keeping with our luck of late, strikes the foot of the post and rebounds back into the arms of the grateful Dutchman.

Moments later Radzinski's off again, this time down the left wing, from where he launches a gem of a cross to the far post. Rooney's made a great run and finds himself unmarked, with the whole goal to aim at, but he makes a complete mess of what should be a straightforward header and it's hacked to safety by the Fulham defence. The home side break almost immediately, and the last action of the half sees Sean Davis crack a volley towards the top corner of the Everton goal, only for the amazing Nigel Martyn to leap full length to tip it around the post.

At half-time Mike and I catch up and get talking about the African Nations Cup which is being played at the moment - Joseph Yobo's still out there - and the obscure managers who make their living doing the rounds of football's lesser lights. Mick Wadsworth managing the Congo is the obvious one, but Mike tells me he once interviewed a bloke called Stephen Constantine who is presently the coach of the Indian national side. Apparently the highlights of his CV are a playing career that peaked at Stevenage and a spell managing the mighty Nepal. There are loads of fellas like him throughout the Middle East and Africa; they're football's equivalent of the brickies on *Auf Wiedersehen Pet* - 'have bibs and cones, will travel'.

Incredibly, Nyarko ambles out after the break despite a first half that was worthy of another shirt-swapping, but Everton start on the attack and only a last-ditch block from Moritz Volz prevents Kilbane from opening the scoring. It's odd that since the turn of the year we've not played particularly good football but we still keep creating chances. Unfortunately our finishing seems almost apologetic.

Ten minutes into the half there's a lull in play and I decide to take the opportunity to answer the call of nature. Wouldn't you know it, I'm halfway down the stairs when I hear a muffled cheer that can only mean one thing.

I complete my ablutions nonetheless and as I make my way back to my seat a lad in our row looks at me and jokingly says, "It's your fault". It seems I'm not the only person who subscribes to the branch of chaos theory that states that if a man urinates in West London it will start a chain reaction that culminates in a Ghanaian dithering in a field, thus allowing a man from Japan (Junichi Inamoto) to kick a ball into a net.

Shortly after this setback, Nyarko and Radzinski are removed and replaced by Steve Watson and Francis Jeffers. Fulham look comfortable though, especially now they're in the lead, and the Everton players can't even get close to Steed Malbranque. He surely won't be playing here for that long; I just hope he doesn't end up at Liverpool, who have been linked with him in the past. There was a time when I'd hope that Everton would sign pearls like him, but the reality of our present situation is that, despite the fact that we've got the kind of huge support that's here tonight compared to the handful of people who come to watch Fulham, there's no way we could afford a Malbranque - and that's if he would even consider coming to Goodison.

As the clock ticks down, Everton are reduced to knocking long diagonal balls for the tall wingers, Kilbane and Watson, to fight for in the air. It's not pretty, but as at Goodison, the Fulham players start to look nervous in the face of a clumsy yet wholehearted barrage.

In the final minute a long, straight ball down the middle tempts van der Sar off his line. Fatal.

He attempts to punch clear but Jeffers bravely hurls himself into the danger area and gets the slightest flick on the ball, sending it dribbling towards the goal line. Everyone's on their feet, and as a result it's impossible to get a clear view of the goal below us. I see two defenders sliding in to try and make a clearance and for a split second my heart sinks, but then suddenly it feels like I'm on the bridge of the Starship Enterprise as bodies pile backwards and forwards amidst an almost terrifying noise.

I take this to mean that the ball has actually crossed the line.

The Fulham players and supporters are stunned, they can't believe that this has happened again, and as the fourth official raises his board to indicate four minutes of injury time it's clear that Everton smell blood and want to win this before it goes to extra-time. Perhaps the players know that they can't maintain this level of intensity for another half an hour.

First Jeffers strikes a shot on the turn that flies narrowly over, then Rooney shows a flash of sublime skill to extricate himself from a tight situation by the corner flag before floating yet another perfect cross to the far post. Kilbane's the spare man this time, connecting with a firm header towards goal but once again, thanks to a combination of standing punters and Loftus Road's general pokiness, I can't see what's happening. It turns out later that Jeffers attempted to head the ball over the line but failed to get enough purchase on it. In short, we once again spurn a glorious goalscoring opportunity.

The referee blows the whistle to signal the end of normal time and the Evertonians, who will always respond to a side who are trying, sing our one song, "Everton, Everton", until they are hoarse. How could the players fail to be lifted by this?

Within seconds of the restart Rooney has the ball on the edge of the Fulham box, surrounded by white-shirted defenders. There appears to be nothing on for the England centre-forward, but he spots a run by Jeffers and slips a perfect 'reverse ball' into his path, leaving him with only van der Sar to beat. Jeffers does almost everything right: he takes one touch, draws the Dutchman, shimmies, and then lifts his left-footed shot over the bar. Ooh, nearly. The breakthrough has to come soon, surely?

Unfortunately not.

Fulham and Everton both sense that the home side have ridden the storm. They begin to get hold of the ball again and gradually we start to run out of steam. It's only little things - a missed tackle here, a weak clearance there - but they all add up and gradually the momentum shifts towards Chris Coleman's side. Malbranque, almost inevitably, receives a square pass from Boa Morte inside the Everton box and the sublime Frenchman shows our strikers how it's done, sliding the ball into Martyn's bottom corner and dumping us out of the cup.

We try to raise ourselves for another comeback, but no one really believes it's going to happen, as yet again we're reminded that in the long run the side that can keep hold of the ball will nearly always come out on top at this level.

However, as we rendezvous in O'Neill's we realise that we're not the most disappointed supporters in London tonight. Tottenham, at White Hart Lane, were 3-0 up at half-time against ten man Manchester City and somehow managed to lose 4-3. Even Everton would struggle to top that, although you'd never bet against it.

It's three o'clock when we eventually get home and we're all feeling a bit pissed off, especially one of the loose cannons, Albie, who was apparently turned away from Loftus Road by the police and spent virtually the whole of the match trying to find his way back to the boozer. Bob's tip for remembering the name of the rendezvous seems to have backfired spectacularly as Albie spent an hour and a half asking bewildered West Africans the way to "that fucking big alehouse in Shepherd's Bush - Jonjo's".

One of the best things about football is that after every disappointment there's nearly always another game just around the corner, giving you the chance to put things right. In all honesty though, if you were picking a fixture to lift your spirits after going out of the cup, you probably wouldn't choose to face Manchester United, Everton's guests on Saturday.

Thursday 5th February 2004
Luis Boa Morte has now made his complaint official to the FA.

Friday 6th February 2004
Niclas Alexandersson has signed a pre-contact agreement with IFK Gothenburg, saying of Everton, "I've really enjoyed my time here, but you obviously want to play football and the past year has been hard for me. But overall, I've had a fantastic time. Everyone at the club has been great, especially the supporters."

That has to be one of the most diplomatic statements of all time, or extremely tongue-in-cheek.

Saturday 7th February 2004
"I'm not staying for any more of this, I'm going to Orry's, I'll watch the second half on the Norwegian."

"Behave Gaz, we could be about to witness history here. If Everton lose eight-nil do you not want to be able to tell your grandkids you were there?"

"No I fucking don't. I'm going for a pint and then I'm getting the early train back to London, I'll see you at Southampton."

And with that, Gaz, the degenerate Welsh lawyer, joined hundreds of other Evertonians who walked out of Goodison in disgust after watching our team produce one of the most gutless forty-five minutes in living memory. Manchester United are three-nil up at the break, but that scoreline doesn't do them justice. Ruud van Nistelrooy and Louis Saha, with a brace, have taken advantage of amateurish Everton defending to score the goals, but in truth both players could have easily had more.

What's most galling is that Alex Ferguson's side haven't even had to work for their lead. They've had the complete freedom of midfield, while their defenders have faced little threat from Everton's front pairing of Duncan Ferguson and Francis Jeffers.

Now I'm a massive fan of David Moyes, but his decision to play Jeffers ahead of Rooney and Radzinski, who are both on the bench, borders on disgraceful. Unlike some people, who haven't forgiven the way he left Everton, or his reaction when he scored against us at Highbury, I have no axe to grind with Jeffers; I just know he isn't as good as the other two players vying for his place in the side.

When we get back to our seats, ready to take our second-half whupping like men, it comes as no surprise to see that the two lads who sit in front of us have also decided to 'beat the traffic'. To our constant amazement they normally leave about five or ten minutes before the end of every match, no matter how delicately poised it is. As a result they missed three of the highlights of last season: Radzinski's injury-time clincher against Southampton and Wayne Rooney's last-minute winners against Villa and Arsenal. That last one, Rooney's first senior goal against the undefeated Gunners to make him the youngest ever top-flight scorer, is one of the greatest Everton moments of all time.

"Were you there when Rooney scored that goal against Arsenal, dad?"

"Er, no son, I was just pulling out of the Vernon Sangster car park. I'll never forget seeing it that night on *The Premiership* though. Happy days lad, happy days."

Anyway, David Moyes, unsurprisingly, makes a treble substitution. He could take any three of the outfield players off and no one would bat an eyelid, they've all been that rank. He plumps for Alessandro Pistone, who made Darren Fletcher look like Tom Finney, Francis Jeffers and Steve Watson. On come Radzinski, Rooney and Gary Naysmith.

Within a minute Tony Hibbert plays a ball into space and the unselfish Radzinski hares after it, forcing the usually unflappable John O'Shea to concede a corner. Naysmith then delivers a near post corner that Duncan Ferguson flicks on for the stooping David Unsworth to force over the line at the far post.

There's some consolation anyway.

We're waiting for United to reassert themselves again, but they seem to be retreating into their shells. The rain is lashing down now and Rooney's got the bit between his teeth, driving at a rattled defence who are punting the ball anywhere and then arguing amongst themselves.

WHAT'S OUR NAME? EVERTON!

It looks as if the youngster's pulled another one back for us when he forces his way through a crowd of United players and lets fly with a dipping shot, but Tim Howard stretches out an arm and flicks it behind for another corner. Naysmith's delivery to the near post is spot on again though and O'Shea, while concentrating on trying to block Ferguson's run, heads the ball into his own net.

Three-two and the Champions are now, to coin a phrase, shitting themselves.

The United supporters' first-half demands for Everton to 'bring on the fat kid' seem to be backfiring as Rooney shows just why he deserves to start playing regularly in his proper position. He tears the back out of Wes Brown and flicks a cross with the outside of his right boot that tempts both Ferguson and Kilbane to attempt overhead kicks. They both unfortunately fail to make contact, but the incident inspires the Goodison crowd to further heights of hysteria as the atmosphere in the grand old stadium positively crackles.

With fifteen minutes on the clock, Fletcher fouls Kilbane and the Blues are awarded a free-kick by the touchline, thirty yards out. Gravesen swings it to the near post, Kilbane makes a late run, the ball smacks off the Everton player's head and flashes past the helpless Howard and into the back of the net.

Three-three. Unbelievable. How can one of the most abject halves of football ever witnessed be followed immediately by the most tense, rousing thirty minutes imaginable? How?

My nerves are raw and I feel physically shattered; no one has sat down since the second goal went in.

Now at this point I wish I could say, in Warner Brothers fashion, 'That's all folks', or in the style of French cinema, 'Fin', but this is Everton. The players, like the fans, are goosed. They're trying to summon one last push to snatch a winner that will equal Manchester City's midweek heroics, but the very act of drawing level, of feeling like we've made it off the hook, seems to have released the pressure in the stadium. That frantic edge has gone and United, like Muhammad Ali with a split glove, have cleared their heads. With Paul Scholes and substitute

Cristiano Ronaldo finding more space, Alex Ferguson's men begin to probe as the heavy-legged Blues start to sit deeper, mindful of preserving their hard-earned parity.

As we approach the final minutes Martyn makes a vital stop from a low Scholes drive, and we breathe a sigh of relief. We look set for a famous point.

As if.

Ronaldo, all corn-row haircut and pointless step-overs, finds space on the left edge of the Everton box and for once looks up and delivers a decent cross to the far post. Neither Alan Stubbs nor Tony Hibbert has picked up the run of van Nistelrooy and the long-faced Dutchman nods home the winner from close range.

I actually find myself kicking my chair like some sort of deranged person. Imagine Basil Fawlty attacking his car with a branch and you will get the idea of the sort of impotent rage I'm trying to convey.

On the pitch there's mayhem; it's difficult to tell what is exactly happening, but the stewards are all out along the front of the Paddock where Ronaldo seems to be getting involved with several less-than-chuffed fans. At the same time the rest of the United players are celebrating in front of the Family Enclosure, which is also in uproar.

An offside Rooney misses an open goal in the final seconds before Neale Barry blows his whistle to end one of the most astonishing games any of us is ever likely to witness.

"A lifetime of supporting Everton summed up in ninety minutes," is Ste Connor's verdict.

And if all that wasn't bad enough, someone informs us Everton only took 1,200 tickets for Wednesday's game at St. Andrews, and that they've all sold out. We're snookered.

Sunday 8th February 2004

Almost inevitably a load of people have reported the Manchester United players to the police, claiming they swore and made offensive gestures to the crowd.

I said it after the first game of the season: all this reporting of players is a horrible modern phenomenon.

WHAT'S OUR NAME? EVERTON!

Chris Coleman, speaking on Radio 5, says that he would like Luis Boa Morte and Duncan Ferguson to meet up, shake hands and put an end to the alleged racist abuse incident. Some people are taking it as a sure indication that Ferguson is innocent, but I can't help feeling that perhaps Coleman thinks that even if his player's telling the truth they can't prove it, so there's nothing to gain.

Now I might be way off beam here, but I also get the impression that perhaps racist abuse occurs on the pitch a little bit more than we're led to believe. Considering racism is meant to be taken deadly serious, Boa Morte doesn't really seem to have had much support. I really wouldn't be surprised if the prevailing attitude in football is, 'Oh, so he called you a black cunt, big deal, it happens all the time; we all turn a deaf ear and get on with it. Stop rocking the boat.' I might be totally wrong there, but that's the impression I get.

Tuesday 10th February 2004

While the vast majority of people are in agreement that the reporting of United's players to the police on Saturday was needless and over the top, some of the articles in the national press, particularly by Martin Samuel of *The Times* and Oliver Holt of *The Mirror*, are scathing in their criticism of the Everton fans and staunch in defence of the United players.

Now, just to reiterate, no one really thinks that players should do a stretch breaking rocks for putting two fingers up at the Paddock, and I, for one, would never be bothered to report a player to the club or the FA. Once the game's over and you're back in the pub it's all forgotten about. However, it's interesting to see the press taking such a firm stance in favour of the players in this particular case. The events at the end of Saturday's game are not without precedent, yet I don't remember Liverpool fans being branded 'mean-spirited hypocritical fools' when they fabricated a spitting incident involving Wayne Rooney and reported that to the police.

Martin Samuel doesn't think that the United incident should even go before the FA, which in effect says that it's okay for players to swear and gesture at supporters. That's fine by me - bring it on, as busty glamour model Jordan is so fond of saying - but why have they never suggested this before? Or is it only okay when it's Everton fans at the receiving end?

Wednesday 11th February 2004

It's the morning of the game against Birmingham at St. Andrews. Bob, Weavers, Alan Welsh and myself have tried to call in every favour, shamelessly ringing people we've not spoken to in months to ask has anyone got any spares. I've even had my mum asking the kids in her school if their dads have got any. So far we've got one between the four of us.

We're going to chance it anyway, but the problem with Birmingham City's ground is that there isn't really a specific pub nearby - a Brummie equivalent of the Springbok at Fulham or the Drayton at Arsenal - where you'll be guaranteed to find the Evertonians and possibly pick up a ticket.

"Throy feather moyn stand ploys."

We've had no joy picking up tickets for the Everton section, so I've drawn the short straw and have to try and convince the girl in the St. Andrews ticket office that I'm not a Scouser infiltrating their end. I therefore mumble my one rehearsed line and thrust the cash at her. I actually sound like Inspector Clouseau doing an impression of Barry from *Auf Wiedersehen Pet* but she starts sorting the tickets out all the same. Magic.

But she only gives me two, and a load of change. Not unreasonably she must have misheard me. I've not rehearsed anything else though; I'll just have to wing it.

"Sorree luv, but oi arsed for throy, yow've ownly given me two."

Some little urchins nearby start giggling at my Pipkins impersonation, but maybe because of the obscuring properties of the plexiglass separating us, the ticket girl doesn't flinch. In fact she apologises profusely and hands over the third ticket, no problem. Marvellous.

We're now on to the second phase of Operation See The Match Without Getting Lynched By The Zulus - that is to find the right gate and actually get into the ground. Over ten minutes it takes us - perhaps it's a throwback to the days when you wouldn't have even dreamed of going in the Birmingham end, but it's like Fort Knox, with railings and barbed wire all over the place. In fact, by the time we do find the entrance and make our way to our seats at the back of the stand, we hear a massive cheer that can only mean one thing: Everton have conceded an early goal.

It's true, Damien Johnson has scored for the home side. That's hardly the most auspicious start, but on the plus side at least we're not sitting with a load of Burberry-clad cavemen. In fact where we're sitting, just by the press box, the atmosphere is most convivial. The make-up of the crowd and the slightly rickety stadium put me very much in mind of Everton and Goodison. I like it.

What's happening on the pitch, however, I like considerably less.

David Moyes has stuck with the team that started the second half on Saturday, but there's none of the drive and commitment that produced three goals against the champions. Gravesen's seeing plenty of the ball in the middle of the park, but as soon as we cross the halfway line our attacks just seem to peter out. Birmingham are hardly pulling up trees, but they don't have to; they're one-nil up, comfortable, and biding their time.

And the biding is over five minutes before the break when Stan Lazaridis picks up the ball on the halfway line, gets his head down in his own inimitable style and sets off on a run at the Everton defence. Now the rubber-faced Aussie is not the most subtle of footballers - give him a stretch of grass to run into and he'll have a bit of a gallop, but he's never going to mesmerise anyone with his footwork. So why, oh why, do the Everton defenders keep backing off him? If one of them makes any semblance of a challenge, he'll panic and toe-poke the ball through to the keeper or out for a goal-kick. But no, Everton's rearguard seem to think they're facing Marco van Basten in his pomp. In fairness to the wholehearted Lazaridis, his finish - that finds the top corner of Nigel Martyn's goal from the edge of the box - is worthy of the Dutch legend, but he should never have been given the time and space to even contemplate having a dig.

Two-nil at half-time and Everton haven't had a sniff of goal. People have taken half-days off work to come and watch this; the players could at least get their knees dirty.

We go for a half-time pint and once again soft ollies here has to do his Jasper Carrott impersonation. There's more than a few big moody-looking black lads in Stone Island woolly hats by the bar so I don't really want to test the limits of Brummie hospitality, hence I whisper, "Two points of lager and a point of bitter plois."

The young lad serving arches an eyebrow and leans forward, asking, "Are yow whispering so yow downt get sussed with that rubbish accent, Scouse?"

I just nod.

"Now worries mate," he says, laughing and handing over the ale.

After that our only danger of blowing our cover, like Bugs Bunny when his tail sticks out from under his saucy nurse's outfit, is if we leap up at an Everton goal.

Fat chance.

Five minutes into the second half, Alan Stubbs makes a balls up on the edge of the Everton box, Robbie Savage finds Mikael Forsell in about a hectare of free space and the sickly-looking Finn - who, when he smiles, looks the double of the sensible shoe-wearing tennis ace, Martina Navratilova - is allowed to take about eight touches before driving home a low shot.

We wait for another twenty-five minutes or so, in which time Everton show little sign of improvement, before deciding that we might as well, yes, you guessed it, beat the traffic.

After watching that, I'll be delighted if we don't get relegated. We've still not won a league game this year and our next game, a week on Saturday, is at Southampton, who will batter us if we play anything like we did tonight. The next game after that's at home to Villa, who are playing well lately. It's feasible that we could be in the bottom three after that.

Woe is me. Or 'wow is me' if I'm staying in character.

Thursday 12th February 2004

A recent report by the IFC stated, amongst other things, that racism is still a problem within football, and that there are real concerns over the way clubs manage their finances. The report also recommended a salary cap, but it's difficult to see clubs buying into that. The Manchester Uniteds of this world can afford to pay players sixty and seventy grand a week, that's why Ruud van Nistelrooy and Roy Keane play for them and not Lincoln City. Why would United support a scheme that would erode their advantage?

And even if a salary cap was introduced, the rich clubs would just find ways of getting around it and making extra payments to the players. You only have to look at the unscrupulous double-dealing that is rife within the present transfer system to know that would be the case.

Ultimately clubs will have to enforce their own wage limits, as the only alternative will be to run up huge debts and eventually go out of business. Clubs like Everton are already facing up to that new reality, although obviously that doesn't sit well with everyone. Speaking to the *Echo*, Everton's chief executive Michael Dunford said:

"I think our board in recent years may have received some criticism from certain sections for not spending more, but you have to look at the Leeds United situation - do you go for the dream? The dream inevitably costs and who picks up the eventual bill? While we are all ambitious - nobody is more ambitious than Bill Kenwright and the board of Everton - there has to be a degree of prudence. If you spend money you don't have in most cases it ends in tears."

Friday 13th February 2004

It just gets worse. Not only are the FA to interview Duncan Ferguson over the Boa Morte incident, but now Greater Manchester Police have had a complaint from a woman saying that Wayne Rooney spat in her face last Saturday night.

Rooney was out in the ludicrously named Ampersand nightclub in Manchester celebrating Kevin Campbell's thirty-fourth birthday. His agent obviously denies the claim and says that it was the other way around: the woman spat at Rooney. Whatever the truth of this latest tawdry incident, didn't anyone question the wisdom of going out near Manchester straight after playing a somewhat fraught game against United?

I hate footballers.

Saturday 14th February 2004

It's FA Cup weekend, therefore no game for the Blues. The Manchester derby is the highlight of the day for us neutrals and it doesn't disappoint. United welly City everywhere despite having phoney hardcase Gary Neville sent off for sticking the head on Steve McManaman.

Less hilarious than the dismissal of the spiv-muzzied son of Neville Neville is news that Li Tie may have broken his leg while training with the Chinese national side.

Sunday 15th February 2004

The *Sunday Mirror* have run a big two-page spread that says Wayne Rooney to Manchester United in the summer is a done deal. It's easy to dismiss stuff like this, as these stories are inevitable whenever someone good plays for a side outside the top four or five clubs, but deep down it is unsettling.

If someone did come with an offer of twenty or twenty-five million pounds would the Everton board turn them down? Few people are convinced they would.

In the short term it would certainly alleviate our financial woes, but what then? We could possibly go out and buy some new players, but none of them would be of the calibre of Rooney - if they were then surely Manchester United would have already bought them instead.

No, if Everton let Rooney go, at the age of eighteen, when the Everton fans have only had the opportunity to see glimpses of the great player he is set to become, then it could prove the final straw for many people. Rooney represents hope, and hope is the one thing that keeps us coming back week after week. We've had years of watching strikers like Brett Angell, Stuart Barlow and

Ibrahima Bakayoko and then all of a sudden, despite our lack of money to go out and buy quality, we've got the England centre-forward, one of the most exciting young talents in world football, and he's a mad Evertonian. That's what you hope for during the darkest times, that something like this can happen, that a genuine superstar will fall into your laps like a gift from above. So to cash in at the first opportunity, in an attempt to paper over the deep cracks that have been caused by the gross mismanagement of the past, will simply leave the supporters thinking "What's the point?"

Tuesday 17th February 2004

All the papers are full of Rooney 'off in the summer' stories now, following on from the *Sunday Mirror*'s lead. There is nothing concrete in any of them, but understandably the speculation has got Evertonians extremely agitated despite David Moyes making a statement on the official website saying that Rooney is not for sale. He adds that unless the Board are saying something different behind his back then they are in agreement, Rooney's going nowhere.

I should feel reassured, but I don't.

At least Li Tie's injury isn't as bad as first feared though.

Wednesday 18th February 2004

It's an evening of international friendlies, starting with the Republic of Ireland against Brazil and then England versus Portugal. Both games are rubbish to be honest. Brazil bring their full complement of superstars over, to the delight of the Lansdowne Road crowd, and the Irish players repay them by booting them all over the place. Our very own Kevin Kilbane plays in central midfield and gives a display that would be best described as 'tigerish'. He doesn't half do some running; he'll be shattered for Saturday.

Niall Quinn's commentary is the most entertaining aspect of the game, which ends scoreless, as he gushes over the Brazilians as if he's watching Tostao and Rivelino for the first time. It's not like when I was a kid, when you had to wait four years to see the

South Americans with their big hair, Che Guevara beards and obscenely tight shorts - Roque bleeding Junior's playing here for heaven's sake, and he's getting turned inside out by Clinton Morrison.

"Ooh, this is an education watching this," coos the ex-Man City target man whose haircut is so unfashionable it has actually come back into fashion in an ironic kind of way. It's difficult to tell exactly which bits he finds so illuminating; perhaps it's Kleberson wellying shots into the stands or Roberto Carlos' unerring ability to hit the wall with his free-kicks. One small mercy is that Quinn at least refrains from saying that the Brazilians all learnt their skills on the Copacabana, and that football was the only way out of the slums for them.

The England game is equally poor. Wayne Rooney, who has two rather disturbing stripes shaved into the side of his hair, partners Michael Owen up front but neither receive much decent service. Personally, I wouldn't play them both together; I'd have one or the other alongside Emile Heskey instead. Heskey's not much of a footballer - he wouldn't make it into the line-up of a top side - but he performs a certain role well for England and Liverpool that makes life easier for the rest of the team. All this allowing Rooney to roam is no good against decent opposition; he just ends up in the way of other players or miles away from the action when the ball's in the box.

It finishes 1-1, with England's goal credited to their best player by far, Tottenham's Ledley King.

Thursday 19th February 2004
The wonder of modern communications in this ever-shrinking world. It has taken almost five days for Everton find out the real extent of Li Tie's injury and now we're back to the original diagnosis: his leg is broken and he will miss the remainder of the season.

Compared to his first season in English football, this one has absolutely stunk for our Asiatic anchorman, he's had no luck at all.

Another player not enjoying his second season in the Premiership so much, Wayne Rooney, wasn't the only English player to give an indifferent display last night but he is the only one who *The Sun* says must leave his present club if he's to improve. Fancy that.

Friday 20th February 2004

The club say they are not entering the InterToto Cup this summer, as it will interfere with David Moyes' preparations for the new season. No doubt that's true, as we never entered last season, but the fact also remains that if we put ourselves forward this time there's every probability we'd face the ignominy of not actually qualifying for the ultimate in Mickey Mouse tournaments.

We really can't afford to lose at Southampton tomorrow.

Saturday 21st February 2004

We're making good time. Eddy, making up for the fact that he had to be dragged out of bed, has got his foot down and we've just passed Stonehenge. At this rate we'll be in the pub before one o'clock.

"Apparently all the stone was from Wales," Weavers tell us. "I saw a documentary on the telly about it. They reckon it might have taken them years to transport it here."

"It probably did," says Bob. "That M4's a fucker at the best of times."

"Shit!" yells Eddy, as he pumps the brakes in a manner that suggests we're either about to collide with a small woodland creature or we've just passed a copper.

Luckily for Bambi, it's the latter. A number of ripped ciggy packets and other items of incriminating detritus are shoved down the back of seats as a police Volvo overtakes us and signals to pull over.

"Get out and talk to him Eddy, it fucking stinks in here," we order our still crumpled-looking driver, but the ploy doesn't stop the angry-looking copper marching straight past him, yanking the door open and leaning in.

"Who threw that fucking litter?" he screams, like a man possessed. In fact he sounds not dissimilar to the copper on *Withnail and I* who famously shrieks the immortal line, "Get in the back of the van!" If you've not seen it, don't worry about it.

There's a bit of a bemused pause until Alan Welsh confesses to throwing a used tissue out of the window.

"That's my pet hate that is," the bulging-eyed lawman continues. "No wonder the countryside's covered in shit. Drop as much litter as you like up in your own part of the country but don't fucking come down here and start doing it. Do you understand?"

Again, a pause. He's going to make us do it, I can tell. He's going to demand a reply.

"Well, do you?" If the pitch of his voice gets any higher he'll crack the windscreen.

"Yes, sorry," we all sort of mumble like scolded teenagers. Anything to get him and his thankfully under-performing olfactory senses out of the car.

Satisfied, he returns to Eddy, waiting in the police car. He knows we're going to the football so takes his time, giving him the full works: license check, breathalyser, a sixty-nicker ticket for speeding, three points and a long drawn-out telling off. Things have obviously been going far too smoothly for us on the transport front of late.

This really hasn't been the greatest start to an important day, although things do continue to get worse before they get better, much better, before they ultimately get worse again. Bear with me.

Once we're in Southampton and in the vicinity of St. Mary's we sling a load of ale down our necks in a boozer named the Old Farmhouse. Presumably it's called that because it used to be a farmhouse, and presumably the farmer and his family were all quite short. Either that or they were constantly smashing their heads on the doorframes, as I do when we leave for the match. It's a proper, full on, top of the head smacker that is so loud that people on the other side of the street hear it and wince.

I'm doubled over uttering a string of curses, some of them in ancient languages not spoken since before the birth of Christ, and trying to hold the top of my skull in place while my mates just roll about laughing. I don't really blame them though, banged heads are almost as funny as fat people tripping on pavements and kids getting hit by swings.

When we get to the St. Mary's Stadium and see the queues for the visitors' turnstiles, I think I'm still suffering from double vision - they're massive. Everton have brought loads today and yet there are only three turnstiles on. Ridiculous, especially in a supposedly state-of-the-art new ground.

Now I know you should get to the ground in plenty of time and all that, but there are always going to be people who don't, for whatever reason, and they expect to miss a few minutes at the start of the match. But nearly twenty minutes?

There's a lot of pissed off punters trying to get in, although to be honest I'm more concerned with counting my jarred fillings than anything else when all of a sudden, just like at Birmingham, we hear the crowd erupt, signalling a goal.

"Oh, for fuc…" I'm stopped mid-moan by a load of banging on the corrugated metal directly above us - the back of the Everton section. It must be a goal for us.

The bloke in front if us is instantly on his mobile phone to someone already in the ground.

"Rooney's scored," he confirms, and the angry mob is suddenly jubilant.

At quarter past three we finally get to our seats with Everton one-nil up and absolutely flying. The remaining half hour of the first period, played in glorious, hazy sunshine, is life-affirming stuff.

Joseph Yobo's back and he looks like a young Marcel Desailly, while up front Rooney is making a mockery of his midweek critics. The Southampton players can't get near the youngster, and only his strange decision to cross instead of shoot, following a rampaging run down the left, prevents him from doubling his tally.

The passing is all crisp one and two-touch stuff and the movement is superb. Tobias Linderoth's been recalled to partner Thomas Gravesen in that problem central midfield position, and despite his long absence he looks as committed to the cause as anyone.

FEBRUARY - BURNING DOWN THE HOUSE

Just over half an hour in, our total dominance is rewarded with another goal. Rooney chases down Antii Niemi, the Saints' keeper, and forces him to concede a throw-in deep in his own half. It's worked to Gravesen - the Dane is having one of those games where he seems to have hours on the ball compared to everyone else - and his inswinging cross is given a deft flick by the head of Duncan Ferguson.

Bottom corner. Two-nil. Birmingham City is suddenly a distant memory and I'm so happy I even forget about the pain in my shattered frontal cortex.

You put up with all the cack for moments like this: we're cruising, the weather's lovely and we can all enjoy a nice pint at half-time. The simple pleasures really are the best.

And then, with a minute or so to go until the break, just as we head for the bar, a little cloud peeps up over the horizon. It shouldn't really spoil our enjoyment, supporters of any other club would probably laugh it off or sing an ironic song, but we're Everton, and if you follow Everton long enough you just get a sort of sixth sense about these matters.

What happens is that the irrepressible Rooney again bursts into the Southampton penalty area, draws the keeper, but instead of shooting, rolls the ball into the path of the inrushing Ferguson. The big fella's unmarked, about twelve yards out, and he's got the whole of the goal to aim at. If he toe-pokes the ball straight ahead, it goes in and we're three up at the break, but he tries to side-foot it back across goal instead. He gets it all wrong and the shot curls rather embarrassingly into the crowd.

Look on the bright side we tell each other, if ever we can afford to miss sitters it's today. Not only are we still two up, but managerless Southampton have been really poor and don't look remotely capable of any sort of fightback. Gordon Strachan left the Saints recently and there are all sorts of ructions between their chairman, Rupert Lowe, and their supporters who are furious at plans to reinstate the objectionable Glenn Hoddle.

For the second-half the caretaker manager, Steve Wigley, sends on two substitutes, James Beattie and Fabrice Fernandes, who change the course of the match. In my darkest moments I fear they may have changed the course of our season too.

Where Everton were playing with such élan in the first period they now seem cautious and inhibited. Beattie - never an international footballer, but a handful at this level - is putting himself about and winning free-kicks. Mindful of defending their advantage the Everton players start to drop deeper, bringing pressure on themselves, and less than fifteen minutes in they fail to clear their lines, despite several opportunities to do so, and Kevin Phillips scores from close range.

It's one of the most deflating type of goals - one of those scored at the far end of the pitch at an away match when there's loads of players in the box obscuring your view. You can tell something's going on, and it's probably not good, but there's a brief moment when you think that the shot might have been saved or whistled narrowly wide. Then three sides of the ground go berserk and you're left to hang your head between your knees for a short while before gathering your thoughts, sitting up straight and screaming, "For fuck's sake Everton, sort it out", or something along those lines.

There's no way we're going to keep these out for another half an hour though; our confidence is too brittle. Some people bravely try to get a chant of 'Everton' going but it never catches on in situations like this. And that's not just a surly Everton thing, no crowd really gives it loads when their side are getting battered, not even the likes of Manchester United who pride themselves on their singing - they were stunned into silence at Goodison when Everton were fighting back in the second half the other week.

The truth is the inspiration has to come from the players first - if they win some tackles and push forward a bit that gets the crowd going and both parties then feed off each other's enthusiasm.

Luckily for us, Rooney still has a bit of spark of his own left, and while we grimly await the inevitable, he has other plans. Again he drives at the heart of the home defence, looking for space to have a dig at goal, but the retreating red and white shirts seem to have crowded him out and nicked the ball. It breaks loose though and only squirts out as far as Steve Watson who eases it back into Rooney's path, allowing him to take a touch, look up, and then hammer a shot into the roof of the net. It's at Niemi's near post but the power of the drive leaves him absolutely no chance.

Rooney whips his shirt off and goes crackers in front of the adoring Evertonians while Ferguson picks up the discarded garment and twirls it around his head. From the despair of being certain that Southampton were going to equalise, to utter ecstasy - all in a matter of seconds.

Anyone who suggests that Everton would be better off selling Rooney so we can buy Nicky Butt or Sean Davis or build a new stand, or whatever, just doesn't get it. This is what it's all about, moments of pure uninhibited joy, not moaning that Manchester United make more money out of selling sausage rolls on matchdays than Everton have taken through the gates, ever, or because Northampton Town have got more executive boxes than we have.

There are twelve minutes to go. We're three-one up and that goal against the run of the play, after the home side had dragged themselves back into the game, must be sickening for them. All we've got to do now is keep it tight and avoid doing anything silly.

Four minutes later it's three-two.

There doesn't seem to be that much danger as David Prutton picks the ball up just outside our box, but then the over-eager Linderoth dives straight in with a hasty challenge. The replays on the telly later show that the foul was just outside the penalty area, but that's little consolation as the referee points straight to the spot and Beattie converts with ease.

The clock's ticking down though and we're still in the lead. Southampton have had their bit of luck with the penalty; surely we're going to take a vital three points.

We're into the final minute when Tony Hibbert lets a ball drift over his head and the Saints win a corner. They've got everyone up and as the ball's whipped over I feel almost serene, so certain am I that Beattie or some other big grock is going to head it home. But I'm wrong; it's headed away at the back post and drifts harmlessly out towards the far touchline.

We all breathe a collective sigh of relief.

And then Fernandes picks the loose ball up, cuts back inside and lets fly with an outrageous, curling shot that smacks the inside of Martyn's right hand post and ripples the back of the net.

Three-three.

Just. Fuck. Off.

Sunday 22nd February 2004

I still feel sickened every time someone mentions yesterday's game. The only consolation was that the Hampshire police hadn't set a *Smokey and the Bandit*-type roadblock for us as we sped home.

Even Liverpool getting knocked out the FA Cup by a hopeless Portsmouth side, live on the telly, doesn't do that much to lift my spirits, and when ten man Leicester City come back from 3-1 down to go 4-3 up at White Hart Lane I'm convinced that I'm the centre of some huge cosmic prank, especially given that Leeds drew at Manchester United yesterday as well.

The only side who must feel more aggrieved than us are Blackburn. Their keeper, Brad Friedel, scored a last minute equaliser against Charlton only for the Addicks to then go straight up the other end and snatch an injury-time winner. Ouch.

Monday 23rd February 2004

David Moyes, while rightly praising Wayne Rooney's two goal performance on Saturday, said that only Chelsea or Real Madrid could afford him. Personally I read that as an example of how highly he rates him and how he doesn't want to sell him, after all Chelsea are owned by a billionaire who is splashing money around as if it's going out of fashion while Real Madrid have broken the world record signing fee on several occasions while assembling their squad of 'galacticos'.

However, some people are interpreting it as a 'come and get him' message. Even I'm not that paranoid, and quite frankly all such speculation should be put on the backburner for now. Worry about it in the summer, no one can move anywhere until then anyway. What matters at the moment is Everton staying up in the Premiership.

I keep thinking about that Ferguson miss. There were others in the game, and in plenty of other games for that matter, but being the pessimist that I am I keep thinking of it in relation to that film *Sliding Doors*, the one where the outcome of one small incident changes people's lives forever. A tad melodramatic, I know.

Tuesday 24th February 2004
It turns out that Merseyside police now want to speak to Alex Ferguson about the conduct of his players at Goodison.

I doubt anyone's arsed any more.

Wednesday 25th February 2004
It's very rare that I end up arguing with anyone about football: life's too short and you're never going to make anyone change their mind. I especially can't be bothered arguing with Liverpool supporters - the fact is that most of the ones that I know, like Peter Hooton, are sound, and we share similar views on most things.

Today is the exception though.

The morning papers are full of stuff about the graffiti daubed on the walls of the Reds' training crowd. Gerard Houllier's under pressure at the moment, especially after cup defeat on Sunday, so the 'Houllier Out' is not that surprising, but 'Hope you die of AIDS' is a bit strong by anyone's standards.

"Good morning paint daubers," is my greeting on entering Partizan's office at LIPA.

"That will be Everton supporters that, won't it," is Peter's rather startling reply.

"What? How do you work that out? Evertonians want that silly cunt to live forever."

"No Liverpool supporter would write that," he replies indignantly.

"Frig off, since when did Anfield become this bastion of fair-minded liberalness? And why would Everton supporters write 'Houllier Out'?"

"They've just done that to cover their tracks and make it look like Reds."

It goes on like this for a while. He says I'm blinkered while I accuse him of being a conspiracy theorist who refuses to accept that Liverpool fans are capable of being anything other than little angels.

"It was probably Chelsea," is my final low blow.

Well, he started it.

Thursday 26th February 2004

Michael Dunford's done a big interview with the *Echo* about Everton's finances. The upshot of it is nothing we didn't already know: things aren't as bad as they were but money is still tight. He does make a pretty strong case for moving grounds - our thirteen executive boxes as compared to Spurs' one hundred and twenty or even Southampton's forty-seven, tell their own tale, much as it grieves me to admit it. He adds that he sees a groundshare with Liverpool as the best solution though - a no-brainer - but doesn't seem particularly confident of it ever happening.

Friday 27th February 2004

Despite the FA saying that their investigations into Luis Boa Morte's allegations are ongoing, the newspapers are all reporting that Duncan Ferguson will be cleared next week.

Saturday 28th February 2004

"Does anyone want a book? I've just bought these off a smackhead in the street by ours."

It's one of those dead sunny but icy cold days and there's loads of us ensconced in the Stuart when PJ - only about four people in the whole world know his real name - kindly starts dishing out a selection of pristine Everton tomes. He's only a young lad - he spent a spell at Everton with the likes of Tony Hibbert and

Francis Jeffers when he was a kid - but he's got a flat near Goodison and always has his eyes open for the many bargains to be had on the thriving black economy.

"He must have been rattling bad," he adds, referring to the chemically-dependent book vendor. "Because I got the lot for a tenner and that Brian Harris biography's worth fifteen nicker on its own."

Mike Harris - no relation to Brian - is visiting from London and the talk of heroin addicts selling stuff reminds him of when he was a student in Liverpool. Now students are very rarely housed in the commuter belt of any city, but some of the places where these fresh-faced kids get dumped in Liverpool are absolutely ruthless. Mike has countless tales of getting burgled and threatened with decapitation by gangs of local head-the-balls, but he also admits there were times when him and his mates chose to take advantage of the lawlessness of their situation.

"My mate Pete asked the smackhead who lived next door if he could get him a bike once. 'Sure mate, no problem, I'll have you one later' he says, and sure enough a few hours later there's a knock on the door, although I think that's the last time he ever did knock, as I'm sure the cunt turned the place over shortly after, but that's by the by. He says, 'Err, I couldn't find you a bike mate, so I got you this instead.'"

"And what was it?" we ask.

"A trombone."

Alan Welsh turns up at the alehouse and informs us that John, the lad who got pulled driving the van back from Blackburn with no insurance in November, has been to court and received a two hundred pound fine and eight points on his license.

"Add them to Eddy's three points from Southampton," he says. "And we've actually got four more than Everton have on the road this season."

A sobering thought. Well, not that sobering, as we're all absolutely bladdered by the time Everton kick off against Aston Villa, and quite frankly that's the only sensible state to be in to sit through what is a dismal first half.

WHAT'S OUR NAME? EVERTON!

Alan Stubbs returns at the heart of the defence but otherwise it's the same side that performed admirably for much of the game at St. Mary's. However, Villa are a team on the up at the moment; they're always hardworking and physical as well, so it comes as little surprise that both sides cancel each other out for long periods. There's certainly none of the free-flowing football that illuminated the first half of the Southampton game, with Everton's best chance of a goal before the break coming courtesy of a Kevin Kilbane header that drifts narrowly wide.

In truth it's Villa who should go in a goal up, but thankfully Darius Vassell squanders a great chance when he finally finds space in the box but shoots straight at the legs of Nigel Martyn. So much is good about Vassell's game - he always looks impressive for both Villa and England - but crucially he never scores a lot of goals. Again, early in the second half, he takes advantage of weak defending by Everton and shows great strength to put himself right in the middle of goal, about eight yards out, with only Martyn to beat. If he puts his shot a foot either side of the keeper he scores, but to our relief he wallops the ball straight down the middle and is denied by a reflex stop.

As we have found out to our cost several times this season, if you don't take chances like that, especially away from home, you will eventually get punished. Today it's Villa's turn to learn the same lesson.

Tomasz Radzinski replaces Steve Watson with just over twenty minutes remaining; a substitution that proves inspired when the effervescent striker breaks the deadlock. The goal's created by Rooney - he's had a quiet game by his standards but, as we know, he's always capable of producing a decisive moment of class. Breaking down the right, he nonchalantly skips past a despairing lunge from the veteran Ronny Johnsen before clipping a cross to the near post. Perhaps a slight deflection off Jlloyd Samuel deceives the keeper, Thomas Sorensen, but nonetheless Radzinski reacts the quickest to meet the ball at the corner of the six yard box and glance a header into the back of the Gwladys Street net.

Six minutes later the result is put beyond any doubt when some nice control from Rooney and a clever dummy by Radzinski leaves Gravesen with the ball at his feet, thirty yards from goal. He sets off on a jinking run into the Villa box that culminates in Johnsen getting skinned again before the Dane drives a clinical, angled finish past his countryman, Sorensen. It's an absolute beauty - the sort of goal Gravesen's been threatening for some time, although disappointingly for a player of his ability it's only his first of the season.

The Villa fans - and there are loads of them today, which is a rarity - begin to stream out. They didn't see their burgeoning young team win on this occasion, but at least they got their money's worth, singing all the classics about the dole and stolen car stereos for most of the match. They really are the crushing bores of the Premiership.

But that's enough about them, let them fester in their resentment at missing out on the City of Culture while we bask in a hard-fought victory on a day when the results went our way elsewhere. We've climbed above Blackburn and Manchester City, into fourteenth place, but crucially Wolves and Leicester played out a nil-nil draw. That leaves Wolves, the team third from bottom, five points behind us. We're by no means out of the woods with eleven games left but we've certainly relieved the pressure and should approach our next match, at home to Portsmouth in a fortnight, with a certain degree of confidence.

Sunday 29th February 2004

Apparently Colonel Gaddafi wants to buy a Premiership club and Everton is one of a handful he is 'eyeing'. We'll just have to add him to the list of celebrity benefactors who have been linked with us in the past, including Bernie Ecclestone, Paul McCartney and the Sultan of Brunei.

I wonder if the Colonel's seen Gravesen's goal yet?

March

Ceremony

Monday 1st March 2004

Everton are playing a friendly against Bray Wanderers in Dublin tomorrow night. The likes of Rooney and Gravesen, players who have been playing a bit of international football and have even more to come with the build up to the European Championships, are being given a rest, but it's still most of the senior squad travelling over.

It seems ironic that we announce a friendly on the same day that Sepp Blatter, the president of UEFA, states that he's spoken to Sven-Goran Eriksson and they agree that the Premiership should be reduced to between sixteen and eighteen teams because there is too much football being played.

Tuesday 2nd March 2004

Thomas Gravesen will miss the next game, against Portsmouth a week on Saturday, through suspension. The win against Villa has left me feeling oddly bullish though; I think we'll cope without him for one game. It's not as if Moyes won't have plenty of options, especially after a number of the fringe players get a run-out over in Ireland. The Blues win easily with two goals from Francis Jeffers and one apiece for James McFadden and Nick Chadwick.

Chadwick is apparently set to go back on loan to Millwall for a while, so it's doubtful he has any more part to play for Everton this season, but I can see McFadden getting the odd game. I hope so - everyone likes to see a bit of wing wizardry now and again.

MARCH - CEREMONY

Wednesday 3rd March 2004

Apparently Merseyside Police are investigating a death threat sent to Gerard Houllier a couple of weeks ago. When I read the story I immediately send an e-mail to Peter Hooton asking him what he makes of the fact that the letter was written in blue ink.

An even more shocking piece of news is that Manchester United have appointed Walter Smith as their assistant manager until the end of the season. Words fail me, almost. The man's clueless about coaching - he looks smart in a club blazer and apparently he always gets the ale in for journalists, but that's it. There's a rumour that when he was at Everton, training consisted of giving the players a bag of balls and telling them to get on with it - if television cameras were expected he'd go and put a few cones out. That's what I heard, and the performances of his teams on the pitch rarely indicated anything to the contrary.

Thursday 4th March 2004

Another Everton youngster, midfielder Steven Schumacher, has gone out on loan. He joins Oldham for a month as David Moyes continues his policy of farming the young reserves out to gain first team experience. Leon Osman is at Derby at present, and apparently playing well and scoring a few goals, while the Scottish keeper, Iain Turner, is at Chester City and wants to stay there until the end of the season.

Just when you thought we'd had enough scandal for one season, nine Leicester players have been arrested in Spain in connection with an alleged sexual assault. Apparently the Midlanders were over there for 'warm weather training'. Do they think the fans are stupid? These mid-season 'training camps' are just piss-ups at the club's expense.

Saturday 6th March 2004

Some of the Leicester players in Spain have been released altogether while others have got bail, but three of them - Paul Dickov, Frank Sinclair and Keith Gillespie - have all been charged with the rather sinister sounding 'sexual aggression with

penetration' after three German tourists staying at their hotel in
La Manga said the players broke into their room and attacked
them.

Next Saturday's visitors to Goodison, Portsmouth, get gubbed
5-1 at home by Arsenal in the FA Cup. The commentators are
full of praise for the South Coast side's fans as they sing "We
Want Six", etc. Apparently it makes you a great supporter if you
think it's funny seeing your side getting twatted.

Tuesday March 9th 2004

In what must be the most pointless piece of investigative work
ever, the FA compliance unit - whoever they might be - are to
interview Francis Jeffers about the Ferguson and Boa Morte
incident. That story the other day saying that the case looks set
to be dropped was obviously a load of rubbish.

Are the men from the compliance unit going to put Jeffers in
the sweatbox like on *NYPD Blue*? Good cop, bad cop and all that,
trying to get him to break and reveal just what was said on that
pitch on that January afternoon?

Probably not.

Wednesday March 10th 2004

Sam Allardyce admits he's interested in David Unsworth.

Elsewhere, those three Leicester players are still being held in
Spain. We play at the Walkers Stadium a week on Saturday -
some of the chants are going to be interesting to say the least.
Surely we'll have at least a McVicar-style chorus of 'Sex case,
sex case, hang him, hang him'.

And Duncan Ferguson has received planning permission to
build twelve luxury flats in the grounds of his two million pound
Formby home. It's nice to know that he'll have something to fall
back on when he retires.

Thursday March 11th 2004

There are loads of Marseille fans in Liverpool city centre ahead
of tonight's UEFA Cup game against the Reds. Far from
bringing a touch of Gallic chic to Church Street and Clayton

Square it's more like a scene from *La Haine*. They are a bunch of bad scruffs, with many of them sporting what look like those bomber jackets favoured by bouncers, but worn inside out to expose the bright orange, highly flammable lining. Unless Lacoste start putting the crocodile on the inside of their jumpers and tracky tops I can't see that particular fashion ever catching on over here.

Friday March 12th 2004

The last three Leicester players have been given bail and allowed to return to Blighty. Some recently released Spaniard interviewed on the radio reckons that whilst inside they were teaching football skills to the other inmates. Sociologists and prison reformers are always saying that people pick up bad habits when in the nick, so just watch, there will be loads of Spanish cons scoring own goals and attempting clumsy offside traps now after a week confined with Frank Sinclair.

Meanwhile, in what amounts to just about the most pointless gesture ever, Leicester announce that the players will no longer be allowed the solitary alcoholic beverage that they used to get in their lounge after the game.

Just watch those East Midlands crime figures drop now.

Another Everton player is to go out on a month's loan. This time its not one of the kids but the vastly experienced Scot Gemmill - he's off to join his old Scotland boss Craig Brown at Preston North End.

Saturday 13th March 2004

The stars are out on Goodison Road today. While selling the mag we spot Patrizio Pascucci - remember him? - Ian Snodin and local DJ, Kev 'Seedy' Seed. Let's face it, who wouldn't want to be around for the stellar occasion that is Everton versus Portsmouth?

David Moyes has gone on record as saying that this is potentially the biggest game of the season - if we win, we go eight points above Harry Redknapp's side and more or less dispel any doubts about the drop. On the other hand, if Pompey secure their first away win of the season, we will be right back within reach of the most likely relegation candidates. So it's full house Goodison with it all to play for.

And it's woeful.

With Thomas Gravesen suspended, Moyes resists the temptation to make wholesale changes to the line-up, preferring instead to put Alex Nyarko in as a straight replacement alongside Tobias Linderoth. It doesn't take long for even the most fervent 'Gravosceptics' to realise just how heavily we rely on the Dane, as we struggle to retain any sort of meaningful possession whatsoever. Luckily Portsmouth are no better - they only have one real chance in the first half, when Steve Stone shoots wide following a defensive error by Alan Stubbs - but it hardly makes for riveting entertainment.

Nyarko is anonymous, Tony Hibbert's having another nightmare, Steve Watson's face is so red he looks like an extra from *Scanners* after ten minutes, and the movement from Duncan Ferguson and Wayne Rooney up front leaves an awful lot to be desired.

Kevin Kilbane has one fierce shot palmed over by Neil Hislop in the Portsmouth goal, but most of the action seems to involve prolonged bouts of head tennis in midfield. After only half an hour, Ferguson is withdrawn due to a hamstring strain and replaced by Tomasz Radzinski, who has a chance to open the scoring just before the break when a cross flicks to him off Rooney. In keeping with the general quality of the play though, the Canadian's volley ends up somewhere near the back of the Park End Stand.

The only thing to cheer us up at half-time is a text from Gid, who sits at the side of the Park End nearest to the away fans, reporting that the weird, tattooed Jerry Sadowitz lookalike, John Portsmouth Football Club Edwards, has been lifted by the rozzers.

Harry Redknapp's obviously pointed out to his players that if they are ever to win away from Fratton Park in the top flight then today's the day, as they are definitely more adventurous after the break. The wily Eyal Berkovic runs the game for the first twenty minutes of the half, so it is a bit of surprise and a relief when he's replaced with the sinister looking Ivica Mornar. However, the big Croatian striker almost justifies his introduction immediately with a shot across the face of Nigel Martyn's goal and a free header that lands on the top of the net.

He really should have scored with that second chance and, as I seem to keep saying, if you waste opportunities you get punished.

There seems to be little danger as Radzinski and Linvoy Primus chase a punt into the corner, but the lumbering defender panics and the Canadian steals possession before slipping the ball into Rooney on the edge of the box. The England number nine hasn't had a great game by any stretch of the imagination, but all of a sudden he explodes into life, operating on pure instinct as he shapes to shoot and then drags the ball wide of John Curtis and Arjan de Zeeuw. Before either of them can react and put in a challenge, Rooney's already drilled a low shot into the bottom corner of the net.

The Portsmouth fans have been well chuffed with themselves throughout, singing 'Who nicked my stereo?' and, shamelessly, *You'll Never Walk Alone*, and Rooney seems to have taken umbrage judging by his celebrations. He runs the whole length of the Bullens Road with his hand cocked to his ear before leaping up in front of the away section in what some might describe as a rather aggressive manner. A few programmes get lobbed at him but, to be fair, no one reports him to the police.

With Portsmouth now all over the place and needing to push forward for an equaliser, their painfully slow defenders are left exposed to the counter-attack. Rooney almost scores two more goals identical to his first, cutting to the right and driving in low shots, but he fails to put the game out of reach as both efforts finish narrowly wide.

It's a rousing finish to what was otherwise a dreadful game. Most importantly though, it ends one-nil to us and the consensus of opinion is that at this stage of the season it's results that count far more than style.

WHAT'S OUR NAME? EVERTON!

Sunday 14th March 2004
It's good to see that Walter Smith has wasted no time in steadying the ship at Old Trafford - United lose the Manchester derby 4-1.

Monday 15th March 2004
Apparently two bricks were thrown at the windows of the Portsmouth team bus as it left Goodison on Saturday. A tad harsh that, especially as they're still the only side generous enough to give us the full six points this season.

Tuesday 16th March 2004
Duncan Ferguson's hamstring strain is not thought to be too bad, although he is doubtful for Saturday's game at the Walkers Stadium. Past experience tells us that where the lanky property tycoon is concerned 'doubtful' means 'he may reappear some time next month if you're lucky'.

And a bit of transfer speculation, we haven't had any of that for ages, and for once it's actually about a player coming to us, not where Wayne Rooney is set to play next season. Our number one transfer target is apparently the versatile but out of favour Inter Milan defender, Jeremie Brechet. I could crush a grape.

Wednesday 17th March 2004
Everton's pre-season trip to China has been cancelled for the second year in succession. The planned visit apparently coincides with the start of the Chinese domestic season - something that a cursory glance at the fixture list could have cleared up ages ago, surely?

Last summer the tour was called off because of the outbreak of the deadly SARS virus. I remember walking past a Chinese chemist on Renshaw Street at the height of the epidemic and seeing in the window one of those crappy dust masks you get from B&Q for when you're doing a bit of sanding. The opportunist proprietor had written 'SARS' in felt tip on the box and was charging the princely sum of five pounds for it. Extortionate or not, it must have been effective as there wasn't a single case of the disease reported anywhere in South Liverpool.

MARCH - CEREMONY

Thursday 18th March 2004

Duncan Ferguson is set to return to the team for Saturday's visit to Leicester. It's also thought that Paul Dickov will be back in the Foxes line-up for the first time since returning from Spain.

Friday 19th March 2004

Ray McKay has sent a spoof letter to the *Echo* bemoaning the proposal to erect a monument to chubby songstress Kerry McFadden in Warrington. He proposes that it would be more fitting to honour Joseph Priestley, the inventor of carbonated water, or Chris Evans, the ginger media mogul who brought us such shows as *TFI Friday*, *Don't Forget Your Toothbrush* and *Boys & Girls*. He finishes by making the observation that there isn't enough bronze in the world to make Kerry's bust.

Sending stupid letters to the *Echo* is now a longstanding tradition; every week there's a couple that slip through the net. Some are dead obvious, especially the 'Rooney is rubbish, sack Moyes' type ones from Reds, but some are a bit more subtle, with often only the name, be it Roger Waters or Bernard Sumner, as the giveaway.

The first one I sent was complaining about people on the internet starting rumours about footballers taking drugs. I got a 'fair tackle' from the Anfield Iron, Tommy Smith, for that one, and I felt he opened up a bit to me with his comments about how the anonymity afforded people by the worldwide web is a dangerous thing. He obviously failed to notice that the letter was signed 'Billy and Charlie Sessions'.

I got a bit cocky after that and got sussed when I wrote in as Mr F. Reebase of Burtonwood, proposing a brass band at Anfield to liven up the atmosphere before games. "I play an instrument myself and nothing livens me up more than an afternoon on the bugle," was, in hindsight, over the top.

Saturday 20th March 2004

It's ten years since I attended Leicester's De Montfort Universty; but in that time Narborough Road has hardly changed at all. Luigi's, the Sicilian hairdressers, is still there - he once famously shaved LECESTER into some fella's hair before the play-offs - and the Huntsman pub opposite is still a bit grim.

It's a strange city really, the only character it has comes from the Asian community and the students; everyone else seems to give the impression of being slightly pissed off all the time. It's probably got a lot to do with their weird 'not quite Brummie' accent. They put 'ohh' at the end of their words i.e. they pronounce the name of their city as 'Lestohh' and nearby in the East Midlands is 'Derbohh'. They don't pronounce their 'g's either; hence the other big city down the road is called 'Nottinum'. When I first arrived there in 1990 the locals were in love with City's winger Tommy Wright, and the Filbert Street terraces used to ring out with the now legendary 'Ooh, Tommoh Raaaaart'.

I used to go and watch the Foxes sometimes, and I was there on the last day of the season in 1991 when they beat Oxford 1-0 to stay up in the old second division and I think I was the only person who didn't get on the pitch at the final whistle. I was slightly bemused by their outpouring of emotion for nothing more than ensuring survival - little did I know that I would find myself in their shoes twice in the decade to come, going mental as Everton escaped relegation by the skin of their teeth in what are now simply known as 'the Wimbledon' and 'the Coventry' games.

We leave The Huntsman just after half past two, walk down Narborough Road and then turn right onto Upperton Road, the one that takes you up to where the old ground used to be - the new one has been built about 100 yards further back. Just over the brow of the little canal bridge - the one that looked like the Golden Gate Bridge when I took magic mushrooms all those years ago - there are a number of police vehicles parked across the road and an area of grass embankment that drops away to the left has been cordoned off by yellow tape that snaps and cracks in the strong wind. At first it looks like the scene of a car crash but there's no glass or any of the other tell-tale signs, so we can only deduce that there's been some fighting. It's unusual for trouble to be this close to the ground though, the chances of getting lifted are too great - the town centre would seem much more likely for any run-ins with the infamous Baby Squad.

We scuttle past, slightly mystified, and pay the scene no more heed for the time being.

They're in the process of putting up all sorts of flats where the old ground used to be so it all looks a bit scruffy and half-built at the moment, but they've finished wide concrete boulevards immediately around the new stadium and I imagine when the whole thing is done it will look quite smart. At least it's still in the city and still feels part of the community that built the club in the first place, unlike somewhere like the Riverside which is out at the arse end of nowhere; or the Reebok, just another unit in a shopping complex.

As for the Everton line-up, Duncan Ferguson actually does return to the side, as does Thomas Gravesen in place of Alex Nyarko. James McFadden also gets a rare start as well due to the fact that Kevin Kilbane is away at the bedside of his expectant wife.

Let's be honest, neither of these sides are renowned for their slick football at the moment and with the wind swirling around the stadium so strongly that the ball won't even stay still for goal-kicks, it's never going to be 'a great advert for the game'.

The home side have got the wind at their backs in the first half, and as a result we're finding it difficult to get out of our own half. Micky Adams has got two monsters, Trevor Benjamin and Marcus Bent, on the wings, and his sole game plan appears to stick high balls up into the corners and get them to battle for them. The first half hour is nothing but niggly fouls, clearances into touch and chants of "You couldn't score in La Manga".

Some fat cretin in the Leicester section is wearing nothing but shorts and a jester hat. He's up and down every couple of minutes to display his tattooed torso and gesture at the Everton fans. At one point the Leicester supporters start to chant 'Rooney' while pointing at this half-wit who, loving the attention, does a little dance. Lord save us from wannabe celebrity fans whose lifetime ambition is to get featured on *Soccer AM*. We used to always knock Geordies for this whole 'shirts off' thing, but it seems everyone's at it now.

WHAT'S OUR NAME? EVERTON!

The game springs to life when Bent heads a Muzzy Izzett corner against the Everton bar and then bundles home the rebound. The home fans go berserk, the Everton players look at each other in disgust and then the referee, Barry Knight, signals for a free-kick. I have no idea why.

After a let-off like that against a side as poor as Leicester - and they are rank - you might expect us to go on and take advantage, but that would just be too simple. No, we go and get our captain sent off instead.

Now I've said it before, Duncan Ferguson gets some unmerciful stick off defenders and instead of being protected by referees, he gets punished for battling on instead of throwing himself on the deck and whinging. A clash with Nikos Dabizas, as they both challenge for a high ball, earns him his first yellow card with Mr Knight unwilling to take into account the fact that balls are hanging in the air for ages thanks to the ridiculous wind; mistakes are going to be made. It is a harsh call, but where Ferguson is his worst enemy is in the way he reacts. Crafty fuckers like Alan Shearer moan constantly but they also try and keep the referee on their side. Ferguson, on the other hand, refuses to even be summoned over and just stands with his hands on his hips, obviously giving Knight a mouthful of abuse.

A lot of these refs are petty, officious bastards but, like it or not, they're in charge and there's nothing to be gained by deliberately pissing them off, especially when you've got such a physical style as Ferguson.

Everyone in the stadium knows what is coming next. A few minutes after the booking, Ferguson tangles with Steffen Freund and Knight is quicker on the draw than Liberty Valance. A second yellow. Off.

Ferguson goes ballistic and goes for Freund, who, admittedly, has been niggling at him and constantly whining to the ref. Ferguson grabs the German and literally tries to wring his neck as the other players attempt to prise them apart. The Scot's coup de grace is a theatrical 'up yours' gesture to the Leicester fans as he eventually marches towards the tunnel.

It's not something you see every day.

Despite being reduced to ten men for the last few minutes of the half it's us who nearly take the lead when Rooney embarks on a mad run that ends with a shot just off target.

At half-time, Ray McKay and Gaz the lawyer look ready to start fighting over whether Ferguson was an idiot or just hard done to. It gets you like that sometimes.

As we make our way back to our seats, Gaz bumps into one of his mates, Bez, who asks if we know anything about the lad who got killed. That certainly stops us in our tracks. At first we think someone must have been stabbed but Bez says he's heard that a sign or an advertising hoarding blew down and killed an Evertonian on his way to the ground. That would explain that cordoned off area on the canal bridge - hopefully it's been exaggerated a bit though; the thought of someone dying in such a random way like that is horrible.

Despite being down to ten men, David Moyes can see that the best form of defence is attack. Micky Adams would like nothing more than for us to fall back to the edge of our box and allow them to bombard us, so Tomasz Radzinski is introduced in place of McFadden. The Scot had a really poor first half, a pale shadow of the player who looked set to take the Premiership by storm when he first arrived. He would do himself a lot of favours if, when things aren't going his way, he would keep it simple and just ensure that we keep hold of the ball. As it is, he tries to flick it past players at every turn, and if he can't then get to it he just seems to give up and shrug his shoulders. That's just not good enough at this level.

Maybe it's down to the extra mobility of Radzinski, or perhaps just the fact we've now got the wind behind us, but Everton look far better despite the numerical disadvantage. The two strikers are making clever runs off the back of the defenders and Rooney is twice denied great opportunities thanks to extremely dubious looking offside decisions.

Les Ferdinand is withdrawn by Leicester after an hour; he retires at the end of the season so his tormenting of Everton is finally over. Some of the Blues acknowledge the fact that he's been a magnificent player over the years and give him a round of applause while others, mostly the younger element, merely scream, "Fuck off Ferdinand, you wanker".

On seventy-seven minutes it's the turn of another magnificent player, Wayne Rooney, to score yet again. It's almost a carbon copy of the one he scored against Portsmouth last week, with Radzinski once again chasing a ball down the left and poking it inside to Rooney on the edge of the box. We know the drill from here on in: he shapes to shoot, lets the ball run across him and then smacks it hard and low. He doesn't find the corner this time but his shot still goes underneath Ian Walker and into the back of the net.

What must it feel like to be Rooney as he slides on his knees in front of that boiling mass of Everton fans and just kneels there with his arms outstretched, soaking up the adoration? It feels crazy enough up here in the stands; it must be completely overwhelming down on the pitch, being the focus of that much unbridled emotion. No wonder players sometimes do crazy things.

We're brimming with confidence now and Leicester haven't got a Scooby. With five minutes to go we should really double our lead and put the result beyond any doubt when Gravesen picks the ball up in our half, spots a gap at the heart of the Leicester defence and drives straight through it. The Dane reaches the edge of the home side's box as well, but just as he's about to shoot the ball is nicked away by the lunging Ricardo Scimeca. It only breaks to Rooney though and he immediately sets up Radzinski who has time and space to pick his spot. The Canadian is never at his best when he has time to think and weigh up his options and in this instance he merely curls a tame effort straight into the midriff of the mightily relieved Walker.

Leicester don't look like opening us up at all until deep into injury time when Dickov lays a ball off to Scimeca who leathers it, only for the under-worked Nigel Martyn to brilliantly tip it onto the post and out for a corner.

Come on, concentrate, this is the last kick of the game and we deserve the three points for competing so well with only ten men. Steve Guppy floats the corner to the back post where Bent rises the highest, just as he did in the first half, and sends a header goalwards. There's a pause for a second, Linderoth's guarding that post and looks like he might have stopped the header, but the ball catches him on the hip and then, like an exhausted cross-country runner, it seems to summon the extra energy to throw itself just over the line.

It's Southampton all over again; as soon as Rooney touches the ball for the restart the referee blows the final whistle.

We trudge away from the ground, distraught. There are even more police on the bridge than before and an eerie hush descends, despite the thousands of people filing past. The rumour about the accident must have spread.

It's only when we're back in the car and put Radio 5 on for the results that the news is confirmed: a forty-year-old Everton supporter was killed by flying debris on his way to the Walkers Stadium at twenty-past-two.

It's a strange feeling as we drive home - we don't even know his name after all - and if I'm totally honest I think a lot of people are thinking how easily it could have been them or one of their friends, as the bloke who got killed was just walking along to the ground like the rest of us, looking forward to the game. It just forces home the capricious nature of death and the fact that it is always closer to us than we care to recognise.

Monday 22nd March 2004

The man who was killed on Saturday was named Bernard Murphy. Everyone still seems a bit shocked.

Wednesday 24th March 2004

Not surprisingly, the FA are charging Duncan Ferguson over the shenanigans at Leicester on Saturday. He hasn't got a leg to stand on considering the picture of him wringing Steffen Freund's neck, like Homer Simpson with Bart, has been in just about every newspaper this week. He must be looking at something like a five match ban. Thanks to the sending off alone he will miss the away game at Newcastle next week. For good measure that's also the first match of Rooney's two-game suspension, received for accumulating yellow cards. Just when we felt that we'd settled on our first choice strike partnership as well.

Everton have distanced themselves from a pantomime, *Snow Blue and the Seven Blue Noses*, that is due to open at the Royal Court next week. Their reasoning? It just isn't funny. No shit, and it sounds a positive hoot. Thankfully the living legend that is Howard Kendall has withdrawn from it as well. No one needs the money enough to be in something that has a character called Count Houllio trying to steal Dixie's boots and kidnap Wayne Rooney, surely?

Thursday 25th March 2004

While things aren't exactly peachy on the disciplinary front, some good news for Wayne Rooney is that the charges against him for allegedly spitting at that girl in Ampersand - still ludicrous - have been dropped due to a lack of evidence.

Paul 'jittery' Gerrard has gone on loan to Nottingham Forest until the end of the season when his Everton contract expires. I used to think he looked mustard when he played for Oldham but a few hideous clangers for us just shattered his confidence completely. I still have nightmares about one against Newcastle when he came flying out of his goal for no good reason, almost decapitated Abel Xavier, and allowed the mutant Craig Bellamy to walk the ball into the net.

To his credit, some woman I used to work with had known him since he was young. She always insisted he was a lovely lad and used to tell me off when I swore at the mention of his name. Bless.

Saturday 27th March 2004

Everyone seems quite subdued in the Stuart today. A load are feeling goosed after going to see a Shack gig that never finished until the early hours, while I'm trying but failing to put a brave face on a chest infection. There's also the fact that games against Middlesbrough are rarely worth getting emotionally moist over. Someone does lend me a pirate copy of the Oscar-winning *Lost in Translation* though, which is slightly exciting.

The lack of enthusiasm for today's game doesn't just seem to be confined to the Stuart; all around the ground the atmosphere seems flat. Perhaps it is the opposition or maybe it's just because, although we're far from mathematically safe on thirty-three points with nine games to go, we seem destined to limp to safety and no more. Who knows, it feels crap anyway.

There's a minute's silence before kick-off in honour of Bernard Murphy. Both sets of supporters observe it perfectly while the players stand, heads bowed, on the centre circle. You never get over that eerie feeling when so many people are silent like that - it's a mixture of sadness and also a certain amount of tension. I almost feel relieved when the referee blows his whistle and the cheering starts.

Anyone hoping for the football to lift their spirits must be sorely disappointed, as it is yet another shocker of a game.

David Moyes said in midweek that despite the trouble at Leicester, Duncan Ferguson will remain Everton captain when he is available for selection. He isn't banned today but he is still missing, apparently through injury. Whether that's really the case or not, you just wouldn't know.

Anyway, little Tomasz Radzinski's up front with Rooney but the rest of the team don't appear to have noticed, the number of high balls they keep lofting forward. Middlesbrough, for their part, are industrious and neat in midfield, but for all the prompting of Gaizka Mendieta and the determined running of Juninho, their forwards, Joseph-Desiré Job and Massimo Maccarone, get very little change out of Joseph Yobo.

All the speculation in the newspapers is about whether we are going to keep hold of Wayne Rooney, but it seems likely that there will be even more clubs sniffing around our Nigerian stopper come the summer. There isn't a team in the Premiership, or even Europe for that matter, that he wouldn't get in. He's better than Kolo Toure at Arsenal and much better than any of the central defenders at Manchester United, Rio Ferdinand included.

An Alan Stubbs header and a Rooney shot deflected over the bar by Danny Mills are the 'highlights' of the first half. The second period is little better, with neither side showing any imagination whatsoever until as late as the seventy-eighth minute when Yobo breaks up yet another Boro move and swings a long pass out to Kevin Kilbane on the left-hand-side of midfield. The Irishman sees Radzinski making a run in behind the visitors' defence, and immediately knocks a deft volley into his path. The back-pedalling Chris Riggott tries to close down the angles as Radzinski drives into the box but the young defender, wary of a right-footed shot, leaves the striker just enough space to get the ball out of his feet and drill a left-footed effort inside Mark Schwarzer's near post. No doubt the pundits would describe it as 'a great striker's goal'.

Boro haven't looked like scoring all match, although in fairness we've hardly peppered their goal with efforts, but you can tell they're going to draw level as soon as the game restarts. I don't know what it is exactly, probably just an air of pessimism brought on by all the late goals we've conceded lately, but it's like the crowd, the players, everyone, knows we won't hold out for the last ten minutes.

In the end it only takes Boro five minutes to get a goal and take a point.

The Everton players are incensed when the referee, Steve Bennett, not only penalises Steve Watson for a foul but also calls him over, dragging him away from his defensive duties, and then indicates for Boro to take the free-kick while he's out of position. Why doesn't he just go the whole hog and float the kick over to the far post for them himself?

However, despite Bennett's dubious refereeing, Boro only manage to force a corner and if we defend it properly then that particular incident would be forgotten. Unfortunately for us, the kick is lashed in low to the six-yard box where it bounces around before a Yobo clearance rebounds off the unfeasibly wiry Job and into the net.

A shite end to a shite afternoon.

Lost in Translation is rubbish as well.

Monday 29th March 2004

The soaraway *Sun* is at it again; they're obsessed with Wayne Rooney. Apparently there were ructions at the lovely Colleen's eighteenth birthday party at the Devonshire House hotel on Saturday night. Police were called, according to Britain's favourite daily, to break up a Wild West-style brawl.

This most unpleasant of tabloids is constantly trying to paint Rooney and his family as a bunch of Jerry Springer guests and, to be quite frank, it's downright unpleasant. No teenager deserves to have the sneering stuff written about him that Rooney has. He can hardly be accused of courting the attention, and in many ways that seems to be his downfall. One thing that the press do not appreciate is being told that they're not important.

Tuesday 30th March 2004

Kevin Campbell has recovered from a back injury and is set to play at St. James's Park on Saturday. Both Duncan Ferguson and Wayne Rooney are suspended so we could certainly do with someone to partner Radzinski.

No one fancies us up there at all. The Geordies got beat at Bolton on Sunday but they're a different proposition at home. They've slipped to fifth in the table, just behind Liverpool, so they will be desperate to get three points and keep the pressure on for the fourth Champions League spot.

Hardly any of the usual suspects are travelling up for this one. A load are going to Ladies Day at the Grand National on the Friday, so they will be skint and in no fit state for anything, while for Bob the Saturday is obviously his busiest day of the year. Weavers, the only one of us still with a one hundred per cent attendance this season, is also doubtful because his girlfriend is expecting their first baby. What sort of excuse is that though? It's not as if he's delivering it or anything.

Some people.

Wednesday 31st March 2004

The Sun are like a dog with a bone where the Rooneys are concerned. According to Martel Maxwell, their showbiz reporter, there is a lot of bad blood as a result of the fighting on Saturday night - so much so that Wayne's dad has offered to get in the ring with the lovely Colleen's arl fella. Here's just a snippet of what they've written:

"A family pal said: 'Wayne Snr is spitting blood. He says Anthony punched him a couple of times. He wants to settle the score the old-fashioned way, in the ring. They know what they are doing, but it won't be pretty.'"

Both families are from Liverpool, where it is traditional to settle disputes with a punch-up.

The pal added: "The fight is called a 'straightener' - it's used for two men to clear the air.

"No weapons are used and when the fight is finished the feud is never spoken of again."

Has the world gone mad? Could *The Sun* dream up any more clumsy regional stereotypes?

"They come from London, where it is traditional to wear a pearly costume and sing 'Roll out the Barrel'. They always look after their own, they're good to their old Mums and it's safe to leave your front door open."

And while we're on the subject of violence, Duncan Ferguson has, unsurprisingly, pleaded guilty to the FA charges concerning his antics at Leicester. However, the Boa Morte racial abuse charges have finally been dropped due to a lack of evidence.

Duncan, incidentally, is from Scotland, where it is traditional to drink whisky, wear a string vest and be extremely careful with your money.

In the evening, young Wayne plays extremely well for England in their 1-0 defeat by Sweden in Gothenburg. For some reason, Sven-Goran Eriksson plays all sorts of Herberts who have got about as much chance of going to Euro 2004 as there is of me getting a Liver Bird tattoo.

The poor Scots get beat at home by Romania, despite a good goal from James McFadden. The exasperation of the Scottish reporters and pundits when they talk about the manager, Berti Vogts, is dead funny. He's like the Teutonic Houllier, the way he says that the team played well when they were quite clearly gash. They were also lucky that the Romanians felt sorry for them.

April

Down In the Tube Station at Midnight

Thursday 1st April 2004

Everton do quite a good April fool on the official website, revealing a mock up of next season's kit with a red and yellow liver bird on the front, supposedly in recognition of our City of Culture status. Apparently quite a few people take the bait and e-mail the club to express their consternation.

I laugh at them and go back to tending my spaghetti tree.

Bernard Murphy's funeral was today at St. Aloysius church in Huyton. David Moyes and Everton chairman, Philip Carter, were both in attendance.

Friday 2nd April 2004

You can tell the summer is on its way, with all the usual nonsense in the news about Glastonbury tickets. As ever, there are more and more measures in place to prevent people reselling tickets at inflated prices. It's strange that in this unashamedly capitalist society of ours, the ticket tout is viewed with such contempt. If, for instance, you buy property and sell that on for a healthy profit, you don't get castigated. Far from it in fact, you get your own programme on UK Living.

Why anyone would want to spend a fortune to go to Glastonbury is a mystery to me anyway. I prefer to recreate the experience at home by watching it on telly, eating half-cooked vegi-burgers and then pooing in the garden. I also leave my front door open so the neighbours can come round and steal all my stuff.

WHAT'S OUR NAME? EVERTON!

Apparently Kevin Campbell's a doubt for tomorrow now. David Moyes, impressed by James McFadden's performance for Scotland in midweek, says he might give him a go up front.

We're going to get battered.

Saturday 3rd April 2004

'I'll pick you up nine o'clock' said Alan Welsh's late night text message. So I've been waiting quite a while, with my butties made and my hat and coat on, when him and Eddy roll up at 10.30. Actually, 'roll' isn't the right word, following their full day and night of excess at the fleshfest that is Ladies Day at the National. With their sunglasses on, their tentative movements and their constant pained expressions, they resemble two heavyweight sluggers at a post-fight press conference.

Thankfully, the M62 is clear and we make great time, even taking into account a stop at some grotty services for a Burger King meal that Richard Harris and George Best tuck into like a pair of pitbulls with a fallen postman.

We park by a pub quite near to the ground, the Leazes Inn, and I give Gaz the lawyer a ring. He's up here with his girlfriend Bev, who is a Newcastle season ticket holder. As it turns out, the pub she's taken him to is right over the other side of the ground from us, so we arrange to meet for a pint at half-time, but not before Bev warns us not to go into the Leazes Inn if we want to get home alive.

"Fuck that, I'm in no state to go walking around looking for anywhere else," says Eddy, already halfway through the door.

I half expect the jukebox to stop, snooker balls to stand still, and even the Arsenal and Manchester United players to take a break from their FA Cup semi-final for a minute to shade their eyes and peer out at us from the big screen that dominates the room. Fortunately for us, Bev's overreacted totally; it's a perfectly friendly, busy matchday alehouse full of hassled bar staff, families in replica shirts and old fellas eating cooked breakfasts.

A sort of standing feature of *When Skies Are Grey* down the years has been the taking the piss out of Geordies. You get the impression that it mystifies a lot of them, as they take pride in the fact that the media have painted them as 'everyone's favourite second team', essentially on the back of the fact that when Kevin Keegan was their boss they played some very attacking football, but ultimately won nothing.

The thing is, we've not got anything against people from Newcastle per se - in fact we've all got good mates from that neck of the woods - but quite frankly it's almost impossible not to attack the pompous, self-aggrandising attitudes of some of their fans.

For a start, they're obsessed with the notion of being a 'big club'. They never shut up about it. Talk about football with the ones who come on to the *WSAG* messageboard to trot out all the usual shite about shellsuits and smackheads, and they will quickly start spouting statistics about average attendances, how many replica shirts they sell, and what the turnover of the club is.

The reason for this insecurity is quite plain: despite being the only club in their city and having the substantial financial backing of the Hall family, their history, particularly post-war, contains very little silverware. In fact a Fairs Cup win before I was even born was the last time they won a trophy. They're always the bridesmaid, and it really rankles that a club like Everton - a club that has to split its potential fanbase with the most successful club in Britain - has a roll of honour the envy of all but a handful of other clubs in the country.

As I said though, there are plenty of sound Geordies, just as there are sound people who support every club - with the exception perhaps of Bolton - and I know for a fact that many of them cringe when they see tattooed clowns with their shirts off or, even worse, the Neanderthal who once told a telly reporter, "I love Newcastle United me. I've got a wife and two kids and I love Newcastle more than I love them. I know that's a terrible thing to say but I mean it."

We watch the end of the semi-final on the screen - United win one-nil - while Alan and Eddy nurse pints of shandy and fight to keep their Whopper Meals down. It's a laugh a minute, this.

Last time we came up here it was for a midweek League Cup game when Rooney was awesome and we eventually won a penalty shoot-out, a rarity for the Super Blues. We were distinctly livelier on that occasion, and spent a couple of hours before the game in a seedy little gaff called Idols Bar. This minging boozer was below a shopping centre - which is almost as bad a sign as a Stanley Racing portakabin in the car park or an angry Alsatian on the roof - and featured 'exotic dancers' who were introduced by some barmpot with the same delivery style as darts commentator, Sid Waddell.

He had us in stitches as he announced, "Alreet lads, noo it's time to get the fanny on" before some emaciated-looking victim of domestic abuse came out and gyrated in a singularly unerotic fashion to the chart hits of the day.

"Look at the nipples on that!" he screamed, as if proclaiming a nine-dart finish to clinch the Embassy. "Champion!"

One thing you have to concede to the Magpies is just how good their stadium is. Personally, I think it's the best in the country, looking equally impressive inside and out. Two of the stands are absolutely frigging enormous, and we're in the corner between them, right near the top. It's a great view of the action, if not a little detached from the atmosphere, but first you've got to get up there. I swear someone's ticker is going to give out climbing these stairs one day - they seem to go on forever. I like to think I'm reasonably fit, and I'm getting tired; Alan and Eddy meanwhile start to make disturbing guttural noises when we're no more than halfway up. By the time we reach the summit, we're expecting to be wrapped in foil blankets and given a Mars Bar by the St. John's Ambulance people.

"Naysmith you cunt," the bladdered old bloke in the row behind me shouts as I take my seat. "You stupid bastard, pack that in."

"What's up mate?" asks his equally inebriated colleague. "They're only warming up."

"That fucker, Naysmith, he's doing my fucking head in," he slurs. "Instead of just chipping the ball up to Martyn he's trying to twat it in the bottom corners. How's the goalie supposed to warm up like that, the twat?"

His mate squints down towards the goalmouth nearest to us - albeit about six hundred feet below - where Martyn is indeed being sent scrambling around his goalmouth.

"That's not Naysmith, that," he reports. "That's the mascot."

When everyone around them stops laughing, the more myopic of the two then begins a tirade at ex-Everton player Gary Speed that continues, pretty much unabated, for the rest of the game. The Speed saga is a long one, but he left under a cloud - don't they always - and despite being a boyhood Evertonian, he is greeted by chants of 'Gary, Gary, Gary, Gary Shithouse Speed' whenever we play Newcastle. To give this balloon behind me his due, his insults are more inventive, especially, 'You humpty-backed bastard' and 'I hope your kids walk backwards'.

Speed famously never travelled to an away game at West Ham - the incident that finally precipitated his move from Everton - and it obviously still grates with this loon.

"I fucking went all the way to West Ham," he wails. "And I had to sit with all them Cockney thugs who were trying to kill me while you just sat at home on your arse you, Speed, you humpty-backed bastaaaaard!"

It's going to be a long game.

In fact it's going to be a very long game. In only the fifth minute, Alan Shearer heads a ball on for the toad-like Craig Bellamy to chase. David Unsworth, in for the injured Alan Stubbs, has time to welly it clear or touch it back to the keeper, but does neither. Instead, he tries to be too clever and ends up completely misjudging the whole situation, allowing Bellamy to push past him and round Martyn before rolling the ball into an empty net.

Needless to say, it's hard enough getting a result up here without handing them a goal on a plate.

The expected black and white onslaught doesn't materialise though, and within fifteen minutes we're level. Thomas Gravesen wins a loose ball in midfield, feeds Kevin Kilbane, and he in turn sets Tomasz Radzinski away down the left. He's really dangerous in this position, as he cuts into the box, thanks to his pace and, well, let's be honest, his willingness to 'emphasise fouls'. We expect him to shoot but he spots Gravesen's run to the edge of the box and squares for the Dane to slide in ahead of Kieron Dyer and plant a low finish past Shay Given.

We're obviously made up, but I can't help noticing the muted celebrations of the players; they don't seem to have much belief in themselves at all. Perhaps I'm reading too much into their body language from this distance, but I don't get the feeling that we're going to push on and get something from the game.

Less than ten minutes later, another passage of insipid defending by the Blues allows Darren Ambrose to attempt a cross to the far post. Before it gets that far though it inadvertently strikes Kieron Dyer in the face and, from the edge of the box, bounces up and over Martyn and into the top corner of the net. Dyer himself looks as bemused as anyone by this freak effort.

The half ends with us 2-1 down.

We go and meet Gaz for a pint and gather around one of the television screens to watch the big race at Aintree. The concourse is absolutely mobbed as my horse, Hedge Hunter, falls at the last, and Ginger McCain's Amberleigh House wins a thriller.

Unfortunately, what then happens around us is a lot more disappointing than my lost tenner.

It's widely known that Everton have something of a reputation for racist chanting that harks bark to the dark days of the seventies and eighties, but thankfully nowadays you will never hear the mass monkey chants or shouts of 'trigger trigger' at Goodison or any other Premiership stadium. However, it's become quite clear that we still have an insidious element that, while not made up of card-carrying National Front members, really doesn't have a problem with songs that are derogatory towards black people.

Do other clubs have similar problems? I don't know, and quite frankly I don't care. I don't support any other club and I don't have to listen to their fans singing about Djimi Traore being a 'coon' or Emile Heskey being a 'slave'. Similarly, is it society's problem? Not when it's being sung at an Everton match it isn't.

It's 'Follow, Follow' that gets an airing here - not the Rangers ditty, but one that refers to Emile Heskey as a 'monkey' - but it isn't just a handful of wellied sixteen-year-olds belting it out, there are plenty of older fellas joining in too. The place is chocker and this song is booming. Gaz asks some teenager immediately behind us what he thinks is so funny about the song, and the little sheep immediately clams up.

Then, after several choruses of this, from somewhere near the back of the concourse comes 'I'd rather be a Paki than a Red'. Not as many join in this time, but there are still more than you would think in this day and age.

I can't believe this is what we've come to. Or maybe, if I'm honest, I can. The fact is I've had plenty of arguments with people in the past who, incredibly, don't think that the Heskey songs are actually racist - they believe that they're just a bit of harmless fun. So maybe I shouldn't be at all surprised that some now feel emboldened enough to sing naked, unequivocal hate songs.

You're always going to get the odd tit-head who will think he's being funny or risqué in an alehouse - I'm sure every club has those - but this season, especially away from home, it feels like someone has let the evil genie back out of the bottle.

I'm fucking appalled, and I find it hard to concentrate on the second half.

In the opening moments we win a corner and as the ball breaks in the box Joseph Yobo almost notches his first ever goal for Everton, with an awkward volley that bounces up off the turf and beats Given, only to clip the top of the crossbar. You don't need me to point out the irony of the 'Joey Yobo' chants as the Nigerian jogs back to the halfway line.

Five minutes later though, the normally unflappable defender, who has struggled to deal with the wily Alan Shearer all afternoon, completely misjudges a loose ball towards his own goal and falls over, allowing the ageing striker to advance unopposed and take on Martyn, one-on-one.

The result is inevitable. Shearer, one of those players, like Roy Keane, you kind of dislike but admire in equal measure, wheels away and celebrates with his customary raised arm.

Newcastle don't look anything like a top side though, and Everton, now we're three-one down, start to knock the ball about a bit. Steve Watson looks like he's pulled a goal back as well when he heads home a Gravesen cross, but a dubious-looking offside flag denies him. With ten minutes to go, however, substitute James McFadden does well to force a corner that Gary Naysmith launches to the far post. Newcastle's defending is slack, allowing Yobo to finally get on the score sheet, sauntering in unopposed and nodding the ball home.

Again, despite the Evertonians' urgings for the team to get forward and grab an equaliser, there is a lack of real forward momentum, despite long periods of possession. It's hard not to wonder how big a difference Duncan Ferguson, and particularly Wayne Rooney, might have made against the extremely unconvincing Magpies.

Any hope of grabbing a point at the death is extinguished when Shearer latches on to a blocked Lee Bowyer shot and cracks home his second goal of the day.

"I've spent well over two hundred quid betting on horses, drinking ale and watching Everton this weekend," says Alan Welsh as we file away from the ground. "And has it made me happy?"

"I don't know, has it?"

"Has it fuck."

Sunday 4th April 2004

According to the official Everton website, the Blues played better than Newcastle yesterday apart from our defending and our finishing. That doesn't really leave much, does it? As the old saying goes: 'If my auntie had a dick she'd be my uncle'.

Millwall win their semi-final to book a place in Cardiff against Manchester United, more or less guaranteeing them entry into the UEFA Cup. Like everyone else, I'd probably joke about Europe not knowing what's in store for them, given the Lions supporters' reputation, but after the Nuremberg Rally at St. James's yesterday, I don't think I'd have a leg to stand on.

Monday 5th April 2004

Duncan Ferguson's been given a four match ban by the FA. Everton are considering whether to appeal, despite the fact that they have no chance of winning, as it would postpone the ban until the last four matches of the season, allowing him to face Tottenham this Friday and Leeds on the Tuesday. It all depends on Ferguson's fitness though; if he doesn't recover soon from his latest injury then it will be better to not appeal and simply get the ban out of the way, freeing him for the last three matches of the run-in.

Tuesday 6th April 2004

Everton have decided very quickly that Duncan Ferguson's injury will probably mean him missing games so they announce their decision not to appeal against his ban. That means our striking options are still severely limited for Friday's potentially awkward game against Tottenham.

In the evening, Arsenal and Chelsea play the second leg of their Champions League quarter-final at Highbury. The Gunners tried to be clever, resting players against United on Saturday, and subsequently they lost. That seems to have knocked their confidence, and they ultimately lose this massive tie to a late Wayne Bridge goal. It shows how quickly things change in football - less than a week ago the treble seemed more than possible for Arsene Wenger's side, but now they've only got the league to play for.

'Only', heaven preserve us.

Wednesday 7th April 2004

I'm facing a moral dilemma. A couple of months ago, when we were all a bit bladdered, I said that I fancied Deportivo La Coruna for the Champions League. Bob the Bookie, who is never off duty, offered me 20-1 and I took him up with a fiver. At that juncture no cash actually changed hands - he's good like that - and he never wrote it down. That was after Deportivo finished their group stage but before they played - and conquered - the mighty Juventus. In the first leg of their quarter-final though, they got torn apart, 4-1, by AC Milan. At that point I still hadn't given Bob the fiver, but neither of us had actually mentioned the bet since we first had it and, if I'm honest, I'll admit that I was just going to keep shtum. After all, he was pissed when he took the wager.

Which brings me to my dilemma.

In tonight's second leg, Deportivo put four goals past Milan, with no reply, to book themselves a semi-final place against Porto. They look sensational, well capable of beating the Portuguese and either of the other two semi-finalists, Chelsea and Monaco.

Now that I stand a fair chance of collecting a ton, do I remind Bob about a bet I was going to conveniently overlook ninety minutes earlier?

Thursday 8th April 2004
Fuck it, I ring Bob and remind him of our bet, although I do jokingly tell him about my selective amnesia.

"No problem," he tells me. "They won't win it anyway so I've just earned a fiver."

Well that certainly took the wind out of my sails.

Friday 9th April 2004
I've got a bit of a cob on. We're not playing until eight o'clock on Good Friday, but while it seems that the rest of Merseyside is on an all-day bender, we've got *WSAG* issue 108 to try and peddle on the street.

It's a particularly good edition in my opinion, but in parts it is critical of sections of our support - more specifically, the ones who sing racist songs. That's not an issue, not by any means - I wrote one of the more strongly-worded articles myself - but we could have perhaps picked a less feisty issue than this one to put a Liver Bird on the cover.

Evertonians are touchy when it comes to symbolism you see, hence the club's April Fool joke with the shirt. Only recently, Redmond sold a t-shirt to some lad who asked for a carrier bag to put it in. Being the helpful soul he is, Phil offered him a Tesco bag, only to see him recoil in horror, like a vampire from a shaft of sunlight.

"I'm not fucking carrying that around," said the lad.

"Why not?" asked Phil, wondering whether he had some objection to Tesco's stance on GM foods or free-trade coffee beans.

"It's got fucking red on it."

Some people take things too far. That said, any Evertonian who buys anything from Phil Thompson's DIY store obviously wants kicking through the streets and battering with big sticks. You've got to draw the line somewhere.

Nick, the cover's designer, says that the idea with the Liver Bird is that it is a symbol of the city, our city; why should the other shower monopolise the symbolism and the heritage? It's a perfectly noble and rational concept, made much easier for him by the fact that he doesn't have to stand on the street and explain his work to people who have been drinking since noon. That's what Redmond and I gripe about anyway.

Fair play to Graham Ennis though; we said, "You're fucking joking?" when we first saw it, but he backed Nick up and said he was willing to argue about it with anyone who objected.

But amazingly no one does. Evertonians must be more open-minded about this sort of thing than Phil and I thought. Either that or they don't see the cover until later because we're handing the issues over to them face down.

While we're selling by the players' car park, some bloke with a limp and a flat cap approaches us, hands over an article he wants us to include in the next issue and then starts on a tirade about what's wrong with the way the club is run. I must confess that I'm only half-listening - after all I'm trying to simultaneously take money off people while keeping their attention from the cover of the mag - until he starts screaming abuse.

"Fucking here are you? You fucking big lanky waste of space."

I'm taken aback, after all I've been called that before, but then I realise that he's actually looking over my shoulder and addressing someone through the railings behind me. I turn around to meet the gaze of an indignant-looking Duncan

WHAT'S OUR NAME? EVERTON!

Ferguson. It's quite clear he thinks I was the one doing the shouting, as Flat Cap is hobbling off like his life depends on it. Great, of all the Everton players to harangue it has to be the one who is hard as nails and has loads of even harder mates. I have visions of getting the Steffen Freund treatment through the railings, but thankfully Ferguson decides not to pursue the matter.

All the omens point towards a draw for this match. We haven't beaten Spurs for an absolute age and we invariably play like a bag of shite when we're on the telly. On top of that we've got yet another experimental strikeforce, with James McFadden playing up front with Tomasz Radzinski. It comes as a pleasant surprise then when we absolutely batter Tottenham from the first whistle.

The first goal comes on a quarter of an hour. A short corner is worked to Thomas Gravesen who crosses towards Steve Watson, whose flick-on is kneed over the line by David Unsworth at the back post.

Less than ten minutes later we're two up. I remember in the summer when we were being linked to every Tom, Dick and Harry, there were people advocating a move for Sheffield United's Michael Brown as he's apparently 'better than what we've got'. He eventually moved to Spurs and, alongside Jamie Redknapp, he's being made to look a rank amateur by Gravesen. A mazy run by the Dane is halted by a foul just outside the Spurs box. It's a great position for a strike on goal, but no one is that confident, given the fact that we haven't scored directly from a free-kick all season. It continues to be a night of defied expectations though, as Gary Naysmith curls a beauty over the wall and into Kasey Keller's top corner.

Spurs are stunned. Gravesen and Linderoth are in total command of midfield, and the Tottenham central defenders, Antony Gardner and the awful Gary Doherty, can't relax for a second thanks to the non-stop pressure from Radzinski and McFadden. Robbie Keane and Jermain Defoe, meanwhile, are completely isolated up front as Everton keep picking up possession and launching wave after wave of attacks, to the delight of the buzzing - or merely bladdered - home crowd.

By half-time it's three-nil. Another free-kick, in exactly the same position as the one Naysmith scored from, sees the same player stand over the ball with Gravesen. This time the Dane smashes the ball straight at Keller, but the unusually nervy-looking American spills it into the path of Joseph Yobo, who stabs home his second goal in a week.

Tottenham have a better go in the second half, but Everton, despite dropping the pace slightly, never look in any danger until the seventy-fifth minute, when Stephen Carr completes a determined run down the right with an excellent finish past Nigel Martyn. Any hopes of a rally are short-lived though, as McFadden picks the ball up straight from the restart and Carr, who has hardly finished celebrating his goal, hauls him down. The goblin-faced full-back receives his second card of the night and the game is effectively over.

McFadden, unlucky not to get on the scoresheet - it really will be some celebration when he eventually does - receives a standing ovation when he is replaced by Francis Jeffers with ten minutes to go. Then, at the final whistle, the whole team receive an ovation in recognition of possibly our best performance of the season.

Back at Orry's, while enjoying a well-earned pint, I feel a rough hand upon my shoulder. For a moment I fear it's an angry Duncan Ferguson, come to seek retribution for Flat Cap's outburst. Luckily though, it's only PJ, clearly full of holiday spirit.

"What the fucking hell is that?" he demands, brandishing the cover of the mag.

Sunday 11th April 2004

Not everyone was thrilled with Friday night's events at Goodison. Apparently Francis Jeffers went ballistic when it was announced that he wasn't in the starting line-up. According to reports, he had a massive slanging match with David Moyes and then, despite being given the chance to apologise on Saturday morning, stood by his assertion that he would never play for the manager again.

Arsene Wenger has stated that this is a matter for the player and Everton. He does not expect Jeffers back at Highbury until his loan spell is over.

Obviously the decision's already been made that we won't be pursuing our interest in the striker, hence the decision to overlook him in favour of McFadden, so all Jeffers can do is try and put himself in the shop window and try and attract some interest from other clubs. I'm not an experienced agent, but I'd guess that acting like a brat and then effectively ruling yourself out of the rest of the season is hardly the best way to go about it.

Monday 12th April 2004

Chelsea get beat 3-2 by Aston Villa live on the telly. We play at Stamford Bridge on Saturday - it's yet another one of our bogey grounds, but in all honesty, despite the fact they're second in the league and in the semi-finals of the Champions League, they really don't look that fearsome. The team of Gianfranco Zola, Gus Poyet and Dan Petrescu used to pass the ball to death and absolutely ruin us down there, but this lot Claudio Ranieri has assembled look ordinary at times, despite the amount of money he's spent.

The tickets for Stamford Bridge cost a disgusting £42. As a result, there are very few of our mates who fancy it, especially given that the pubs in Liverpool will be screening it on the foreign satellite channels.

Tuesday 13th April 2004

The White Bear, in Batley. The best away pub in the country, bar none. It's only ten minutes from Elland Road but it's a bit awkward to find, and as a result we're the only football fans in here for the second season running. In fact, we're the only punters in here, full stop.

We've got the pool table to ourselves and the landlord even recognises us from last time we were here. You can't half tell you're in Yorkshire though, especially when you ask him what crisps are on offer. There's no deep breath followed by a litany of exotic flavours here, oh no. There's no sweet Thai chilli, honey and mustard, sea salt and ground black pepper. In fact you're liable to get funny looks if you ask for anything as cosmopolitan and downright effete as prawn cocktail.

"Plain," is all there is. No explanation or excuses either.

Other than the paucity of the bar snacks though, it is a great little pub.

We get so comfortable that we leave it very late to get to the game. Due to the lack of time, we end up breaking our golden rule and sticking Gid's car on the bit of scrubland that masquerades as a car park, just by the railway line. The other year, one of the freaks who collects the money told us it was 'the fastest emptying car park in Elland Road'. He lied. It can literally take hours to get away from here, as these fluorescent-jacketed bastards pack the cars in like sardines and then fuck off, leaving every man for himself.

As well as the parking issues, there are loads of reasons to dislike Leeds, yet it's one of my favourite away matches. A lot of people will be delighted if they get relegated, especially after they lorded it up when they were spending money they didn't have, but I'd like them to stay up. It's not just because I like the trip up here either; after watching Everton's relegation battles over the last decade I kind of admire the way Eddie Gray's side have started to make a go of survival. They're still crap like, but they've dragged themselves off the bottom, and we play them on the back of two consecutive victories, against Leicester and the wobbly looking Blackburn. I imagine they fancy their chances against us.

There's a ridiculous amount of police stationed by the entrance to the away section, and they're performing extremely thorough searches, complete with metal detector sweeps, on a load of young lads getting off an Everton coach. Why the police are geared up for a riot I don't know, but obviously I don't look that dangerous, as they usher me straight through past yet another youth having his Paul and Shark baseball cap rigorously examined.

"It's all Everton," someone tells us as we take our seats.

They're not wrong either; we're all over Leeds, much to the displeasure of the home crowd. They're away to Arsenal after this game, so they're banking on three points here. On twelve minutes their survival hopes are given an almighty dent when none other than Wayne Rooney, returning after his two-match suspension, scores here for the second season in a row. The one he rattled in last year won us the game - the first time we'd triumphed here in the league for over half a century - and was perhaps more significant for many Evertonians than his more famous effort against Arsenal. For me and many other Blues, when Rooney skinned Erik Bakke and Lucas Radebe and then cracked home that goal, everything changed. Suddenly anything was possible. Seriously, we felt that if this fearless teenager could lead us to victory at Elland bleeding Road, then all bets were off.

A year later and we're getting almost blasé about his talents. No one is in the least surprised when, after Gravesen cunningly picks him out on the edge of the box, Rooney makes himself just enough space to drill a low shot inside Paul Robinson's right-hand post. From behind the goal you can tell it's in as soon as it leaves his boot.

Minutes later, Leeds should be two behind when Gravesen picks out Tomasz Radzinski and the Canadian's shot beats Robinson, only to cannon back off the foot of the post. The rebound's then cleared to safety before Rooney can slide in and poke it home.

From that moment, it's like a switch is thrown and the polarity of the pitch is reversed. For the next seventy minutes or so the action, which has all been directed towards the Leeds goal, flows towards Nigel Martyn as the home side completely take over. It's one of the most instantaneous and dramatic turnarounds I've ever seen in a game - even our fightback against Manchester United required a half-time bollocking.

It's incredible that we manage to hold on to our lead until the interval, such is the pummelling we get from the Yorkies. It's not particularly pretty - there are a lot of balls just twatted in the general direction of Mark Viduka and Alan Smith - but it's enough to put Everton firmly on the defensive.

No one epitomises Leeds more than the snidey, wet-mouthed Smith, but you have to admire his determination here. Admittedly he moans and cheats like a junior Shearer, but let's face it, there's a lot at stake. He looks certain to score on more than one occasion, but ex-Leeds favourite Nigel Martyn is again in outstanding form.

The second half continues in almost exactly the same manner, except this time, less than five minutes in, criminal defending by Alessandro Pistone allows James Milner to turn and shoot from the edge of the box. Even Martyn is powerless to stop this effort as it nestles in the same corner as Rooney's strike.

Leeds now have forty minutes to push on for the winner and three more vital points. Their crowd are understandably raucous, the momentum is with them - it has been for most of the night - and another goal seems inevitable.

But Martyn is having none of it. With a number of his teammates missing presumed dead in the face of the white-shirted barrage, he just grows like some energy-sapping beast from a Japanese cartoon. The more they throw at him, the bigger and stronger he becomes. You can almost hear the sound of flinty Yorkshire hearts breaking as he makes one particular flying stop from a Smith volley.

Every keeper we've had since Neville Southall has had to live in the Welsh legend's shadow and, in all honesty, none have come even close to matching the almost impossibly high standards he set.

Until now that is. Obviously Southall did it for over a decade, so Martyn's never going to be revered in the same way as the man many consider the best Everton player they have ever seen, but still he's undoubtedly made of the same stuff. He has the same authority and air of defiance that Southall had; it's not something you can teach or pick up through practice, you've either got it or you haven't. And no one can deny that Martyn's got it, especially on nights like tonight. It's such a shame that we didn't sign him until now. We actually almost did sign him before he went to Leeds, but that's another story altogether.

WHAT'S OUR NAME? EVERTON!

At the end of the game, with the scores somehow still level, he receives a round of applause from both sets of fans, despite the fact that he's almost single-handedly denied his former employers two priceless points. From the Evertonians' point of view it was almost worth seeing the rest of the side perform so badly just to get the chance to witness a great player in action.

And at least it gives us something to talk about while we wait for the fucking car park to empty.

Wednesday 14th April 2004

The big news is that Umbro are going to be manufacturing our kit next season and we have some sort of distribution deal with JJB Sports. To be honest I find it hard to get as excited as some people do over a piece of scratchy, flammable nylon made in some Far Eastern sweatshop and sold at around 1000% mark-up. On anyone, other than people playing football, they look shite, and they're an utter rip-off.

And talking of rip-offs, there's a rumour doing the rounds on the worldwide web of lies that Alan Stubbs has been telling people that Wayne Rooney to Manchester United is a done deal. Some versions have him going for a straight twenty million quid, while others have Nicky Butt and Ole Solskjaer thrown in for good measure. Apparently Everton are going to make some eye-catching signings first, and then sell him once they've got all the season ticket money in.

Thursday 15th April 2004

Today's the anniversary of the Hillsborough disaster. Everyone has their own memories of that horrible day; personally the thing I remember most clearly was the relief when we heard that my two uncles were alright. It took a while longer for the full horror of the events to really sink in. Even now it's difficult to comprehend how something like that could happen to people on a day out to watch a game of football.

According to one paper, David Moyes has already had talks with Jay-Jay Okocha about bringing him from the Reebok to Goodison in the summer. The part of my brain that enjoys conspiracy theories, and doesn't dismiss rumours out of hand, can see how the ball-juggling Nigerian would certainly qualify as an eye-catching signing.

Meanwhile, Francis Jeffers has issued an apology, saying that his outburst was all down to the fact that he is frustrated and just wants to do well for Everton. I don't think anyone's really got any time for him now though, although the manager has accepted his statement and will include him in the squad for Chelsea.

Moyes has a reputation for being harsh, but no one can say he isn't fair as well.

Friday 16th April 2004

Leeds, so combative against us on Tuesday, are torn apart by Thierry Henry at Highbury. The Frenchman, who has taken football to another level in terms of the combination of ability and athleticism, scores four goals as the Gunners essentially clinch the title with a five-nil win.

Leeds remain third from bottom, six points behind us - as long as we do nothing stupid we'll be fine - but they're still well within striking distance of Portsmouth and Manchester City, who have gone into freefall.

Saturday 17th April 2004

"You're havin' a larf aintcha?"

It's 12.30, we're stuck in traffic in London and we are breathtakingly lost. This cabbie, stopped next to us, isn't really helping much.

"This is Islington and you want to get to Chelsea? You're gonna have to go right through the city. You've got no chance."

"This is Harvey Weavers' fault," declares Eddy. "When he's old enough I'm going to batter him for this."

Harvey is, of course, the new baby of our normal travelling companion. He was born on Thursday and these balloons, Eddy and Bob, were out until all hours of the morning 'wetting the baby's head'. I suppose I must bear some blame for letting Eddy navigate in this state - once we missed the turning for the M40 we were doomed.

We spot a sign for an NCP car park and make the decision to cut our losses, stash the motor here and get the tube from the nearby Angel underground station.

The bloke manning the barrier at the car park tells us that it's nearly full but we can use the handicapped spaces. When we eventually find them, an absolutely drop-dead gorgeous young black girl pulls in next to us.

"Is it definitely okay to park here?" she asks.

"I think so," I say, straightening my jacket and leaning an elbow on the roof, ever so casually.

She smiles, not something you see very often in London, and she's just about to say something else when she's cut short by a strangled, coughing noise followed by a horrible, wet slapping sound.

I turn around to see Eddy, hands on knees, spewing his egg McMuffin all over the floor. I take that as my cue to McFuck off, abandoning my burgeoning relationship with the young beauty. Crimson with embarrassment, I don't stop walking and I don't look back until I'm in the nearest pub.

The tube can be a bit daunting when you're a little worse for wear, especially on a hot day like today, but despite looking a bit pasty, Bob and Eddy put a brave face on it and we get as far as Edgeware Road without incident. It's only just turned two o'clock when we board the overland train bound for Fulham Broadway, a mere five or six stops away. The carriage gets a bit chocker, but it's no problem, we'll be alighting soon. And then, just as we approach West Brompton Station, the whole train judders to a halt.

At first there's still a low hum, as if the engine is just having a quick breather before merrily whisking us back on our way, but then that cuts out and the whole contraption seems to let out a mellow sigh before settling wearily on its springs. In the words of that cabbie, you're having a larf aintcha?

As the experienced London travellers get themselves comfortable, turning up the volume on their iPods or fishing out a copy of the latest *Harry Potter*, we just shoot each other resigned looks. It's starting to get really hot and I've got that feeling that I always associate with being in an office following three pints of Stella at lunchtime. My eyes and tongue feel all rough and gritty, and my temples are starting to throb as this godforsaken train - a train that seems ignorant of the fact that an extremely expensive game of football starts in about twenty-five minutes - is showing no sign of moving.

Eventually, after what feels like half a lifetime, an almost comically nasal voice comes over the public address to inform us that we will very soon be on our way. It's true, and incredibly we manage to only miss the game's kick-off by a couple of minutes - that's almost early by our standards.

The Lower East Stand, where the Everton fans are situated, is an absolute fucking rat hole. How they can justify the prices is outrageous, although if stupid gets like us keep paying it then I suppose there's not really much incentive for them to drop them. Surely Roman Abramovich, top of the *Sunday Times* Rich List with his seven billion quid, can stretch to getting a plumber out to take a look at the khazis though. While most of us are guilty of harking back to the 'good old days' a bit too much, one thing that you really don't expect in this day and age is to have to hike your kecks up like Max Wall to keep them out of rancid pools of piss.

Honestly, if ever you wanted to see a microcosm of a capitalist society then look no further than a football ground like Stamford Bridge, proudly boasting its corporate facilities, hotel rooms and restaurants on the surface, while down below the plebs are being fleeced and living in filth.

The game itself does little to justify the hefty price either. Frank Lampard, one of the Premiership's players of the season and easily Chelsea's best, clips the bar with a shot early on, but for all the big names in the home side's line-up they're again far from fluent. With all the good players they have, Chelsea are always going to be challenging for honours, but you need a bit more than that to elevate you to the very top: you need some great players and also a great coach who can produce a side that's more than just the sum of the parts. Arsenal have those things and so do Manchester United, despite their recent slump. Chelsea don't have an Henry,

WHAT'S OUR NAME? EVERTON!

Pires or a van Nistelrooy, and in terms of the way they play, Claudio Ranieri changes the line-up so often that it's no surprise that they rarely produce flowing, instinctive football.

Even lowly Everton more than match them for forty-five minutes today. In fact, we should go in at half-time at least one goal ahead. Wayne Rooney's the main thorn in Chelsea's side; Marco Ambrosio has to dive full length to keep his free-kick out of the top corner and then, following a goalmouth scramble, unwittingly blocks a close range shot from the youngster.

We offer less going forward in the second half, but for all Chelsea's possession they lack inspiration in the final third of the field. Adrian Mutu has turned out to be a dud, and strikes little fear into the Everton defence, while the normally dangerous Jimmy Floyd Hasselbaink gets little change out of the rock solid Joseph Yobo. As the second half wears on, Nigel Martyn is called into action a bit more, but nothing like at Elland Road. As the game meanders towards a goalless draw, there are only really three real points of interest.

1. Lampard hits the woodwork again, and Hasselbaink fails to cash in on the rebound.

2. During a lull in the 'action' some gimp in the Matthew Harding Stand, dressed in wraparound shades and sporting both a Hoxton-fin type haircut and a hip-hop style sweatband, stands up and starts doing the tried and tested 'Calm down, calm down' hand gestures towards the Everton section. Not only is he doing this but he's also looking around at the other Chelsea fans with a dead chuffed look on his face. It's almost like he's read a *Daily Star* pullout on 'How to Act Zany at the Footy'. Honestly, he really thinks he's the funniest man in the world. A young lad in a Lacoste tracksuit at the end of our row turns to him and shouts, "Sit down Pop Idol", which is far more amusing, obviously.

3. The booing. Francis Jeffers comes on for the last ten minutes and gets booed by the Everton fans, despite Thursday's apology. I would never boo our own players, no matter who they are, but I'm sure it comes as no surprise to Jeffers that people are pissed off with him. At the final whistle though, with honours even, the Chelsea players get booed off the pitch. I'm not sure whether I

find their supporters fickle for this - after all they're playing in the Champions League semi-final on Tuesday - or whether I admire the fact that they're being so discerning; with all the money they've spent they should be able to play better than what they've shown here. Ultimately I couldn't care less though, it's another good point for us at a ground where we have taken some right thrashings in recent seasons.

Now all we have to do is get home.

Sunday 18th April 2004

I was so knackered by the time I got home last night that I fell asleep and missed *The Premiership*. Watching the repeat this morning the thing that stands out is the dire straits Manchester City are in. They lost 3-1 at home to Southampton, leaving them only two points above the relegation zone. A new ground and the signature of Steve McManaman have hardly done them much good.

Everton's last game of the season is at City as well. We could send them down, which would be hilarious, but also quite terrifying. I might brush up on my Noel Gallagher accent before then, just in case. I hope it's better than my Brummie one.

Monday 19th April 2004

Derby are desperate to keep Leon Osman, whose loan spell finishes this Saturday, but manager George Burley seems resigned to the fact that David Moyes wants him back at Goodison. His time at Pride Park seems to have done Osman the world of good and it will be interesting to see if he gets a chance in the Everton side before the end of the season. With every league place being worth somewhere in the region of half a million quid though, Moyes is unlikely to be too experimental with his team selections.

Tuesday 20th April 2004

Despite their pledge not to discuss contracts until the summer, it's reported that the club are already in talks with Tomasz Radzinski, as well as Thomas Gravesen, over extending their current deals. That's great news. After all, it's just as important to keep hold of your best players as bring in new ones.

Chelsea blow up big style in the Champions League, losing 3-1 to ten-man Monaco. After Claudio Ranieri's lunatic substitutions cost them the game, I'd just love to see the faces on the 'Claudio Must Stay' campaigners now.

Wednesday 21st April 2004

Where does the time go? Already the club are planning the pre-season friendlies and have announced that we are to face Sheffield Wednesday on the third of August. It only seems like yesterday that Weavers was trying to bunk into Rochdale.

Deportivo draw 0-0 at Porto in the away leg of their semi-final. Good news for my wager.

Thursday 22nd April 2004

A bad day for Ron Atkinson.

Saturday 24th April 2004

Spring has sprung. It's a glorious day but the football is heinous.

Blackburn are desperate to get themselves away from the relegation zone after a dreadful season, while Everton's players seem to think that we're already safe. When Thomas Gravesen gets injured in the twentieth minute it is impossible to see where any sort of creativity is going to come from.

One of the most limp and lifeless games we've seen all season - and there have been a fair few - seems destined for stalemate until John Stead, Rovers' new signing from Huddersfield, glances home an Andy Cole cross.

So, a one-nil home defeat by Blackburn leaves us looking anxiously over our shoulders at Leeds United. The powers that be at Everton must be wishing they'd picked a different time to announce a twenty per cent hike in the price of season tickets.

Sunday 25th April 2004

An indication of just how piss poor we've been this season is that Portsmouth's televised victory today takes them above us in the league, with a game in hand. Luckily though, that win comes at Elland Road, where Leeds look like doomed men, a far cry from the aggressive, defiant team who all but battered us into submission last week. With three games remaining, they are seven points behind us but with a much worse goal difference. Their only real hope is to catch Manchester City, who are a mere three points ahead of them. City's big consolation is that Everton have the look of a team who will roll over on that final day, if it comes to that.

Arsenal clinch the league with a draw at Spurs, of all places. They are more than worthy champions, playing a brand of football that is almost ahead of its time.

Monday 26th April 2004

It looks like the knee ligament injury that Gravesen sustained on Saturday will keep him out of our remaining three games at Wolves, at home to Bolton and then at Manchester City. Kevin Kilbane damaged his hamstring as well, making him doubtful for the run-in too. If James McFadden is after a chance to prove his worth then this is it. Leon Osman might be returning to Goodison at just the right time too.

I think most people will just be happy to see the back of this season now, and judging by many of the comments on the internet, a lot of people, pissed off with the team and the increase in season ticket prices, aren't going to be in a hurry to renew next time around.

Saying that, it's like this at the end of almost every season. After a couple of weeks without any football - and especially if we make a few new signings - everyone will be impatiently awaiting the publication of the new fixture list.

Tuesday 27th April 2004

A lot of people are still seething over the price rises for next season. I'm not happy, obviously - no one wants to pay more for anything - but it's difficult to see what alternative the club had.

We want Everton to compete with the rest of the Premiership in terms of attracting players - or at least keeping hold of our best ones - but our ticket prices have traditionally been amongst the very lowest in the top flight.

Something's going to give eventually.

Don't get me wrong, I think going to the match is an utter rip-off, but unless all the clubs get together and decide to stop paying players obscene salaries, then the price of tickets is going to continue to be driven up.

What makes it even more frustrating is that they could cut wages by half as well if they wanted to, and not a single player would leave the game and take up another profession. It will never happen though, obviously, as clubs and their fans are desperate to see the best players in their colours and not those of their rivals. That desperation produces tunnel vision, and the clubs end up paying forty or fifty grand a week to utter gobshites.

Everton are raising their prices merely to stand still. They must wish they'd done it last summer when there was still a real feel-good atmosphere around Goodison. The truth is, people don't mind paying to watch winning football. And while the club must have calculated that the market can sustain this price rise for the time being - there's still a residual faith in Moyes and Rooney - eventually people are going to start drifting away if we have another poor season like this one.

Friday 30th April 2004

Some good news at last. David Moyes is confident that Wayne Rooney will sign a new five-year deal in the summer. Crucially though, he's not set to put pen to paper until after the European Championships. That means there's no way Evertonians will be able to enjoy the summer tournament now; they'll be too worried about covetous clubs, at home and abroad, preparing bids for Rooney if he does the business against top class international opposition.

Is it selfish to hope he gets sent off in the first game and misses the rest of the competition? Probably.

May

Safe From Harm

Saturday 1st May 2004

"Look at what you get for three and a half quid," says Ste Connor as he tucks into a vast fry up.

We're in a pub called the Red, White and Blue on the outskirts of Wolverhampton. Well, when I say 'we', half of our travelling party are - two carloads of us departed from the northwest this morning, and the rest are in the next alehouse along. We'd all originally driven past the Red, White and Blue without stopping, because it looked so downright manky, but as we pulled into the next pub a load of comedy teenage hooligans came out and started gesticulating at passers-by as they moved off down the street. Another two dressed in the regulation Stone Island coats and Acquascutum baseball caps were stood in the doorway, so, despite the other carload chancing it, Redmond turned us around and drove back here.

The thing is, we haven't played Wolves for that long that no one is sure where the best place to drink is. All we do know, from mates who support Liverpool and Manchester United, is that there are always scores of head-the-balls around Molyneux looking to fill opposing fans in.

In this case then, discretion seems the better part of valour.

As Ste demolishes his cooked breakfast, my mobile phone goes; it's Alan Welsh and he's laughing his head off.

"It's fine in here, you bunch of shithouses," he says. "It's all families having meals. The barman said they get away fans in here all the time and there's never any trouble."

I can hear Kel, Weavers and Eddy shouting comments in the background.

241

"Eddy says you probably did the right thing," continues Alan. "There are some big kids in the Wacky Warehouse who definitely look like they're up for it."

We're not going to hear the last of this one for a while.

As we look for a space up by the ground, we drive past one of the coach parks and see the police holding all the Evertonians back. One of Gaz's mates rings us to say that all the Blues who came by train were herded together and marched to the ground for twelve-thirty. They then had to twiddle their thumbs for an hour before the bar even opened. When Wolves go down - and it could be today if we beat them or Manchester City beat Newcastle - no one will mourn their passing.

Most people just want a good drink and a pleasant day out when they go to away games, and you're fine at virtually every ground in the Premiership. The lower divisions are a different story though, and it tends to be sides that come up like Wolves, or West Brom last season, whose hooligans feel they have a big point to prove.

If you've read any of the ever-increasing number of books written by skins from up and down the country, you will already know the usual stuff about codes of honour and how if it's just hooligans fighting hooligans - or 'lads', to use the proper nomenclature - then it's not doing anyone any harm.

Obviously it's all bollocks.

The fact is, ignoring the instances of innocent people getting hopped on and battered all the time, the skins don't exist in a vacuum. We all get treated like shite by the police, and are restricted to where we can get a drink because of the threat of trouble. The celebrity hooligans should at least be honest about that, instead of trying to perpetuate the myth that it's all good, clean fun.

We all know people who have been into that caper at some time, and I remember a while ago someone asked me whether I had ever been involved myself. The temptation when asked something like that is to be all vague, as if you've got some dark stuff in your past that you don't like to talk about - perhaps even intimate that you were a bit of a 'Stanley-merchant' - but I had to be honest and admit that I've never even 'bounced around' or 'gone toe to toe' at the match in my life. Ultimately, beyond all the oft-discussed cultural aspects of hooliganism or 'the casual scene', I can't get my head around the bit were I'd have to punch people because they support a different football team to me.

More to the point, I dislike the idea of them punching me back.

And talking of punching, David Moyes must feel like giving some of his players a dig in the mouth on days like today.

Wolves are shite - you may remember that the likes of Paul Ince and Denis Irwin were embarrassing at Goodison - and in the first half we must carve out at least five or six clear-cut chances.

Unfortunately we only convert one, less than two minutes into the game.

With Kevin Kilbane and Thomas Gravesen injured, there's been an almighty reshuffle of the midfield, with Alex Nyarko, Lee Carsley, James McFadden and Leon Osman, fresh from his exploits at Derby County, all starting. And it's none other than Neon Leon himself who justifies his selection by getting on the end of a McFadden cross and glancing a near-post header past Paul Jones. He is absolutely elated, and so are the Evertonians. Everyone likes to see a youngster come through the ranks and do well.

The home side are desperately slow at the back and Everton look liable to tear them apart with every attack. However, a succession of one-on-ones with Jones are wasted thanks to piss-poor finishing by Radzinski, McFadden and Rooney.

And what happens when we waste chances away from home? That's right, the other team eventually get their act together and twat us.

Ten minutes into the second half, McFadden once again tries to be too clever in midfield and gives that ball away far too easily. Before you can say 'turn your collar down you tit', Henri Camara has blasted the equaliser, an absolute screamer, in off the underside of the bar.

The fact that we know just how poor Wolves really are only makes the ensuing pasting all the more unpalatable. Joseph Yobo, David Weir and Nigel Martyn do their best to repel the waves of clumsy but determined attacks from the home side, but they get virtually no protection at all from our midfield. Nyarko's loping about like Bambi, while the leaden-footed Carsley never actually gets close enough to the ball to put a tackle in. No wonder we're fucked when we have to rely on the likes of these two.

The young lads like Rooney, McFadden and Osman - who visibly tires after an hour - are far from blameless either. Instead of concentrating on just getting hold of the ball, they're trying to be too clever with their ambitious first-time passes and naïve dribbling. As a result, they're constantly conceding possession and putting us under pressure.

At least Radzinski keeps trying to hold the ball up and show for his teammates. Unfortunately, his determination backfires as he's harshly penalised when he battles gamely for a loose ball out by the right touchline. He's still fuming as the free-kick is launched into the Everton box. We're all fuming when the huge Carl Cort leaps highest to plant the winner past Martyn.

There's still five minutes remaining when that goes in, but it's perfectly obvious that there's not even the remotest chance of a comeback from a spent Everton.

At the final whistle the news that Manchester City won means that, despite their victory, Wolves are down. In theory, Leeds United could still catch us if they win their three remaining games, starting tomorrow at Bolton. That scenario does also depend on us failing to take a point from either of our last two matches, but at the moment that seems entirely feasible.

"There's going to be murder," says Gaz when we meet him at the exit. "A big mob of Everton have just headed off towards the coaches."

As if to emphasise the threat of insurrection, a police helicopter is hovering low over the area Gaz is talking about. Luckily our car is parked in the opposite direction to the trouble, down by the train station.

Redmond and I get separated from Gaz and Ste Connor as we trudge back with the equally glum Wolves supporters, and we're conscious of the pockets of teenagers congregating by the entrance to the subways and eyeing up everyone who comes past.

MAY - SAFE FROM HARM

We don't fancy getting ambushed down there, so we head up some steps and along a main road that is being patrolled by stern coppers with angry-looking Alsatians.

We're just about to cross over when we notice four lads peel away from a set of railings and station themselves behind us. Again, like the little firm at the alehouse earlier, they've got the full pantomime hooligan costumes on, with one nugget even wrapping a Burberry scarf around his face, Intafada-style.

There are basically two directions to go from the crossing we're on: down a hill towards the car park or straight towards the city centre. As the traffic stops, Redmond and I make out as if we're going down the hill, where it's pretty much deserted and these twats will be free to jump us. They're still trying to act all nonchalant - they don't realise we've clocked them - but they're spreading out in order to try and stop us getting on our toes when the Kung Fu starts. Halfway across the road though, we switch direction back towards the town centre, and before our would-be assailants can regroup and decide what to do, we're mingling with the crowds of regular, gold shirt-wearing punters.

We get back to the car with no further incident, but you just know that some poor, unsuspecting bastard is going to get volleyed everywhere by those rats.

By half past six we're back at the Butchers Arms, celebrating Alan Welsh's thirty-sixth birthday and putting the miserable events of the day behind us. Apart from Ste Connor that is, as he appears to have got more than he bargained for - namely a severe case of food poisoning - when he paid three and a half quid for a breakfast at the Red, White and Blue.

"The cook must have been a Wolves fan," we joke, somewhat unsympathetically, as he turns the colour of a widow's net curtains and projectile vomits for the third time.

Sunday 2nd May 2004
Ste isn't the only Evertonian feeling sick, as Mark Viduka has put Leeds ahead at the Reebok.

Luckily the big pumpkin-headed Australian then goes and gets himself sent off.

WHAT'S OUR NAME? EVERTON!

Youri Djorkaeff equalises at the very start of the second half, before Leeds fold completely and concede another three.

That's them down and us safe. The cameras keep zooming in on some kid in the Leeds end crying his eyes out. My God he's ugly. He somehow manages to look like both Warren Clarke and the dancing baby off Ally McBeal.

At least we know we're playing in the Premiership next season, but it's hardly cause for celebration. It feels like we've stayed up almost by default, we've been that poor. We all know there isn't going to be much money for Moyes to spend in the summer either, so the majority of the squad will be the same players who have failed to cover themselves in much glory this time out. Groovy.

Tuesday 4th May 2004

Tomasz Radzinski's contract negotiations are not as straightforward as we were led to believe. Everton have offered him a two-year deal, but he's after a three-year one. I doubt he's that keen to stay anyway. If we buy another target-man - we're still meant to be after Dmitry Bulykin as a replacement for Campbell and Ferguson - then Radzinski is going to end up playing second fiddle to Rooney again. Does he really want to do that at the age of thirty?

I'd like him to stay though; I still think there are things about his attitude and his application that put Rooney to shame a little bit. He still gets criticised for his erratic finishing but, just like Gravesen, he's another who won't be fully appreciated until he's not around.

My bet with Bob's gone up the Swanee. Porto beat Deportivo La Coruna in the Champions League semi-final second leg.

Wednesday 5th May 2004

It's unusual for David Moyes to mention money but today he said, "Anyone looking at the Everton manager, whether it be me or previous ones, would say they require some support and, to be fair, for the two close seasons I have been here the board have tried to give me that. There is no reason to suggest they won't try and do it again. But we are getting to the point where the level of investment we need is getting greater and greater."

God only knows where that investment is going to come from. Thinking way back to the game against Leeds at Goodison, we looked like a team on the up then while the Yorkies already seemed doomed. There was a definite feeling of 'there but for the grace of God' that day. Now though, faced with the prospect of starting next season with pretty much the same squad, there's the horrible, creeping feeling that maybe we're still on the same road as Leeds - it's just that they were a bit further along it when Steve Watson scored that hat-trick last September.

Only time will tell I guess.

Thursday 6th May 2004
The new kit's revealed. Apart from the welcome change to white socks it looks just like the old one to me.

Friday 7th May 2004
David Moyes is to be offered a new four-year contract despite the fact that his current deal still has two years to run. If only one person ties their future to Goodison this summer then I hope it's him. There have been some ridiculous articles on the internet, blaming our poor season on the manager, but anyone with half a brain can see that he's the one holding the whole thing together.

I'm contemptuous of the majority of the chancers and bullshitters in football, and I don't think I give praise cheaply, but I genuinely admire Moyes. I wouldn't swap him for anyone.

Saturday 8th May 2004
"Fuck off Dunford! Fuck of Dunford!" A lad several rows down from us in the Park End is screaming so hard it looks as if he's about to have an aneurysm. Just why he's hollering that at the Everton players as they commence their customary end of season lap of 'honour' is beyond me. Perhaps he thinks one of them might pass the message on to our Chief Executive in the bar. Whatever feels good I suppose.

WHAT'S OUR NAME? EVERTON!

It's not quite the end of the season - we've still got the utterly pointless trip to Manchester City next week - but it is the last home game, and in what is becoming something of a tradition, we have been defeated. Last season it was Manchester United, the Champions, who put a slight dampener on our celebrations; this time it's Bolton Wanderers who have not so much peed on our bonfire as rubbed our noses in the soggy ashes.

David Moyes, who looks sheepish as he leads the players around the pitch, recalled Duncan Ferguson up front and gave Leon Osman a start in his favourite position, the centre of midfield, but it was to no avail. We started energetically but, when Youri Djorkaeff poked home the first of his brace on a quarter of an hour, many of our players just sagged and felt sorry for themselves, as ever.

Tomasz Radzinski's introduction at half-time livened them up a bit and he combined with Osman to fashion an equaliser for the otherwise anonymous Ferguson on sixty-eight minutes. With three minutes remaining though, Djorkaeff connected with a left-wing cross and turned home the winner, albeit with a lucky deflection off Steve Watson's hand.

That's twelve points we've lost to just Bolton and Blackburn this season. No wonder Moyes looks gutted.

The stadium's half-empty and the atmosphere is poisonous. A lot of those who have remained are clapping half-heartedly - for Moyes more than anything, I think - while others are booing or trying to get 'sack the board' chants going. The police and stewards even have to break up a little fracas in our end.

This is the worst thing about being shite; people get frustrated and turn on each other. There hasn't been this much discontentment since the darkest days of Peter Johnson's reign as chairman.

And the thing is, people don't want much. It's over fifteen years since we won the league; nine since we won the FA Cup. Evertonians aren't soft, they don't expect that to change overnight, but they want to be entertained, and most of all they want to see the players look like they give a shit.

Selling the magazine before the game we were struck by how busy Goodison Road was, despite the fact that the weather was horrible and season is effectively over. No wonder there's a lot of pissed off people at the end then; they've made the effort to fill the ground but they're rewarded by the likes of Duncan Ferguson mincing about for ninety minutes while we're having the piss taken out of us by Simon Charlton and Kevin Davies.

Osman, Tony Hibbert, Joseph Yobo and Tomasz Radzinski looked as if they wanted to have a go; the rest of them appeared to want the summer to come even quicker than we do.

Sunday 9th May 2004

David Moyes' post-match comments yesterday were: "I used to think that money wasn't everything, that you could work with players and make them better. Some people have had money and it has not been well spent. But I now believe that, at this level of football, you do need money.

"Something will have to give here, I am not going to put the fans through another season like this.

"There is work to do here at the end of the season, and it will be done. I couldn't put the fans through this again. Everton as a club has to do better."

I don't think I've felt this low about Everton for a long time. If the normally upbeat and determined David Moyes seems at the end of his tether then what hope is there for the rest of us? If there are any billionaires out there intending to bail Everton out then they're taking their time in making themselves known.

I hate the business side of football. I hate the fact that the sport sections of the newspaper seem to talk about nothing but how much the players earn, and I hate it even more when I hear fans boasting not about the skills of their players but of the size of their club's sponsorship deals and how many shirts they sell in Kuala Lumpur. However, it's becoming increasingly clear that a club like Everton, so far behind so many of their competitors when it comes to all that non-football bollocks, is going to struggle in the future. I've always had this sort of fantasy that we could plough our own furrow and do things our own idiosyncratic, uniquely Everton way without the need to be like Liverpool, enviously eyeing every horrible capitalist venture that Manchester United have undertaken. And when David Moyes arrived on the scene - turning a load of wasters into European contenders - and Wayne Rooney took the country by storm, I really felt that fantasy could become reality. But I've come crashing back down to earth this season, make no mistake. If things stay as they are, how long can we expect to keep hold of our best players or even our manager? They're only human, they must long to sample a bit of success and the financial rewards that go along with it.

It seems that the jester hats will inherit the Earth after all.

Monday 10th May 2004
As if our financial predicament and lack of prospects needs highlighting, it seems that the Prime Minister of Thailand is set to purchase thirty per cent of Liverpool Football Club for a whopping sixty-five million quid.

Tuesday 11th May 2004
It looks like David Unsworth is on his way to Bolton in the summer. They've offered him a three-year deal, which is what he was looking for. The Trotters have been trying to sign the cadaverous Brazilian cheat, Rivaldo for the past month or so, but he started stalling as soon as other clubs around Europe began to show an interest in him. No doubt Unsworth's signature will come as some consolation to the Reebok faithful.

Wednesday 12th May 2004
Another player who might have played his last game at Goodison is Alex Nyarko. His work permit expires in the summer and there is some doubt over whether he will be eligible for an extension to cover the last year of his contract.

Do they not have a rulebook at the Department of Employment that states the criteria for handing out work permits? It's just that whenever a player needs one there seems to always be a big delay and a load of uncertainty, yet it's very rare that anyone actually gets knocked back.

We've all tried to give Nyarko the benefit of the doubt this season, but quite frankly, despite a promising start, he's been poor, especially away from home. It's an indictment of the whole squad that Moyes has had to give him as many games as he has. He'll hardly be missed if he is deported.

Thursday 13th May 2004

Tomasz Radzinski still hasn't given Everton any indication over whether he's going to accept the two-year deal on the table, and it's said that Fulham are in for him.

People are still really low as we approach the final day and what amounts to a wooden spoon game against City. Even a lot of the lads who drink in the Butchers, and who normally go everywhere to watch Everton, are considering not renewing their season-tickets and just picking their games from now on. Judging by the letters to the papers and the messages on the internet, they're not the only ones who feel that way.

I think most of them will change their minds eventually though. I said at the start of the season that you eventually end up war-weary, but after a bit of a summer break you're itching for the new fixtures, especially if you've made a couple of new signings. Everyone starts off equal and, despite your better judgement, you always start to think, "If we can just steer clear of injuries, and we do sign that highly-rated Latvian full-back…" and before you know it you're striding up Goodison Road with your summer tan and your box-fresh sneakers.

Friday 14th May 2004

Regardless of tomorrow's result at Manchester City, big changes are needed. David Moyes speaks out again, saying: "It's simple really. If we don't manage to get players in this summer, and I'm talking about quite a few, then we will be flirting once again with relegation… and we've been doing that for thirteen years.

"We've finished in the top ten only twice in that time and that's a really poor effort for this club. We are in need of drastic change. It's clear we need to change quite a lot of players around if we are to make any progress."

He's been extremely outspoken lately. On one hand it's good to know that your manager isn't happy with the situation, and wants change as much as the fans, but on the other hand he's upping the ante quite a bit with the board. If they can't provide him with the funds to buy new players, what then?

Saturday 15th May 2004

Since we played Arsenal on the opening day of the season, both clubs' paths have diverged dramatically. The Gunners beat Leicester City today, maintaining an unprecedented record of not being beaten in the league all season. Everton, on the other hand, finish with a five-one reverse against Manchester City, the second worst team to stay up in the Premiership this season.

Our total of thirty-nine points is apparently the lowest we've ever amassed since 1888-9, when the season was only twenty-two games long.

It was another good day out - well, a broken mobile phone and a sprained ankle tell me I must have enjoyed myself a bit - ruined by a half-arsed team. We met some Man City supporters, mates of Kel and Ray McKay, and had a good drink in the Dry Bar and a heavily policed Wetherspoons, before making our way to the stadium. After visiting the Reebok and Derby's Pride Park I've not been a fan of new stadia, but you can't fail to be impressed by Eastlands. It looks great. In fact it reminds me a lot of the artist's impressions of our proposed ground at the Kings Dock.

"It is great," said Hodges, Ray McKay's mate. "But it's not Maine Road. I'll probably get used to it eventually, and I understand the financial reasoning behind moving, but it's still not Maine Road."

Earlier on we'd been discussing the histories of both clubs, and he said something that really hit home with me. He said, "Everton are dead proud of the fact that you've been in the top flight for ages and everything, and you laugh at City because we're a yo-yo club, but those seasons when we were in the lower divisions were great. We were winning all the time and we were going to away games at loads of mad places we'd never been before, and we were everyone's big game so the atmosphere was always fantastic. And believe me, the buzz of a promotion season is like nothing else. Compare that to what? Grimly surviving, and knowing that's the best you can hope for the year after as well? Great."

He really did make relegation sound quite enticing - encapsulating everything that going to the match is meant to be all about i.e. having a laugh and a good day out and watching a good, exciting game of football.

Unfortunately, the financial landscape, and by that I'm basically referring to the money from Sky, means that those days of the yo-yo clubs are more or less over. Many big clubs, and Everton are a prime example, have got themselves in so much debt that their television money is spent before a ball is even kicked in the new season. We struggle to make ends meet as it is, so to lose those Murdoch millions would spell financial meltdown. Many experts have said they will be surprised if Leeds United even exist in a year's time, never mind whether they'll bounce straight back up to the Premiership.

With Hodge's words and my own depressing thoughts still rattling around in my head, I was late getting to my seat, as ever, and missed Richard Dunne committing a professional foul on Tomasz Radzinski. The ex-Everton defender didn't even receive a booking, never mind the red card that was warranted, but even if City had been reduced to ten men it seems unlikely that Everton would have fared much better.

It was the same old story. All over the pitch the players lost their personal battles and made a poor City side look like AC Milan. By half-time, Kevin Keegan's men were three-nil up, thanks to a Paolo Wanchope brace either side of a Nicolas Anelka effort.

Substitute Kevin Campbell headed home a corner on the hour, but in the final couple of minutes both Antoine Sibierski and Shaun Wright-Phillips found the back of the Everton net to ensure the scoreline underlined just how bad Everton were.

Sunday 16th May 2004

So that's it. All over.

I have to admit, it wasn't what I expected when the season started. I don't think anyone did, especially David Moyes. After yesterday's game he reiterated what he has been saying for a while now, essentially challenging the board of directors at Everton to back his plans for change.

"There are no words for that, it just wasn't acceptable for Everton Football Club and it hasn't been acceptable all season and now we have to do something about it.

"It was the last game of the season and there are a few players here now who will not be here when we start again.

"If I am still here I will do what I can but I am certainly not going to be going with the same group of players that I have finished the season with so we will wait and see."

Where did it all go wrong then? Well, our problems certainly didn't start this season. They've been brewing for a long time, and perhaps in many ways the minor miracle that Moyes worked last season helped to disguise the depth of the difficulties the club faces. As he said recently, he believed that he could do the job without major investment, that he could make players better and build a competitive side that way. I know I bought into that ideal along with him.

As I asked the doubters such as my barber at the start of the season though: if we did it last season, why couldn't we do it again? What was stopping us?

I think time catching up with Kevin Campbell once and for all was a big factor. He did really well for us last season and brought the best out of the rest of the players in the team, particularly Radzinski and Rooney. Without him, Moyes was forced to do a lot of juggling with his forwards and never settled on a convincing-looking pairing.

The players' attitudes certainly didn't help either. There were all sorts of rumours about their moaning because training was too hard and too frequent, and the public fallings-out with Francis Jeffers, and particularly Duncan Ferguson, certainly seemed to confirm the talk of dressing room rifts. Given the way that

Moyes transformed them when he first arrived though - after years of Everton players taking to the pitch disorganised and patently unfit - I know I prefer his ethics and attitude to that of the prima donnas in question.

Blame and recriminations don't really get you anywhere though. We always keep coming back to the question of how do we make changes and actually move forward? And honestly, I have no idea. I'm not sure anyone has. Short of someone new coming in with a massive heap of dough, everything else just seems like tinkering around the edges.

So barring the unearthing of our very own Roman Abramovich, things look like they could be pretty tough next season. I pity the poor sod who writes that book!

We have to remember though, no matter how hopeless things can appear, they can change, and change quickly in football. It really doesn't seem so long ago that Everton and Liverpool were the dominant forces in English football, Manchester United were a standing joke, Arsenal were boring, and the idea of a Russian billionaire taking over a club would have been confined to the realms of bad fiction.

And even if the changes we want don't take place in the near future, we'll still be here, because while there's breath in us we'll fight on. And maybe things will get worse before they get better, but those bad times only make the good times that much sweeter. You only have to look back through our history to see that although we've been relatively successful compared to most clubs, the successful seasons are the punctuations between long stretches of mediocrity. But still, even when Everton are terrible, following them is still great. Evertonians are great, the walk down Goodison Road still gives you goosebumps, and if you time your entrance to the stadium just right and you get to the top of the stairs just as *Z Cars* starts, you still get that peculiar feeling in the pit of you stomach. And at the end of the day, when you cut through all the bollocks, that's what it's really all about.

So don't forget. Don't ever forget.

What's our name?

Is right.